Walter Debenham Sweeting, William. ill Ball

Historical and Architectural Notes on the Parish Churches In and Around Peterborough

Walter Debenham Sweeting, William. ill Ball

Historical and Architectural Notes on the Parish Churches in and Around Peterborough

ISBN/EAN: 9783337191801

Printed in Europe, USA, Canada, Australia, Japan

Cover: Foto ©Lupo / pixelio.de

More available books at **www.hansebooks.com**

ON THE

PARISH CHURCHES

IN AND AROUND PETERBOROUGH.

BY THE

REV. W. D. SWEETING, M.A.

Photographs by William Ball, Broad Street, Peterborough.

LONDON: WHITTAKER & Co., AVE MARIA LANE.
PETERBOROUGH: E. T. HAMBLIN.
1868.

[*All rights reserved.*]

Preface.

The title of this book sufficiently indicates its purpose and contents. No pretension is here made to a complete local history. A few materials have been collected from various sources, and so arranged as to form rather sketches of the several churches and parishes, than exhaustive accounts of them. The time at the disposal of the writer has been sufficient only to gather some discursive notes, and to place them in some sort of order, and is quite inadequate to the task of making historical collections even for a few parishes. The deficiencies therefore in the work will, it is hoped, be set down to the modest nature of the task proposed, and not to a clumsy attempt at a more ambitious scheme.

The extracts from registers, churchwardens' books, and other documents, are given verbatim: but the dates, for greater simplicity, have been put according to one uniform plan at the commencement of the extract, and must not be considered part of the quotation. The inscriptions on bells are not numbered according to the recognised rule in works on campanology, and the numbers have no reference to the note of the bell.

The best thanks of the author are due to all those gentlemen who have assisted him in the collection of these notes, many of whom, wholly unsolicited by him, have supplied interesting matter of which he has gladly and most gratefully availed himself. More especially does he owe them to the clergy and churchwardens to whom he has applied, for the kind and ready permission always granted to inspect the documents in their keeping: to Mr. F. A. Paley, for allowing him the free use of his Notes on the Parish Churches in this neighbourhood, the great advantage that has been taken of this permission being itself the best proof of the value attached to it: and to Mr. J. Cattel, for much kind interest and encouragement during the progress of the work, as well as for the solution of many difficulties, and for important information on the antiquities of the district, which no one is better able to impart.

King's School, Peterborough,
    May, 1868.

MARHOLM.

Marholm.

This retired village is situated about four miles from Peterborough. It is very small and compact; in 1791 it had but 15 houses; and the population, which in 1800 was 109, is now 172. Till the 18th cent. the name was spelt MARHAM; in a few instances it was written MARHOLME; and once MARREHAM. It was among the possessions of the abbey, and is so mentioned in a bull of pope Eugenius III. in 1145. The ADVOWSON has always been in the lord of the manor, and has consequently passed through the families of Waterville, Thorp and Wyttilbury, of whom it was bought by the present possessors, the Fitzwilliam family, in 1503.

The Church is dedicated to S. MARY. It is called in old wills Marham Sanctæ Mariæ Virginis. Bridges says it is *probably* dedicated to S. Guthlac; but he was misled by a chantry in the church dedicated to that saint. Market Deeping, Linc., and Astwick, Bedf., have churches dedicated to this saint, of whom some account will be found in the notes on Crowland abbey. In the taxation of pope Nicholas IV. the rectory was valued at 8*l*. In the king's books, 1535, it is put at 9*l*. 2*s*. 2*d*. after deducting 10*s*. 7*d*. for procurations and synodals;* the tenths were 18*s*. $2\frac{3}{4}d$. The two chantries at the same time were valued at 14*l*. and 4*l*. 13*s*. 4*d*. Adam Potts and Bernard Bradyll were the priests. Of these the former was founded by sir Wm. Fitzwilliam for one priest and four old men, who each had 53*s*. 4*d*. These, with the priest's stipend, would make the whole foundation worth 17*l*. 13*s*. 4*d*. This, or part of it, was granted in 1579 by queen Elizabeth to Walter Fish, of London, who in 1580 founded 5 divinity scholarships at S. John's, Oxford. The latter was founded by sir Wm.

---

* Procurations were due when the archdeacon visited the church; synodals, when he summoned the clergy and churchwardens to a synod.

Thorpe in the 14th cent. Its value at the suppression was 5*l*. 9*s*. and Roger Aspden, then priest of it, reported as 'meanly learned,' was allowed a pension for his life of 4*l*. 17*s*. 6*d*.

The REGISTER begins in 1566, the first 33 years having been copied from an older book, now lost. This was done by Wm. Hilles, each page being attested by his signature, and by the marks, without names, of his churchwardens. It commences in the middle of the book, and is continued at the beginning. The following is its heading:

<blockquote>The Reg^r booke belouging to the pish of Marham wherin is recorded the names of all such as have been maried baptized and buried sence the yeare of our lord god one thousand five hundreth threescore and five before the wch tyme is not any names Registred to be found truly coppyed out in A^o Dⁿⁱ 1599 according to the Queen's Maties Iniunction and statute.</blockquote>

The baptisms average 6 or 7 in the year. The second book, given in 1747 by earl Fitzwilliam, extends to 1812. Both are in good order. They have been carefully searched for the family at Milton house, and some of their entries have been re-written, amongst the entries are these:

<blockquote>1610. Joanne the widow of olde Thomas Giles was buried maie 31.
Joane ye wife of old Willm pope buried Septemb^r 12°.
1612. Old William Pope buried Julij xxiii^o.
1699. Dec^r. (the Honble) William y^e (First) son of William Ld Fitzwilliam of Milton.</blockquote>

Fined at ye same time for not burying in Woollen and 50 shillings paid to ye poore of Marham.

The words in brackets have been inserted in a later hand. All burials about this date have a note as to the affidavit that the body is buried in woollen. An act for encouraging the wool trade made this provision; it was passed 1678, and repealed in the present century. In 1657 is one marriage

<blockquote>....by Alexander Blake justice of peace dwelling in Peterborough.</blockquote>

At the end of the first book is a list of collections at the end of the 17th cent. under certain briefs. Many of these are for loss by fire. Some are curious.

<blockquote>1678. Towards ye Rebuilding of ye Churche of St Pauls in London 7*s*. 7*d*.
1670. ....in ye behalf of English Captives in order to their redemption out of Turkish slavery, 1*l*. 19*s*. 10*d*.
1680. ....for same, 9*s*. 11*d*.
1670. ......for Great Food (flood) in ye parts of Kesteven in Lincolnshire, 1*s*. 8*d*.
1672. ....a loss sustained by fire in ye sugar manufacture of London 5*s*. 2*d*.</blockquote>

In the rectory is preserved a bible once chained to a desk in the church. The title is gone, but a calendar remains, after which some 20 pages have been cut out. It is in black letter, and is dated 1611, as appears from the richly engraved title to the new testament. The binding is very thick, having metal knobs, and ropes at the back.

The following inventory of goods in this church was taken 23 Sept. 1558. The original is in the Record office, and a facsimile of the name of this parish in the original document is here given, as a specimen of the writing.

It ij Bells and a setus bell yn ye steple—
It one vestm^t of blake velvett—
It one other of whytt damaske—It a chalyce of sylv^r w^t a paten peell gyltt—It one crose of Latyn*—It ij alt^r clothes—It ij surpless—It a clothe of sey (or fey)—It ij candelstyks of latyn—It one payre of sensars of lattyn—It ij crewets of pewt^r—It one corporas case of grene velvett—It a cope of blake velvett and a cope of blake velvett and a nother of blew damaske yn the hands of my lady ffitzwyllms—It a vestm^t of crymsen velvet and a nother of satyn alrygs (?) widyn ye hands of ye seid lady—It ij harnyses for ij decons of ye same blew damaske widyn ye hands of ye seid lady.

Amongst benefactors, Francis Adyson, in 1585, left by will† 6s. 8d. to the church; and in the same year Tho. Carter left 4d.; in 1556, Tho. Curteys left 3s. 4d.; in 1643, John Wyldbore left his body to be buried in the church of Marham *in Rutland*, and to the poor 6s. 8d. In 1638, Wm. Budd left 10l. in the hands of the earl, who pays 10s. a year. The Merchant Taylors' Company in London pay annually 12l. 13s. 4d. which is divided among the residents in the almshouses, after paying the rent. In 1849, Chr. Hodgson left 50l. to keep the tomb of his father in repair, the remainder to go to the poor. In this and other lists of incumbents those that are ascertained to have died in possession of the living are marked, d. Those who are known to have resigned are marked, r.

---

* A composition metal much used for church plate and ornaments.
† Most of these extracts from old wills have been taken from bishop Kennett's notes, now in the British Museum, MS. Lansd. 1028, 1029.

RECTORS.

1217	Gilb. de Preston.[1]	1542	Ed. Keble, r.
	Hugh de Watervile.		Tho. Messenger.[3]
1271	John de Schardelow.	1546	‡Tho. Britefelde, d.[4]
	John de Doscrile.	1565	‡Tho. Sedgewicke, d.
1313	Adam de Suthwik.	1577	‡W. Hills, d.[5]
1317	Tho. de Veer.	1602	‡W. Lindsell, d.
1322	Tho. de Tyrington.	1613	Tho. Whitfeild, A.M., r.
1341	David de Wolloure.	1642	‡Sam. Green, A.M., d.
1342	Ric. de Sandford.	1670	Purbeck Halles, A.B., r.[6]
	W. de Sanford.	1675	‡Jeremiah Pendelton, d.
1361	W. de Sanford, jun.	1704	‡Paulin Phelips.[7]
1382	Ric. de Grymesby.	1735	Joscelyn Percy, d. [8]
1385	John Noppe, jun.	1756	Kennett Gibson, A.B., d.[9]
1409	Rob. Kinge.	1771	Tho. Layng, A.B., d.[10]
1418	Ric. Taillor.	1791	Christopher Hodgson, L.L.B. d.[11]
1440	John Bokvyle.	1849	‡Jos. W. Harman, A.M., d.
	John Colvile.	1854	Constantine B. Yeoman, A.M., r.[12]
1483	Rob. Wolmer.	1860	Rob. Shapman C. Blacker, A.B.[13]
1511	Nich. Messenger, r.[2]		

For 114 years before Harman the rectors were also curates of Castor. On the external wall of Paston chancel is a tablet to rect. Gibson; and on a tablet in Castor church, rect. Layng is described as an 'elegant scholar,' a 'good man,' and a 'conscientious Minister of the Gospel.' The only memorials at Marholm itself to former rectors are a displaced slab to Jeremiah Pendelton, now lying north and south in the nave; a tablet to Christopher Hodgson on the north wall; and a plain massive cross, S.E. of the chancel, to rect. Harman. In 1592, sir Nicholas Messynger appears as brother and exec^r. of John Messynger of Morcott, Rutl.

The CHURCH is of various dates. The oldest part is the tower, which is massive but very low. Its parapet is but a few feet higher than the chancel roof. It is so exceedingly plain that it is hard to assign a date to it:

‡ Buried at Marholm.
1. Also rect. of Achurch, Northants.
2. First rect. presented by the Fitzwilliam family.
3. Recuperat. versus Edvardum Kebull nuper possessorem.
4. His will is dated 2 Feb. 1564. (MS. Lans. 1208.) He leaves his body to be buried in the chancel of Marham, 'towards the repayringe thereof xxs—to Alice Ravey my old cloke—to every housholder wthin the town of Marham a stryke of barley to be given upon my buriall daye and as much upon my seaventh day............I geve to my ladye Fitzwilliams my best silver spoone..........I make my supervisor Mr. Mountstevinge.' One of the witnesses is Wm. Grene, curate of Paston.
5. Preb. of Peterborough.
6. Adm. to the rectory 12 May, 1670, the same day that he was ordained priest.
7. Also rect. of Woolley, Hunts.
8. Buried at Peterborough cathedral.
9. Grandnephew to bishop Kennett. Buried at Paston.
10. Also rect. of West Deeping. Buried at Castor.
11. Held the living 58 years. Buried at Castor.
12. Formerly vic. of Yedingham, Yorkshire: now vic. of Manfield, Yorkshire.
13. Formerly inc. of Longthorp.

but some features in it seem to point to the early part of the 13th cent. It is lit only by very narrow lancet lights, having pointed heads; these are deeply splayed within, owing to the great thickness of the wall, and at the inside face have round arches. The arch to the nave is now blocked up, and a late acutely pointed door has been inserted: the original stringcourse however (which was of course not continued over the new work), remains on the west wall of the nave, on each side, and the arch itself is to be seen from the tower. It has a round head, and the masonry is earlier than the date above assigned to the tower. Very extensive alterations were made at the end of the 13th cent. The whole church, except the tower, was destroyed; and a new one built, consisting of chancel, nave, and two aisles. At the east end of each aisle was an altar. The pillars now remaining in the church with the arches, and the chancel arch, are of this date. So also is a very beautiful little window now placed at the S.E. corner of the nave, above the recumbent effigy of a knight. It is of two lights, and has in the head a quatrefoil in a circle. The external appearance of this window is well seen in the view. It is hardly four feet in length. The square-headed window to the west of it, of three lights, with net-tracery (so called from its resemblance to the meshes of a net) is about 40 years later. It has thin cusps, which shew that it is early work. The best example of net-tracery in the neighbourhood is the east window of the grammar school at Peterborough: but the Marholm window is earlier than that. The next great change was the enlargement and rebuilding of the chancel. The date of this, within a very few years, is known. In 1534 it was 'newly edificed;' and was therefore built within about ten years from that time. It was done at the cost of sir Wm. Fitzwilliam, extracts from whose will are given below. For so late a date the work is very good. On each side of the chancel are two large windows of four lights each; the E. window has five lights. The lower part of each light is cinquefoiled. The stringcourse, or moulding that runs under the windows, is ungainly; and is the same as that running under the clerestory windows in the nave. Indeed the destruction of the aisles probably followed immediately upon the dissolution of the chantries. This was in 1545. So that about that time the aisles were pulled down, and the new mouldings made similar to those so recently made in the chancel. The nave arches were then blocked up, and windows inserted under them: two of those on the south side being preserved from the aisles. The south porch is still later, probably Elizabethan. It has a very acute gable, which cuts into the moulding under the clerestory windows. It has a round-headed door under a square label, of very debased design. The corner pinnacles of the tower, which are very ugly, may have been added at the same time. The tower and chancel are embattled. Over the priest's door, between the two south chancel windows, there has been an enormous sundial painted. Traces of the letters remain, and the gnomon itself. Its position is clearly visible in the photograph. The buttresses to the chancel are placed diagonally: the tower has in lieu of buttresses those peculiar means of strengthening a building used in early work, which gives the angles an appearance of being overlapped with a thin layer of stone; in this case it is hardly more than six inches in thickness.

Within the church are many features of interest. The piers in the nave consist of semi-cylindrical shafts. Below the capital is a plain fillet surrounding the whole: the capital and this fillet are coloured almost black, against the lighter tint of the pier itself, producing a good effect. The two windows inserted under the blocked arches north of the nave are very poor; they are of the same date as the destruction of the aisles, one of them has plain lights without tracery, but the chamfer above is scalloped in a singular way; the other has four-centered lights, but no tracery. Both have three lights. There are three clerestory windows on each side, of three lights each; all are cinquefoiled, those on the south side being somewhat the larger. A few of the original benches remain: they have poppies with three heads.

The font is octagonal, low, on five shafts. Each face has a flower and leaf in slight relief, more like a pattern on plaister (as is common in Herefordshire churches) than a device on stone. On the west wall is a fresco decaying rapidly. There are three figures; the one to the left is S. Catherine, she has long flowing locks and a wheel in her hand; the centre is S. Andrew, as is shewn by his cross; the third seems to be a woman, but is too much worn to be identified. Against the west wall is visible the weathermould of the old decorated nave, shewing the pitch of the roof, which was removed to give place to the present perpendicular clerestory. The chancel is divided from the nave by an uncouth screen, erected it is said upon no æsthetical principles, but to support the drapery at the funeral of one of the Milton family. The nave roof, though late, is good; the beams are well moulded, dividing the whole roof into squares. The chancel roof is ceiled. On the sill of the S.E. nave window is a curiosity. It is a wooden hoop, hardly a foot in diameter, with two bands crossing each other at right angles above it, and attached to it, forming a sort of open crown. It is coloured black and white. This was once a funeral garland. The ribs were adorned with paper flowers and other ornaments; and it was the custom to carry such garlands at the funerals of unmarried girls, and to leave them in the church as memorials. Several still remain in Derbyshire churches with their ornaments complete.* In the chancel are some remains of the achievements and armour of the Fitzwilliams. The bars that supported them remain, but most of the decorations themselves have vanished. A few banners in rags, a gauntlet and spur, two swords, one of which is kept in the chest, and two helmets, the upper one of which a bird seems to have utilised for a nest, are all that are now left. The chancel windows have borders of stained glass, and fragments of coats of arms, &c., in the central lights. The east window has many Fitzwilliam shields with a golden fleur-de-lys in the centre. In the S.E. window is the rebus of abbot Kirton, a

---

* In Chambers' Book of Days, i, 273, is an engraving of five garlands still hanging from the roof of the church at Ashford-in-the-water.

church standing on a yellow tun, with the letter R on it. It has been turned round so as not to be seen properly from within. He was abbot of Peterborough, and built the new building and the deanery gateway: over the doors of this gateway is to be seen the same rebus carved in stone.

The beams of the belfry have been well restored. There is but one BELL thus inscribed, with ornaments between the words:

TOBY NORRIS CAST ME 1673.

This seems to be intended for a jingling rhyme.

Four MONUMENTS in the chancel possess great interest. The earliest is dated 1534, and is in the N.E. corner. It has a canopy supported by twisted iron bars and stone spiral shafts. At the back are brasses of a knight and his lady heraldically dressed in the Fitzwilliam colours. A scroll with the motto prohibere nephas proceeds from the mouth of each. The inscription is

Syr Wylliam Fitzwylliams Knight decessyd the ix daye of August in the xxxi yere of Or soberayn lorde Kynge Henry the viii in anno Dni mcccccxxxiiii, and lyeth beuried under thys tombe.

An interpolated inscription in the centre, destroying the unity of the memorial, records its restoration in 1674. This knight rebuilt the chancel. He was an alderman of London and sheriff in 1506. He rebuilt great part of S. Andrew Undershaft, in London, at his own cost. He had been one of the retainers of cardinal Wolsey, and received him at Milton house. The following copious extract from his will, dated 28 May, and proved 5 Sept., 1534, is taken from Nicolas's Testamenta Vetusta, p. 665. The name Marham is there erroneously printed Masham. He describes himself as William Fitz William, the elder.

> My body to be buried in the new chancel at Marham in the said county of Northampton, which I have of late caused to be made and newly edified there; and I will that my executors cause a tomb of marble to be made there, with a scripture making mention of my name, as shall be devised by my executors; and I will that wherever I happen to decease within the realm of England, my corpse be conveyed to the said chancel of Marham.....If I happen to decease in London, I bequeath vi. to the five orders of friars within that city, viz. the Grey Friars, the Black Friars, Augustine Friars, White Friars, and the Crossed Friars, to the intent that they shall bring forth my corpse (if I decease there) out of the liberties of the said city, and to have in each of the said places a

trental of masses; to the four orders of friars at Stamford, if they be at my burial at Marham IV *l.* they saying a trental of masses, in every of their places, for my soul and all Christian souls;......to the marriages of poor maidens, *cl.* sterling....to the poor scholars within the Universities of Oxford and Cambridge XL*l.* to be distributed by the advice of two Doctors of Divinity, and XXX*l.* amongst poor people....to the Prior and Convent of Clerkenwell, in London, x*l.* to have a dirige and mass for my soul within their monastery.

West of this is a monstrous erection, so large as to block up one light of each of the windows on the north side. It is to earl Fitzwilliam, 1719, and his wife Anna, 1727. Their images stand erect, and the whole is protected by railings. In a lengthy inscription the earl is described as one

    Qui aulam ornare poterat Ruri latere maluit.

This monument was put up by their only son, earl John, who (for with this pious sentiment the whole is concluded)

    Pietatis ergo et Obsequij hæc parentavit.
    Jacob: Fisher de Camberwell Fecit.

On the south is an altar tomb with coloured effigies to sir Wm. Fitzwilliam and his lady. It is dated 1599. He is represented in armour; according to the inscription he was 'Lord Leiutenant of ye Kingdom of Ireland.' West of this is a small marble pillar, 1646, to a son of lady Fitzwilliam. The curious inscription, deprecating wanton destruction by iconoclasts, is as follows:

    Grassante bello civili.
    To the courteous souldier.
  Noe crucifixe you see, noe Frightful Brand
  Of suptition's here. Pray let mee stand.

In the nave are two slabs to former rectors already noticed. A third, which cannot now be deciphered, seems to be the same as that mentioned by Bridges, as lying in the churchyard, the inscription of which he gives thus:

Hic jacet Johannes Wyttylbyri qui obiit viii. die Maii, Ao. Dni millimo. cccc. cujus aie ppicietur Deus. Amen.

Bridges also speaks of a stone to John Whitfeld, of Yarmouth, dated 1631.

The CHURCHYARD has for so small a village a great number of altar tombs, mostly near the south porch. Two stones only remain of 17th cent. date; one to Joseph Bull, and one to Elizabeth Turner, the latter on a small stone south of the path, both of 1692. At the west end are a great many from the household at Milton. The versification is stranger than usual even on tombstones. An example is appended.

> Engrave no flattery on our stone
> Man is by nature lost:
> Salvation is by grace Alone,
> Then what have we to cost.

This was in 1844. Recently a few simple headstones, that speak by their form to the christian's faith and hope, have been placed about the churchyard.

Castor.

This village is four miles from Peterborough. The noble church is in a commanding position on the slope of a hill, the village itself nestling around it. The name has remained unaltered, except in spelling, from the time of the Romans. Their city of Durobrivæ was on each side of the river: both villages, Castor and Chesterton, bear in their names evidence of the castra, or camp. The only variations seem to have been CASTER, CAISTER, CASTRE; the last being by far the most common. Great part of the camp itself is easily to be traced: and in the churchyard and rectory walls are fragments of Roman masonry.

The living has a special interest for this diocese, since it was for 218 years attached to the bishoprick, and held in commendam with it. The list of rectors therefore for that time, with the exception of an intruder during the commonwealth, is simply a list of the bishops of Peterborough. The dedication of the church, to S. KYNEBURGHA, is believed to be unique. She was the third of four daughters of Penda, king of the Mercians. Their names and careers may be found in MS. Lansd. 1025. She alone, of the four, was married. Her husband was Alfred, king of Northumbria. She founded a convent at Castor, then called Dormumdceastre, and presided over it: here she

CASTOR.

died and was buried. The church she built in the year
650. In the beginning of the 11th cent. her body, and
that of her sister S. Kyniswitha, were removed by abbot
Elsinus to Peterborough. The monks used to keep the
anniversary of their 'translation' on the 7th of March.
A shrine was placed over their bodies: and Mr. Bloxam,
a great authority in sepulchral lore, who read a paper on
the monumental remains of the cathedral at the meeting
of the Archæological Institute, in 1861, was of opinion
that the stone now preserved in the new building was a
sculptured monument erected over the relics of these
saints. It is commonly accounted a memorial of abbot
Hedda, 870: but the details of the stone do not warrant
so early a date being assigned to it. It is certainly not
older than the 11th cent., which date would agree with
that of the removal of the bodies from Castor: for Elsinus
was abbot 1005—1055. A ridge in Castor field is still,
it is said, known as lady Connyburrow's way; an evident
corruption of Kyneburgha. The patronage of the living
was in the convent, till its dissolution: it has since been
in the bishop. Its value in 1254, and in 1291, was
36*l*. 6*s*. 8*d*; at the earlier taxation the sacrist had a
pension of 5*l*; at the later the abbot had a pension of 5*l*,
and a portion of 3*l*. 6*s*. 8*d*; the sacrist had 3*l*. 16*s*. 8*d*.
and the subsacrist 5*l*. In the king's books the full value
was 58*l*. 3*s*. 4*d*, and the only deductions were the abbot's
5*l*. and 10*s*. 9*d*. for the archdeacon's fees.

The REGISTERS are in excellent order. The earliest
dates from 1538. The entries up to 1598 are copied
from an older book, attested on each page by the curate
and churchwardens. This is done in Latin, except once
as follows:

It agreeth with the originall as witnesseth Edward Stokes, Curat, &c.

A great many extracts from this book made by bishop
Kennett, who was rector, are to be seen in the British
Museum, MS. Lansd. 991. On the left of the page is a
column for the year, on the right for the year of the
reigning sovereign. In 1654 the questionable custom
prevailed of giving the ages of brides. There are many
entries of the Fitzwilliam family, their seat being in the
parish. Of others but few possess general interest:

1609. 24 Aug. (buried) Sir Robert Wingfield.
1654. 14 May (baptised) Nathaniel the son of Edmond Spinks Minister.
1656. 12 Dec. (buried) Ann Chaplin widow & gentlewoman.
1709. 10 May. Robert King son of Tho: King privately baptiz'd by a Presbyterian Parson.
1720. 10 Apr. Old Goody Bate of Castor bur.

Amongst unusual christian names occurring in this volume may be cited, Ananias, Athanasius, Israel, Penitent, Vertue. Nathaniel Spinks, whose baptismal register is here quoted, was afterwards rector of Peakirk, and became a celebrated nonjuring bishop. At the end of the volume is a list of collections on briefs for the years 1690—1715. Amongst them are:

1691. 22 Jan. For John Clopton of ye city of Norwiche who sufferred great casualtye by sea 00 03 07
1693. 11 Oct. For the French Protestants 0 10 01
1699. 17 Apr. For ye Vaudois and French Refugees in Switzerland 03 06 00¾
1700. 11 Aug. For ye Captives at Machanes 01 02 10
1701. 14 Sep. For Ely Cathedral .... 00 05 04ob.
1702. 12 May. For Chester Cathedral 00 07 02
1703. 20 Feb. For ye Refugees of ye Principality of Orange 0 11 1½
1704. 13 Aug. For ye wives and children of seamen y^t perish'd in ye storme 0 13 10¼
1715. 13 July. For ye Cowkeeper's Brief .... 02 : 16 : 06

Most of the collections were for churches.

The churchwardens' books are preserved only from about 1770. They are remarkable chiefly for the repeated payments for destruction of sparrows and hedgehogs. As a specimen the following may be taken:

1781. 5 Nov. paid the boys for makeing the Burnfire 6 0
1787. 11 May. P^d Mr Coke for Larg Prayer Books for the church 1 1 0
1798. 18 May. P^d Robert Shelstone for 1 Dozen of spar 0 0 2
Mr Bates Boy 1 Dozen of spar : 1 doz : of Eggs 0 0 3
Mopsey's Boy a young Hedge hog 0 0 2
Perkins Cobley an old d^o 0 0 4

The constable's books are preserved from 1720. Both these and the churchwardens' accounts are being gradually destroyed by the damp. Some of the items are amusing:

1737. 28 Oct. for Returning a worren (warrant) James Dawkins .. 0 1 0
John Clark for wiping (whipping) on him 0 00 6
7 May. Paid to the Molecatcher 1 10 00
1739. 6 Feb. for going to Peterborough Myself and Horse to attend the execution of Elizabeth Winchley 2 0
1747. 1 Dec. For going to foch the boy home in my cart that was left in our feild in the Sno 5 0
1750. 27 Feb. For returning a warrant to prevent ye Cox being holled at on Srove Tewsday 1 0

The storm mentioned among the briefs occurred 27

Nov. 1703, and was most destructive. The first Eddystone lighthouse (the wooden one by Winstanley) was destroyed by it, the unhappy inventor being in it at the time. The fleet just returned from the Mediterranean suffered great loss, and it is to this the brief doubtless refers. The loss of officers and men was given at 1500. Their widows were ultimately pensioned as if the men had died in action.

The custom of throwing at cocks on Shrove Tuesday was very general, particularly in schools: and in some cases the master's stipend was augmented by a tax upon the scholars for providing the sport. In Brand's Antiquities the custom is said to have been retained at Heston, in Middlesex, till 1791. We see the good people of Castor were long before that time, anxious to abolish a custom so cruel.

The inventory of church furniture in 1558, shews how well the church was then supplied. The curate's name was sir John Smyth.

ffirst in ye steple iiij grete bellys. Itm in the same a sanctus bell. Itm two hand belles. Itm two chaleces peell gylt of sylv'. Itm one chalece of sylv' doble gylt. Itm one cross with a fote of cop[1] and gylt. Itm a holy wat' stocke of brase. Itm two small candelstyks of latyn. Itm one cope of black velvett. Itm one cope of tawny velvett. Itm one whyt cope of taffa damaske brodered wth tawny taffa. Itm one other whyt cope of taffa damaske. Itm one other whyt cope of whyt fustyan. Itm one vestment of crymsyn velvett. Itm two dalmatyks of old crymsyn velvett for the deacon and subdeacon. Itm one vestment called the golden vestment. Itm one hole shute[2] of vestments of whyt taffa[3] damask. Itm one good vestment of red and gryne sylke. Itm one olde vestment of whyt taffada mask. Itm one old vestment of crymsyn satyn. Itm one old vestment of red sylke. Itm two vestments of grene dornyx.[4] Itm one pall of corse gold worke. Itm a haugyng of an alt' of red sylke wth a frenge of whyt damask. Itm a rare cloth of whyt sylke. Itm a freng[5] for an alt' of red and purple velvett. Itm a cross staff' of cop and gylt wch was delyvrd on to Doctor ap harry and Sir Thomas holt is his executor. Itm ij kercheffs. Itm a bybell and the paphrases.[6] Itm iiij corporas wth two clothes. Itm iij old red sylke cosbyns[7] Itm iij alt' clothes of diap. Itm vij other of flaxen. Itm iij diap towels whereof Doct' ap harry had one. Itm iiij playne bowels.[8] Itm iij flaxen shets.[9] Itm an old freng for an alt' of red sylke. Itm a crose clothe of sylke. Itm a pyx of copar wch doct' ap harry had and Sir Thomas hys executor. Itm j sens[10] of brase. Itm ij cruetts of leade. Itm ij grayte candellstyks of latyn sold for xviij^{sl} wych was putt in ye pore mens box.

It will be seen from the following list that doctor ap Harry mentioned in this inventory had been rector.

1. Foot of copper. 2. Whole suit, meaning a chasuble and two tunicles. 3. Taffeta, a thin silk stuff. 4. Darnix or dernyche: in the dictionary of the Academy defined as 'drap de Tournay,' Tournay cloth. 5. Fringe. 6. The paraphrase of Erasmus. 7. Cushions. 8. Bowls. 9. Linen Cloths for Holy Communion. 10. Censer.

The only benefaction recorded in the church is that of Mr. Robert Wright, who left lands in Norfolk yielding 52s. a year, for 12 penny loaves to be given every week to 12 poor people. For many years this bequest was entirely neglected; 19 loaves are now given. Many sums have been left by will to the church; in 1499 Rob. Mayden left 4d. to the high altar for tythes forgotten, and to the guild of the Blessed Virgin in Castor his croft on the hill and all its belongings; in 1557 Joanna More left 4d. to the high altar and 8d. to the bells; in the same year Thurstan Kerby bequeathed

> to the high Aulter of Castor a strike of barley and to the bells ii strike of barley. Item I give to the Churche for my buriall iii^s iiii^d. Item I give to the churche a cowe willing that her first caulfe may be rered to mayntayne the churche and releve the povertie in the towne and to the end that ther may be every yere my anniversary kept with masse and dirige and a peale ronge for my soul.

And the will of Rob. Curteys the elder, in 1544, has a clause too curious to be omitted. He leaves his body to be buried in the N. aisle,

> to thighe aulter iii^s iiii^d to the sepulcre lyght iii^s iiii^d to the bells xii^d to the mother church of Peterborough iiii^d. Item to the behove of my paryshe church of Castor x^s. Item I bequeth to Robert Curteys my son vi^s viii^d for to fynde a certen lampe in the church so that yt may at the yeeres ende be made as good by the occupacyon thereof as yt was in the begynninge soo longe as he lyst to kepe itt or else to lett some other have ytt that will occupy ytt of the same manner soo that I wyll nott ytt shulde dekay or peryshe.

RECTORS.

1228 Virgilius, d.	1450 John Colynson, r.
1240 Will. de Burgo.	*Tho. Harby, d.
Pet. de Augusta, d.	1460 Joh. Sybely, d.
1287 Joh. de Affordeby, d.[1]	1466 Will. Wytham, L.L.D., r.
1314 Will. de Melton, r.[2]	1466 ‡Tho. Tanfield, S.T.B., d.[7]
1316 Rog. de Northburgh.	1474 Tho. Dalyson.
1317 Rog. de Nassington.	1477 Tho. Blencho.
1320 Joh. de Aslakeby.	1477 Joh. Palady, L.L.B., d.[8]
1336 Hen. de Edenford.	1490 Hen. Rudde, L.L.D., d.[9]
1340 Alex. de Ormesby, L.L.D.	1506 Joh. Gayton, d.
1345 Rob. Swetman de Dodyngton	Joh. Marys.
1355 Joh. de Wilford.	1543 Augustine Dudley, d.[10]
1355 Gervas. Warde.	1544 Hug. Rawlyns, A.M.[11]
Rob. de Austhorp.	1546 *Joh. ap Harry, L.L.D., d.[12]
1372 Ric. de Leycester.	1549 Will Jeffery, L.L.D.[13]
Will. Borstall.	1561 Chr. Hodgeson, A.B., d.[14]
1378 *Tho. Hervy.	1600 Laur. Stanton, S.T.P., d.[15]
1383 Tho. Pykwell.	1613 ‡Tho. Dove, A.M., d.[16]
1385 Joh. de Langeford.	1629 Warner Marshall, A.M., d.[14]
Ralph Repyngham, d.[3]	1632 Will. Peirse, S.T.P., r.
1416 Will. Kynwolmersh.[4]	1633 Augustine Lindsay, S.T.P., r.
1419 Tho. Whiston, L.L.D.	1634 ‡Fr. Dee, S.T.P., d.
Ric. Raynhill, r.[5]	1639 ‡Joh. Towers, S.T.P., deprived.
1449 Will. Witham, L.L.D., r.[6]	1646 Edm. Spinkes, deprived.[17]

1660 Benj. Laney, S.T.P., r.
1663 Jos. Henshaw, S.T.P., d.
1679 Will. Lloyd, S.T.P., r.
1685 Tho. White, S.T.P., deprived.
1691 ‡Ric. Cumberland, S.T.P., d.
1718 ‡White Kennett, S.T.P., d.
1728 ‡Rob. Clavering, S.T.P., d.
1747 Joh. Thomas, S.T.P., r.
1757 Ric. Terrick, S.T.P., r.

1764 Rob. Lamb, L.L.D., r.
1769 ‡Joh. Hinchcliffe, S.T.P., d.
1794 ‡Spencer Madan, S.T.P., d.
1813 Joh. Parsons, S.T.P., d.
1819 ‡Herb. Marsh, S.T.P., d.
1839 ‡Geo. Davys, S.T.P., r.
1851 *Geo. Andrew, A.M., d.
1864 Joh. Jas. Beresford, S.T.B.[18]

Of the eighteen bishops, whose names are here given as rectors of Castor, brief notices will be found in the notes on the cathedral.

The CHURCH is cruciform. It consists of chancel, nave with aisles and clerestory, N. door and S. porch, N. and S. transepts, the latter with an eastern aisle, and central tower and spire. Nearly all the details of this church are of great beauty; but the Norman work, especially the tower, is by far the richest work of its date in the neighbourhood, and is probably not surpassed by any parish church in the kingdom. We are fortunate in possessing accurately the date of the earlier part of the building. A dedication stone, removed from the Norman chancel, has been rebuilt into the wall over the priest's door. The stone is still quite legible; it reads thus:

<pre>
        XV° KL'
     MAI   DEDICA
   TIO   HVI'   ECL'E
     AD   MC   XXIIII
</pre>

* Buried at Castor.
‡ Buried at Peterborough cathedral.
1. Formerly rect. of Polebrook.
2. There was a vic. of Pightesley of this name 1306—10, and a vic. of Wedon, 1347—49.
3. Preb. of Lichfield and Sarum, also dean of S. Adde, collegiate church, Salop.
4. Presented by abp. of Canterbury: he was dean of S. Martin's, London, and buried in the cloister there. In 1422 he was appointed 'Domini Regis Thesaurarius.' Bridges gives two successive rectors of this same name.
5. Also rect. of Stanwick and Paston.
6. Archdn. of Stow, 1464, dn. of S. Mary, Leicester, 1462.
7. Also rect. of Harpole and Gayton.
8. Rect. of Arthingworth, 1461, Holcot, 1496, Weston Favell, 1470, Blisworth, 1473. Also warden of Wappenham, 1470—90, and there buried, ' nuper Gardianus hujus Ecclesie.'
9. Rect. of Weston Coville, Camb., 1478, Cottingham, 1486, Pitchley, 1487, Downham, Camb., 1490. Also vic. gen. and comm. of Ely diocese. In his will he directs his body to be buried at Bury S. Edmunds ' before S. Christopher.' He left 50l. to Peterborough monastery, and legacies for vestments to Castor.
10. Fuller mentions Dudley as a reputed martyr, 'yet on enquiry, his sufferings amounted not to loss of life.' There was but one martyr in the county, John Hurd, a shoemaker, of Syresham, burnt at Northampton, 1557.
11. He assisted in drawing up articles against Ferrar, bp. of S. David's, ultimately burnt at Carmarthen, 1555.
12. Princ. of Broadgate Hall, Oxf., chancellor of Llandaff and Peterborough, and archdn. of Northampton.
13. Archdn. of Northampton, chancellor of Sarum.
14. Preb. of Peterborough.
15. Dn. of Lincoln, and rect. of Uffington, Linc. Buried at Uffington, where is a monument to him in alabaster and marble.
16. Archdn. of Northampton, preb. of Peterborough.
17. Also rect. of Orton Longueville. Ejected under the Act of Uniformity.
18. Formerly fellow of S. John's, Camb., and precentor of Peterborough.

Free from abbreviations this would read, 'Quinto decimo kalendas Maias dedicatio hujus ecclesiæ anno Domini mcxxiiii;' or in English, 'The dedication of this church was on the 17th of April, 1124.' On this stone Mr. Paley remarks

> Though this date, 1124, is not incompatible with the style of the church, it cannot be relied on, as the last figures seem to have been cut by a later hand, and they are incised instead of standing in relief.

The last figures appear even to have been carved in the present century; for Kerrich* has preserved some etchings of this church, and he remarks that over the south door there is an

> Inscription with a date, of which date only 2 letters M C . . . now remain.

That the date now given on the stone is correct we have collateral evidence. In Gunton, and in the MS. Lansd., this extract from the chronicle is given:

> 1124. Hoc anno Ecclie de Castre solenniter ab Epo. Linc. consecrata est.... Sub eodem nempe tempore quo Alexand. Linc. Epus. ecclesiam S. Petri de Burgo de novo instauratam dedicasse memoratur, presentibus Abbatibus de Thorneia Croylandia Ramesia &c.

The church so consecrated consisted without doubt of a plain cross, with central tower and south porch, and most probably an eastern apse. The Rev. O. Davys, who described this church at the meeting of the Archæological Institute, in 1861, conjectures that the tower was originally capped by a pyramidal roof. When the aisles were added, the outer door of the S. porch was flush with the walls of the aisle, and there it still remains, forming the inner door of the new porch. These aisles also of course abutted against the W. walls of the transepts, so that the windows there had to be blocked. One of these windows in part remains, and is to be seen within the church from the S. aisle. The arch which was opened from the aisle into the transept, cut through part only of one of the transept windows, and enough of it remains to shew the character of the windows throughout the Norman church. They were small and round-headed, and had a double billet moulding all round. A larger remnant of a similar window is to be seen on the N. side of

---

* Brit. Mus. Add. MSS. 6750. The date is about 1795—1800. Other notes and sketches of the church, but of no great value, are to be found in Essex's Collection, Add. MSS. 9769. The spire is there said to be of 'an ill proportion.'

the N. transept externally. The S. door already spoken of is of the same character; it has two rows of billets, and one of nailheads. It is supported by two good shafts with enriched cushion capitals. At the W. end is another Norman window, distorted in the head. Here the junction of the Norman masonry of the nave, with the early English work of the S. aisle, is plainly observable. On each side of the present porch, in the aisle walls, can be seen the weathermould which formed the gable of the original Norman porch. Into the W. wall of this porch is built an old head, part of a Norman corbel table. Under the W. end of S. transept roof is a large corbel table, partly Norman. Near the E. end of the S. chancel wall is inserted a ram's head, which might easily escape notice. Over the S. door is a figure apparently in the act of blessing; it is not possible to identify the object in the left hand. It is of Norman date, and was removed to its present position when the aisles were added. These are all the remains of the Norman church except the glorious tower. This stands on four massive piers, the capitals and bases of which have been restored. Two capitals of the N.E. pier are new, the old ones having been destroyed to make room for a monument now removed into the chancel. The carving on these capitals is very rich and quaint. Here can be seen lions, boars, dragons, hounds, goats, and men. On the N. and E. sides, externally, are visible the weathermoulds that shew the pitch of the roofs: the S. transept retains its original pitch. There are two stages above the roofs. All the walls are covered with rich designs. The ornaments are partly scallops, partly zigzags. The lower stage has windows of two lights, blocked on three sides. They have irregular zigzags of striking design. The upper stage is an arcade of five arches, three being belfry windows. The corbel table dividing the stages has heads like those on the S. transept. The whole is surmounted by a spire of the 14th cent. At its foot is a cumbrous parapet, the corner pinnacles being unfinished. The outline of the tower and spire is not pleasing, for the spire is too tall to be considered as a mere pyramidal capping, such as the Normans used, and far too short for the size of the tower itself. There are two rows of spire lights, the heads being square-sided; the upper row is very near the summit of the spire, and this arrangement, combined with small gabled niches which are between the windows, give the spire a stunted look.

The state of the fabric within is only less worthy of attention than the external work. The aisles are separated from the nave by three arches, those on the south side being the earlier. These have round piers and arches, and the nailhead ornament in the capitals shews the early date of this work, about 1250. The arch to the S. transept is of the same date. Above this arch is the weathermould shewing the pitch of the first aisle roof, this was raised in later times, possibly when most of the windows were inserted. The door of this aisle has round it this inscription cut on the wood:

✠ RICARDVS BEBY RECTOR ECCLECIE DE CASTRE FECIT.

No rector of this name occurs in the registers of the bishop or elsewhere; but Richard Beleby, in the 14th cent. was vicar of Whittlesey S. Mary, and with him this door may be connected. Over the arch between the nave and tower are two coats of arms painted on the plaister, of no antiquity. The nave roof is good though of low pitch. It has been well restored. Angels with outspread wings on the roof itself hold shields. The wall-pieces have smaller figures. Of the transepts that to the south is much the more spacious. It has three windows, one of three lights, with plain circles in the heads. It seems they had originally quatrefoils in these circles that have been knocked out. The eastern aisle to this transept has two windows with plain intersecting tracery. The vestry is now here. An arch opening into the chancel is early English, but later than the chancel, one of its windows having been destroyed when the arch was made. This arch was blocked until the recent restoration in 1851. The chancel is raised five steps. It is completely of 13th cent. date, except the east window, which is an ugly insertion. There are four good lancets, all deeply splayed; the east window had a triple lancet, remains of which are visible without in the deep hollow mouldings on each side of the present window, which terminate abruptly at the spring of the arch. There are two broad sedilia with round arches supported on a corbel, and a double piscina, very richly carved with the dogtooth, with marble shafts and octagonal basons; another cinquefoiled piscina on the N. side has been removed thither, it has a singular little square flue. At the east end of the south side is a segmental arch with part of a floriated cross beneath; opposite is a similar arch, perhaps a credence. The N. transept is raised above the nave floor. It is quite separated from the aisle by a stone screen, restored, which held the image and shrine of S. Kyneburgha. This shrine consists now of open quatrefoils below supporting a series of niches, the central one of which has a pedestal for the figure of the Saint. The whole composition was the reredos behind the altar of the N. aisle. An embattled staircase in the N. transept leads to the bells. The roof is flat and low; above it is a curious chamber, doubtless once occupied by the priest. It has a fair perpendicular roof with wall pieces and corbels, two of which are lost. Good figures remain here, similar to those in the nave roof. Here is a sturdy little chest, some three feet long, once the almsbox. In the N. aisle is a double aumbry, where relics may have been preserved. Here are two decorated windows of three and five lights, with square heads and net tracery. The nave arcade on this side has octagonal piers and pointed arches. At the west end is preserved a fresco. Part only can be clearly made out: this represents the martyrdom of S. Catherine. The W. nave window is decorated, of three lights, and has a foreign look. Each of the transepts has a blocked door. The seats throughout are low and open; in the nave the ancient custom of dividing the sexes is retained.

The belfry arrangements are very good; the birds are kept out by wire. Here are six BELLS, all inscribed, but in two cases the inscriptions are repeated. The first two have plain round discs between the words; the third and fourth have flowers.

1, 2 HENRICUS BAGLEY NOS FECIT 1700
3, 4 HENRY BAGLEY OF ECTON MADE MEE 1700
5 CANTATE DOMINO CANTICUM NOVUM HENRICUS ME FECIT 1700
6 I TO THE CHVRCH THE LIVING CALL AND TO THE GRAVE DO SUMMON ALL HENRY BAGLEY MADE ME 1700

In the view of Castor church from the S.E., which is that given in the photograph, may be seen several features of interest. Of Norman work is the tower, the figure over the S. porch, and the dedication stone over the priest's door in the chancel; of pure early English is the S. door, and the S. wall of the chancel, including the lofty lancet; of geometric work is the S. transept, dating about 1250, the high-pitched roof of which gives it a dignity of external effect far exceeding that of the chancel or nave; while of pure decorated work of the 14th cent. may be reckoned the spire with its open parapet, the S.E. chancel window of 3 lights, and apparently the clerestory windows of the nave. The cross at the west end of the nave, just visible over the roof, is a singular one; it is simply a pointed quatrefoil cut out of a square.

The earliest MONUMENTAL remains are without name or date. Part of a rich cross lies under an arch east of the sedilia; and in the S. transept is a coped coffin-lid, apparently of 13th cent. work, having under a trefoiled canopy a head with hands raised in prayer. There are more recent tablets on the walls to members of these families: Cole, Simpson, Bate, Layng (rector of Marholm), White, Wright. The Rev. Stephen White, L.L.D., whose tablet is in the chancel, was vicar of Lavington, Linc., and rector of Connington, Hunts., for 50 years. He died 1824; his descendants live in the parish. The Wrights have resided here for more than a century. On a stone to a member of this family, in 1786, Horace is quoted in attestation of his virtues,

Multis ille bonis flebilis occidit.

No inscription remains earlier than 1672. Of this date is one in the chancel of a lozenge shape in black marble;

above is a coat of arms, and a wreath in clunch surrounds these words:

Gualfridus Hawkins Thomæ Hawkins de hac Parochia Gen. Filius De Coll. Trin. Cant. olim alumnus Artium omnium præsertim Mathematicarum magister hic nuper sacerdotio fideliter functus, In Cœlis perpetuo filisiter perfuucturus Ascendit. Die Martij 8 A° 1672.*

He must have been curate to bishop Henshaw. Many stones on the floor are inscribed, but there are none very old. There is a singular rhyming one in the S. transept.

The following is on the floor within the altar rails, now in great part obliterated:

Ann Selby d^r of William Coo of Cranford wife of Michael Selby of this place, gent; who exchanged this temporary life for life immortal in the heavens December the 23^d 1695. She often repeated she had rather be a door-keeper in the house of her God than to dwell in the tents of wickedness. So these words were the subject of her funeral sermon by her own appointment.

In the CHURCHYARD is part of a Saxon cross. Near the porch is an old font. In the external S. wall of the church are two low sepulchral arches; a stone coffin, on its side, is beneath one. A good coffin lid with a raised cross is nearly concealed in the grass on the N. side. On the wall of the churchyard are remains of many more: close to the N.W. gate is a very singular one, quite perfect; and in the middle of the wall is one with a black letter inscription, but broken and imperfect.

On 4 June, 1795, the tower was struck by lightning; the clock and 'clock-house' were destroyed; and the damage being estimated at nearly 40l. a rate of 8d. was granted for the repairs. The present clock cost 84l., and was put up in 1818.

---

* This is given not quite accurately in Clement's Church Notes in the British Museum, Add. MSS. 11,425.

Peterborough S. John Baptist.

The ancient parish of Peterborough has recently been divided into four distinct parishes; the church for one of these is the old chapel of ease, at Longthorpe, while for the remaining two new churches have been built. It will follow from this that the notes referring in reality to the four parishes as now existing, will be found for the most part in the account of the mother church: to it all the registers and other documents belong, and to it exclusively all ancient memoranda refer.

The present name of the city has been attained by degrees. Originally MEDEHAMSTED, or MEDESHAMSTED, (a name that seems to describe itself, since MEDE is a meadow, HAM a home, and STEAD a place;) the revived importance of the town after the restoration of the monastery in the 10th cent. is said to have originated the name BURG, or BURGH; in Domesday book it is called BURG; from this it was changed to GILDENBURGH, or the GOLDEN BOROUGH, from the increasing wealth of the monastery; and from this to BURGH S. PETER, from the dedication of the church, and so to its present form. The variation in spelling the last syllable has apparently been guided by the fashion of the time in spelling the common word 'borough.' In a document of the 14th cent. preserved in the Bodleian, (quoted in Gent. Mag. 3 Ser. xii. 60,) giving a few characteristics of English towns, Peterborough has a bad name. 'Orgoyl de Bourk' is interpreted the 'Pride of Burgh;' and we may probably thank the lordly claims of the abbots of that period for the connection. In a well-known rhyme about the various abbeys in the neighbourhood, the same stigma is attached to this place, 'Peterborough the Proud.'

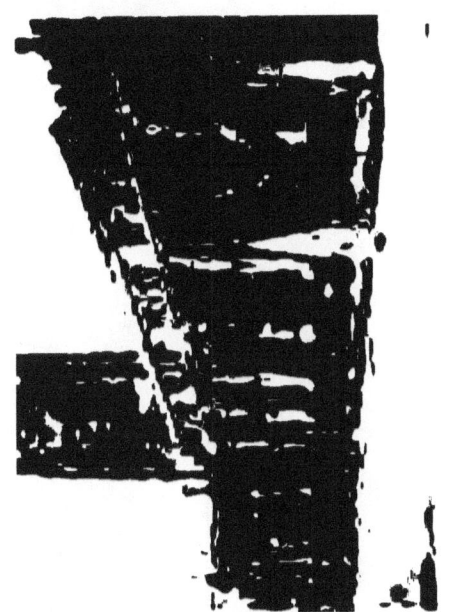

PETERBOROUGH S. JOHN BAPTIST.

The church originally stood east of the minster. The main part of the town was situated there also. The gradual removal of the better sort of houses to the west is said to be due to the erection of the bridge by abbot Martin in 1140. The rectory in 1291 was valued at 36*l*. 13*s*. 4*d*., appropriated to the sacrist of the monastery, and the vicarage at 6*l*. 13*s*. 4*d*. In the king's books this is valued at 15*l*. 13*s*. 4*d*., and the 'improved yearly value' returned to the governors of queen Anne's bounty was 66*l*. 0*s*. 5*d*. There seem to be no chantries founded in this church: but there were several guilds. Wm. Rainer, of Peterborough, whose will was dated 12 Apr. 1525, left for a mortuary his best horse or mare 'after the custom of the town,' and also among other bequests,

<small>To the reparations of the Church of Peterbor. ii^s ; to the gyld of our blessed Lady xii ; to the gyld of St George and St Jamys ii^s ; to the gyld of St John Baptist xii^d ; to the gyld of Corpus Christi xii^d ; to the gyld of the xii Apostles iii^s viii^d.</small>

The patronage of the living was in the abbey till the dissolution; afterwards in the bishop.

The REGISTERS are copious and most interesting. They commence in 1559. As is usual, the entries to the year 1600 are copied from an older book.* The extracts that follow are by no means all that possess great interest.

1561. 10 May. John Masons mayd was drowned in a pond and buryed.
12 Sep. A poor child that dyed in the street was buried.
1562. 3 July. Ellen Marshall that drowned herself in Mulloryes Pils (?) was buryed.
1572. Here left Ball to kepe the book, and then began a loss of names.
1574. Jan. Here began the Plague.
1575. 19 Jan. Julyan Scambler the wife of the Reverend father in God Edmond Scambler Lord Bisshopp of Peterburgh a godly matrone, and mother of all poor widowes and fatherless children, in Peterburgh, relieving their necessities, was buried.
6 Feb. Thomas Talbot the singing man .... was stricken by death very sodaynly and strangely.
1579. 4 Apr. Dorothy Wood ..... was drowned in the towne well.
14 Apr. John Clarke John Hutchinson and Richard Rawlins were hanged and buryed.
1581. 17 Sep. Thomas Radwell did marry Ellen Rogers at three of the clock in the afternoone.
29 Nov. Henrye Stowkes a Schoolmaster and good Bringer up of Youth was buryed.
1583. 14 June. ..... a soare fire in Westgate which burned and utterly

---

<small>* Nearly the whole of the extracts here given have been transcribed by bishop Kennett, MS. Lansd. 991. Many are also quoted by Burns in his 'Parish Registers,' and a few by Mr. Elliot, in a paper amongst those of the Arch. Soc. Northants.</small>

wasted to the number of xx houses to the great impoverishing of the Inhabitants there.

1585.	2 May.	Jollis Mr. Robinson's boy hanged himself.
1587.	31 Jan.	(buried) Agnes Williamson the wife of Sir Thomas Williamson Curate.
1592.	19 Sep.	William that was slayne with a mast of a kele.
1600.	15 Jan.	Agnes garret condemned & hanged for a witch was buried.
1606.	23 Sep.	Michael Pickeryng Gentilman was slayne by John Morton Gent. in a challenge near Borough Berry and was buryed.
1606.		Henry Reynolds came from London, where he dwelt, sicke of the plague, and being receyved by William Browne, died in his house. The said William soon after fell sicke of the plague and died; so did his sonne, his daughter, and his servant. Only his wife and her mayde escaped with Soars. The plague, brought by this means, to Peterborough, continued there till September following. (Reynolds was buried 16 Dec. 1606.)
1610.	24 Jan.	Mistress Alice Swynscoe widdowe a good Benefactor to the town of Peterborough both in the tyme of her lyfe as allso at her death.
1611.	Jan.	Bartholomew Barnabye an ould Fawlkener buryed the 5 daye above an hundred years old.
1615.	5 Sep.	Zachary Barker was buryed .... a poore Labourer mowinge of corne about the syde of Westwood was strucke dead with the thunder, and his cloaths set on fyre, which did scorche his skin in divers parts of his body.
1629.	10 Sep.	(buried) Edward Pond Gent. famous for Mathematical Science.
1634.	15 July.	(buried) Godfrey Capstaffe. A cart run over this man and broke his neck.
1640.	10 Apr.	William Broome being forth and came home late in the night was drowned.
1665.	16 Sep.	About this time the plague was supposed to be brought by a woman stranger from London, who was entertained at the Woodgrounds in the 40 acres. And they whose names have ✠ were some suspected, and some apparently dying of that disease. Most of them buried in the woodgrounds, or at Crawthorne hill, or at the pest house.
1666.		The plague broke out in May, two persons dying of it in that month. in June 57. in July 122. in August 96. of wch 12 died in a day Aug. 2. in September 60. in Octob. 49. in Novemb. 15. in Decemb. 4. in January 3. in ffebr. 2. in March 3. in Apr. following 2. & there the Plague ceased.
1727.	4 Sep.	William Mallason (a Soldier kill'd in robbing an Orchard).
1731.	20 Apr.	Thomas Macklen a Trooper.
1732.	12 Sep.	Margaret the Daughter of James and Isabella .... Black Strangers.
1734.	2 May.	A vagabond woman, whose name I cou'd not learn.
1737.	29 Aug.	Richard Huppax found dead in Dogsthorp field.
1740.	17 Apr.	Richard Paddy from Maxey falling down the Angel Stairs in Peterboro' on his way to Northamp: to vote for Mr Hanbury died on ye spot.
1754.	23 Mar.	Richard Wellton a Vagrant Clergyman.

All these, except one entry in 1581, are from the register of burials.

It will be seen from above extracts how severe were the visitations of the plague in this town. There was a visitation in 1574; another, which lasted for 9 months, in 1606; a third which lasted (apparently with some little intermission) for 19 months, in 1665—6. The necessity of the case generally required immediate burial; accordingly we find evidence not only of the bodies being interred in unfrequented places, as the 'woodgrounds' which was the scene of the first attack, or at 'the pest house,' or in 'the fenwash,' but also of the interments being effected in haste, some who died of the plague being buried in 'a closse' (close), some in an 'orchard,' some in 'their yard.' Gunton was vicar during the last and most severe attack. His signature is appended to each of the pages in the register, accompanied in each case by a thankful ejaculation for his own preservation. These are so simple and so graceful that they are here given.

1. Misericordia Dei hucusque preservatus.
2. Sub alis divinæ misericordiæ latus adhuc.
3. Bonitate Dei sospes.
4. Misericordia Dei superstes.
5. Gratia & bonitate Dei salvus.

The heronry at Milton doubtless was the scene of the exploits of the old Falconer, who died in 1611. The word 'apparently,' under date 1665, is used in a sense no longer attached to it; it there means 'obviously.' The names of Beata and Avis occur. Though these names look unfamiliar they are neither in fact disused. The former is said to survive in Wales: the latter is still borne in Essex, and very probably elsewhere. The registers are not quite perfect. The entries for April, 1604, are lost. So are those for the whole of 1641. None seem to have been made from March, 1650, to August, 1658.

The parish accounts do not seem to have been preserved for years anterior to 1782. The following items in that year shew how lately the custom of collecting money for church repairs by briefs prevailed:

27 Aug. Paid to a Brief for Drayton in Hales Church com. Salop.. 2s. 0d.
7 Oct. Paid to a Brief for Malmesbury Church com. Wilts....... 1s. 9d.

The following extracts from the town books illustrate some of the matters above referred to.

---

1. Preserved till now by the mercy of God.
2. Borne up hitherto on the wings of Divine mercy.
3. Saved by the goodness of God.
4. A survivor by the mercy of God.
5. Saved through the grace and goodness of God.

1614. Rents for stallage at the Market Cross for 1 whole year ...... 3s. 8d.
1615. Money rec^d towards the repair of the Parish Church.
Of Reginald Pancke which was given by his brother William's will to ye repair of ye Church .... 20s.
Of Robert Brightmore of Dogsthorpe being a legacy given by his father for the use of the church .... 14s.
1649. Rec^d under the market cross of several fellows for the use of the poor of Peterborough .... 8s. 6d.
1660. It is ordered that the beadle for the city of Peterborough shall monthly make diligent search in the severall wards of the s^d city after all families and new inhabitants & take notice of their report & places of abode together with what charge they bring with them. And that imm^{ly} make a report thof to the next meeting of Poor within this city. And further he is to take care that no idle persons and mendicants shall trouble or molest any persons at any public houses within the s^d city and for his own performance and observance hereof he shall be allowed Forty Shillings a year and a Blue Lyborg coat with the town Cognizance thereon. He is likewise to have care that no persons whatsoever do absent themselves Voluntary from Divine Service & Sermons upon any public days appointed by the laws of this realm.
1668. Ordered that the Boards wherewith the cleansing houses were built in the time of the late infection be delivered up to Mr. Edw. Guibbon, Mr. Hetley, & Mr. Knowles & by them laid up in a convenient place to be disposed of for such uses as the Governors or any seven of them shall think fit and approve of.
That the sum of £10 be laid out for a stamp & coinage of the public halfpenny with the town arms & the improvement thereof (to wit) for the putting out poor & fatherless children, apprentices, or other charitable uses.
1670. 4 Apr. adjourned to 7 Apr. At a meeting of Governors at 8 in the morning a note was given in by William Panck the sexton that he had rec^d into the town church three score and eleven long deals, fifty-five short deals, thirty-five boulders and spars, and one ladder, being brought from the pest house and now lying in the Bellfrey & not to be disposed of without orders.

It is possible, from the entry under 1649, that the rents at the Market Cross were appropriated to the poor. They were not of very considerable amount. In 1620, 5s. 10d.; in 1622, 5s.; in 1623, 7s.; in 1632, 7s. 10d.; in 1652, 'from the Standers under the cross,' 5s.; and other like amounts are all that were received.

The oldest document, exclusive of the registers, belonging to the church is dated 5 Eliz. It is a charter relating to Yaxley market. The Peterborough men wanted to restrict the Yaxley men to a weekly market on Thursdays between Candlemas and Whitsuntide only. The Yaxley men did not wish to be so limited, and wanted the market the whole year round. This deed confirms the Peterborough view. The large seal of queen Elizabeth is in singularly good preservation. In the vestry room is to be seen an exchequer tally of date 1622.* It is 2 ft. 3 in. long, and except at one end sliced in half. Down the edge are 17 notches and a half. A latin inscription in ink runs down the edge, legible except towards the conclusion. It is here given.

Civibus et Burgessibs de Peterborough in Com pred ex donis s' spontan' vers' tutel et defens Palatinat Hereditar Patrimon pdilecti gen'i potentiss dni Regis Jacobi............

On another side it is dated

xij° Decembr an° Regis Jacobi xx^{mo}

The transaction to which this refers is explained in receipt of which this is a copy:

11° December 1622
Received the day & yeare above written of John Harryman Farrier of Peterborough in the Countie of Northtone the some of seventeene pounds & tenne shillings of lawfull money of England by the appointme^t of Mr Gunton of Peterborough gentleman & is to be paid into the kings Exchequer for & in the Behalfe of the Inhabitants of the said towne of Peterboroughe I say Received the said some   xvij^{li} xst James Pagitt

Among other papers here are five faculties relating to the fabric.

    4 Oct. 1732. License....to build a Gallery over S. Ile of the Church.
    5 Dec. 1744. Faculty for gallery at W. end.
   21 Jan. 1756. Faculty for Burial place granted to Ja^s Delarne, Esq. at W. end of the S. Ile. Vicar to receive £1 1s. on each Interment.
  30 Aug. 1805. Faculty for erecting several seats.
  14 Sep. 1814. Faculty for confirming the sale by the churchwardens of 41 seats in the church amounting to £502.

The existence of some of these faculties made the alterations in 1820 a matter of difficulty. An act of parliament had to be obtained at great cost to legalise the changes. This act received the royal assent 14 June 1819.

In the inventory taken 23 Sept. 1552,† the place is called 'Peterbrogge,' and Robert Rawlins was 'paryshe pryste.' As might be expected the list is a long one.

---

* Accounts in the exchequer were kept by these Tallies till 1834. They were then ordered to be burnt, though many people would have purchased them for curiosities. They were burnt in the stove of the house of lords, the flues were thus over-heated, and the whole parliament house destroyed by fire. An engraving of a tally is given in Chambers' Book of Days, ii. 810; and another in Timbs' Curiosities of London, 286.
† The date of the previous inventories has been given erroneously. They were all made 6 Edw. vi.

ffirst a chalyce of sylv w^t ther patente whereof on all gylte thother pcell gylte. Itm ij sylv' censures ij shipes [1] of sylv.' Itm ij candylstycks of sylv' on crysmatoryc of sylv' one crose of syllv^r pcell gylte. Itm one pyxe of sylv' one Image of the Resurrectyon of syllv^r p gylt—a brokyn cruet of sylv.' Itm vij corpasses one cope of Red tuffhen [2] one of grene tuffcyne one of Red velvet ij of blew velvet—ij of whyte sylke ij of Red sylke and ij of blew damaske. Itm tunacles of Red tuffyen for the pste decon & subdecon w^t other necessaryes. Itm a suet of blew velvet for the pste decon & subdecon w^t all other necessaryes lacking one stoll & fannell.[3] Itm a suet of whit damaske for the pste decon & subdecon w^t all other necessaryes. Itm a suet of blew damaske decon & subdecon w^t out necessaryes. Itm a suet of Red sylke for the pste decon & subdecon w^t out necessaryes. Itm an old black suet w^t one albe lacking other necessaryes. Itm ij whyte w^t albys & other necessaryes. Itm ij vestments of gren sylke w^t albys of other collers. Itm ij tunacles of gren sylke w^t out other necessaryes. Itm ij lyttle copes of gren cruell for boyes. Itm on croscloth of yalow sylke & ij old paynted clothes for the same. Itm iiij old surpleses for the prestes & iiij for clarks. Itm xij olde towels.[5] Itm v alt' clothes of lynen and iij other alt' clothes for other alt.' xvj old paynted clothes for the sepultum Rede & other plass. ij horse clothes one of blew damaske a nother of dyv^{rs} colers. Itm vestments for O^r Ladye alter one of blue damaske wth all necessaryes one of Rede brydys satten laking necessaryes one of grene brydys satten w^t all necessaryes & one of white fustyan w^t all necessaryes. Item for hanging at the alter syde ij for the highe alter one paynted a nother white chamblet ij for Saynt Jonys alter on of tapstery worcke thother paynted ij for o^r Lady alter one of tapstere worcke thother paynted. Itm v Great Bells yn the styple and one sanctus bell one handbell v sacring bells. Itm ij old copes of white damaske iiij copes of grene cruell ij blew copes of sylke w^t byrds on them lyke unto doves. Itm ij vestments for children one rede sylke a nother of grene cruell. Itm a vestment of old white damaske w^t a stoell & a phannell[3] lacking an albe. Itm ij tunacles of the same suets lacking albys stolls & phannells. Itm the sylv' crose was sold by the cosent of the moost parte of the honeste of the towne towarde the charge of ther chirche that was brokyn w^t a pynacle fallyng on the chirche & other necessaryes—to one Dyxon a goldsmythe in the chepsyde to the value of xiij^{li} xiij^{sol} iiij^d.

The altars herein mentioned prove the existence of two at least besides the high altar.

Some of the sacramental PLATE is costly. It is none so old as the above inventory. It has mostly been presented. Mrs. Mary Towers gave a silver paten: a fine flagon is the 'guift' of a donor whose name is skilfully concealed in a cipher, but seems to resolve itself also into the name of Towers: John Dickenson,* in 1703, gave a large silver flagon: and a silver-gilt paten, dated 1735, was given by Maria Walsham.

A list of benefactors can be made out from the boards hung up in the vestry room. Amongst the more important are the bequests of bishop White of 240*l.* for

---

1. Ships, i. e. incense boats.
2. Tiffany, a very thin silk.
3. Fanon, or priest's maniple, worn on the left wrist.
4. Crewel, fine spun worsted used in embroidery.
5. A word in the Castor inventory interpreted to mean 'bowls,' seems from the context to refer more likely to 'towels,' as in the present one.

* He left 20*l.* by will for the purchase of this flagon.

the annual distribution of 10*l.* among 20 poor people who can recite the Lord's prayer, the creed, and the commandments distinctly;* of Rob. Orme for 12 poor people in Lent the interest of 150*l.*; of 100*l.* from John Dickenson for old people; of Ed. English for 40 poor people the interest of 100*l.*; of the same sum from Jas. Lowry for the same purpose. There have been also several legacies of 50*l.* for the poor. Wyldbore's charity, for the poor, the ringers, and a sermon, being distributed according to the will on 15 March, has caused that day to be known in the parish as Wyldbore's day. The school founded by Thos. Deacon is the most valuable of all. Samuel Brocksopp, 1841, left 1000*l.* to the feoffees of this charity, the interest to be distributed half-yearly among the poor. The old wills relating to the church are innumerable.

In 1480, Joh. Tydde left to each of the guilds (already enumerated) 6*s.* 8*d.* except 3*s.* 4*d.* only to that of Corpus Christi, 6*s.* 8*d.* to the bells, 3*s.* 4*d.* to repair the high road, and 6*s.* 8*d.* for the bridge; in 1495, Tho. Mason left to the three guilds two tenements in 'Reten rowe;' in 1498, the sum of 3*d.* was thought a fitting legacy, as appears from the following, which is given in the original as a specimen, all the wills about this date being in latin:

1498. In crastino assumptionis B. Marie Virg. Ego Johes Gregory de Burgo S. Petri . . . corpus sepeliend' in cemeterio Petri & Pauli cum mortuario meo secundum usum ville. Item lego tribus gildis ibidem infra villam Burgi videl. beate Marie Virg. Scti Johis Bapt. & Sctorum Jacobi & Georgij, cuilibet eorum iii^d.

Will. Stevynson, whose will is dated 1 Oct. 1544, had clearly the desire to forget nobody. He bequeaths his

sole to almighty god oure lady and all the hole company of heven my body to be buried in the cathedrall churche and mynster of Peterborough between the sepultures of Master Marshall and John Oddam. I bequeth to the church of Peterb. 12^d, for my mortuarye according to the custome of ye countie, to the hic aulter for tythes forgotten 3^s 4^d, to the reparations of the paryshe church of Peterb. 3^l 6^s 8^d, to be delyvered to the churchwardens for the use of the said paryshe churche. to the reparations of the brige of Peterborough 3^l 6^s 8^d. to every gylde of the said churche 12^d. Item I bequeth to be done at my buryall daye seventh daye and thyrtye daye and for other ordinary charges 6^l 13^s 4^d I will that a Dirige wth a Masse of Requiem to be done in the College by the hole Quere. Item I bequeth to my lord bishop 8^s to his Chapleyn 3^s 4^d every Prebend 3^s 4^d every Canon 20^d every Clarke singer 8^d every Querester 2^d and to the

---

* The terms of the will are explicit; and some difficulty is occasionally found in complying with them.

Vergers and Sextons 4ˢ to every poore house in the said towne 4ᵈ Item I will that a Dirige wᵗʰ masse of Requiem to be song in the paryshe churche of Peterborough with the vicar and his company. And I bequeth to the vicar 12ᵈ and every preste 8ᵈ every clerke 4ᵈ and the children 2ᵈ .

VICARS.

1229 Will. de Watford.	1504 Will. Tempest.
Hugo.	1510 Tho. Wilkinson.
1264 Hen. de Wermingham.	1517 David Smyth.
1269 Ric. de Braibroc.	1522 Ralph Bolham, S.T.P. r.
1290 Ric. de Walmesford.	1542 *Ric. Kay, A.M., r.²
1330 Walter de Horsham.	1555 *Tho. Williamson, d.
Joh. Trygg.	1592 Ed. Wager, A.M., r.
1353 Tho. Daumo.	1618 *Rob. Thirlby, A.M., d.³
1359 Rog. Fraunceys.	1620 *Paul Panke, d.⁴
1372 Steph. Kynesman.	1660 *Simon Gunton, A.M., r.⁵
1373 Adam Warrok.	1667 *Geo. Gascoigne, d.
Tho. Cupper.	1680 Jos. Johnson, S.T.B.
1398 *Joh. Anketill.	1685 David Waldron, A.M., d.
Joh. Boton.	1687 Joh. Gilbert, A.M., r.⁶
1433 Will. Brewster, r.	1698 Isaac Gregory, A.M.
1439 Joh. Hare.	1707 *Will. Waring, A.M.⁷
1467 Rob. Bayston, L.L.B.	1726 *Tho. Marshall, A.M., d.
1468 Joh. Wylde, r.	1748 Joh. Fisher, A.M.
1460 Ric. Chapman, r.	1760 *Joh. Image, A.M., d.⁸
1469 Joh. Carter, r.¹	1786 *Joh. Weddred, d.
1469 Joh. Forman.	1806 Jos. Steph. Pratt, L.L.B., r.⁹
1479 Joh. Welles.	1833 Joh. James, A.M., r.¹⁰
1497 Joh. Gryndell.	1850 Edm. Davys, A.M., r.¹¹
1499 Joh. Affen.	1865 Will. Hill, A.M.¹²

The CHURCH was built early in the 15th cent. It had before stood, as already mentioned, east of the minster. In 1401, the parishioners complained to the bishop of Lincoln that their church was too far off, and the waters frequently prevented their attending the service, and prayed for its removal to a more convenient spot. A full account of the event is given in Bridges, ii. 543. The

---

* Buried at Peterborough.
1. Held variety of preferments. Rect. of Rushton, 1451, of Irthlingborough, 1453, of Woodford, 1462, of Creton, 1486, of Cranford, 1487, of Achurch, 1502, and of Overston, 1504.
2. Made preb. of Peterborough on resigning the living.
3. Master of the King's School.
4. Died 1658; but his successor could not obtain possession till 1660. Mr. Willson took charge of the church during part of the commonwealth time, he was ejected at the restoration, and is mentioned by Calamy in these terms: 'a man of excellent ministerial Skill and Ability: Of signal Piety and Diligence in his Work, and extraordinary Success; doing good to multitudes.'
5. Preb. of Peterborough, 1646, afterwards rect. of Fiskerton, Linc. and vic. of Pightesley. He was the historian of the cathedral. The abp. of Canterbury gave him the living.
6. Author of an answer to the bp. of London's 'Exposition of the Catholicke Faith,' 1686, and of 'Reflections' on his pastoral letter.
7. Master of the King's School, precentor, and rect. of Alwalton.
8. Also precentor of the cathedral.
9. Preb. of Peterborough, and vic. of Maxey. Buried at Ware.
10. Now S.T.P., preb. of Peterborough, and inc. of Glinton; formerly fellow of S. John's, Oxford, Head Master of Oundle School, vic. of Maxey, and rect. of Peakirk.
11. Now inc. of Trinity Church, Leicester.
12. Hon. can. of Peterborough; lately inc. of Trinity Church, Leicester.

bishop gave his license, afterwards confirmed by pope Boniface. The new fabric was completed in 1407, and in that year opened with much solemnity by abbot Genge. But for this date being ascertained, the details of the work, which are of advanced perpendicular character, would have probably assigned a date several years later. The church was rebuilt at the cost of the parishioners, and the abbey gave towards the work the nave of S. Thomas-a-Becket's chapel, the chancel being left entire. It is agreed that the present grammar school is this chancel. The chapel of S. Thomas of Canterbury was begun, according to the chronicle, by Waterville and finished by Benedict, who died 1193. It is manifest that of this erection there are no remains whatever. The date of the existing chancel cannot be earlier than 1350 or 1360; for the side windows are clearly of transitional date, although the east window has flowing net tracery. It seems, therefore, likely that Benedict's chancel was destroyed in order to build a handsomer one, his nave (probably transitional Norman) being left. And so when the rebuilding of the parish church was agreed upon, the abbey might have consented to give the old nave to further the work, but would not permit the new chancel, which had not been standing much more than 40 years, to be destroyed. The church has a chancel with aisles, nave with aisles, W. tower, and S. porch. Both nave and chancel have clerestories, containing in all ten windows of three lights each. The N. door is blocked up. There are entrances to both chancel aisles, and to the tower, externally; there is also a W. door. The E. window is of five lights; all the windows in the aisles are of 4 lights, having plain intersecting tracery. Although the tower, nave and chancel arches, and S. porch, are certainly parts of the original fabric, it seems hard to believe that the aisle windows and clerestories have not been changed, if not rebuilt. The chancel is embattled: two niches are placed in the east wall. The nave has 7 lofty arches, and the chancel is of 2 bays with a blank space beyond. The chancel arch is very spacious, so are the arches from the nave aisles to those of the chancel. The noble proportions of this fine church are sadly marred by the untasteful arrangement of the interior. The ancient open roof of the nave probably still remains above the present ceiling: the roofs to the aisles seem destroyed, as the ceilings there are disposed in so original a manner that no gothic roof can have been adapted to them. The galleries are heavy; they lean upon the pillars of the nave. The pews throughout, though not so offensively high as in many places, are not arranged so as to economise space. Of the set of free seats in the middle it is sufficient to record that it exists. The floor, except one shallow step to the sanctuary, is on one level. The aisles extend westward as far as the tower, but the last bay is not open to the church. At the W. end of the S. aisle is the vestry-room for parochial meetings. Here is a large picture of Charles I. Two curious specimens of ancient embroidery are to be seen here. They are worked up into a cushion, but were once part of an altar-cloth or else of a vestment. They are similar, though not identical. In each case the work is in the form of a cross about 2 feet in length, the width of each arm 5 or 6 inches. In the centre is the figure of our Lord on the Cross, and in the arms of the cross are angels bearing cups. Above, in one, is a dove; in the other, a dove upheld by the Father represented as the Ancient of Days. One has a skull at the foot of the cross. In the division between the aisle and this room is an arch buttress to support the tower. Another exists on the north. This is mentioned by Essex, an architect of the last century. He made sketches and notes of this church[*] in the year 1759. A few of his notes are quoted here. It will be seen he assumes a former church to have existed on the same spot: but of this there is no evidence.

> The settling of ye pillars from ye perpendicular seems to be owing to their Building ye part on ye old foundations and part on ye new in order to enlarge the middle Isle of the Church. The old part being well settled stood firm, but ye new giving way occasion'd ye settlement of the pillars in the manner they now appear. After the settlement of ye pillars happend the upper walls were rebuilt perpendicular and at the same time arch buttress were added within ye Arches adjoin^g to ye Tower to prevent its falling.

---

[*] Brit. Mus. Add. MSS. 6769.

The present appearance of the clerestory certainly confirms the idea of its having been materially altered. And indeed when we remember how much the cathedral suffered in the middle of the 17th cent., we should almost expect the parish church to share its ruin. We have evidence too * that such was the fact, for in 1641, the chancel was 'in decay.' In 1791, says Bridges,

At the entrance from the church into the chancel are eight stalls of oak, after the cathedral manner.

No traces of these remain. He speaks also of some wainscot of Norway oak behind the altar. This has been removed. Mr. Walcott, præcentor of Chichester, in his 'Memorials of Peterborough,' speaks of a picture by sir R. K. Porter, of the 'Transfiguration' as if still remaining in the church. It has been sold. At the east end is a little attempt at colouring. A small room at the end of the N. aisle has been made into a vestry: above it is a pew. The S. porch is a very fine one. It has a stone groined roof, the bosses being well carved, the centre one having a crucifixion. A boldly carved animal is seated on the apex of the roof: the porch stands well out to the street. There is a room above it, to which access is gained by a staircase in the N.W. corner. It is used for the library of the book society, and contains about 3000 volumes. This society has been in existence upwards of a century. Archdeacon Neve was chiefly the founder.

The TOWER at the W. end is fine. It is embattled and has pinnacles with vanes. The clock faces are placed in an unsightly fashion, half above and half below the parapets. The belfry windows are large, of four lights each, transomed. There is a peal of eight BELLS, and a single smaller one, all inscribed. †

1. THE LORD TO PRAISE MY VOICE I'LL RAISE. 1808.
2. WILLIAM DOBSON, DOWNHAM, NORFOLK, FOUNDER. 1808.

---

* Brit. Mus. MS. Lansd. 1026.
† The inscriptions on the peal of eight are from a paper kindly lent: they are given also in Lukis's book on bells.

3. LONG LIVE KING GEORGE THE THIRD, WM. DOBSON FECIT. 1808.
4. GIVE NO OFFENCE TO THE CHURCH. WILLIAM DOBSON FECIT. 1808.
5. OUR VOICES SHALL WITH JOYFUL SOUND MAKE HILLS AND VALLEYS ECHO ROUND. 1808.
6. W^M ELLIOTT, AND FRENCH LAWRENCE, ESQ^{RS}, MEMBERS OF PARLIAMENT FOR THIS CITY, DONORS. 1808.
7. EARL FITZWILLIAM, VISCOUNT MILTON, AND THE REV^D. W^M. STRONG, D.D., ARCHDEACON OF NORTHAMPTON, DONORS. 1808.
8. THE REV^D. JOSEPH STEPHEN PRATT, L.L.B., PREBENDARY OF THE CATHEDRAL, VICAR, STEPHEN SHEPHERD, W^M. SALMAN, AND W^M. SIMPCOX, CHURCH WARDENS, 1808.
9. W HAWKINGS TOBIE NORRIS CAST ME 1675.

The last is the smallest. It is now used for the 'firebell'; its diameter does not exceed 2 feet.

There are no MONUMENTS of very great interest. The floor is literally paved with gravestones, but many are not in their original positions. The earliest seems to be one in the S. aisle, 1731. There are numerous wall tablets. At the W. end are many to the Delarne family, at the close of the last century. Tablets occur with the following names and dates; of more than one date to the same name, the earliest only is given. Cox, 1703; Sambrook, 1759; Dr. Balguy, 1767 (these two on the piers of the chancel arch); Warriner, 'Late a Native of this City And one of its ancient Inhabitants,' 1767; Bowker, 1782; Image, 20 years vicar, 1786; Squire, 1786; Freeman, 1795; Beharrell, 1831; Brocksopp, a benefactor, 1841. Within the altar rails are two large monuments, one on each side, of different coloured marbles; that on the south is to John and Elizabeth Wyldbore, who died 1755 and 1748; that on the north to Matthew Wyldbore, their son, of Trin. Coll. Camb., twice member for the city, 'many years a very useful member of the hon^{ble} corporation of the great level of

LONGTHORPE.

the fens,' who died 1781. At the W. end of the N. aisle is a mural tablet which has been twice used, once for Roger Cooke, and once for Mary widow of some one else, one inscription being painted over the other, the decay of the second partially revealing the first. The burial ground in Cowgate, now disused, was acquired by the parish in 1804.

1358859

Longthorpe.

Till 1850 this village was a chapelry to Peterborough. In ancient records it is written simply THORP; in Domesday it is TORP. The name is a very common one. The word 'thorp' for a village is in constant use—'by twenty thorps'—and it was given frequently to the villages lying near large towns. The Rev. I. Taylor has pointed out that 'thorps' indicate always Danish as opposed to Norwegian settlements, which were 'thwaites.' The word *thwaite*, he says,*

occurs forty-three times in Cumberland, and not once in Lincolnshire, while *thorpe*, the chief Danish test-word, which occurs sixty-three times in Lincolnshire, is found only once in Cumberland.

In Lincolnshire, though spelt as in the present case, the name is generally pronounced 'throp.'

The same thing has happened here as at the mother church. The chapel was in an inconvenient situation, from the gradual removal of the dwellings from its vicinity, and upon the petition of the inhabitants, the old chapel was taken down and rebuilt in its present position. This was done 'at the instance and charges of Sir William de Thorp,' with the permission of abbot Robert de Sutton.† We are thus able within a very few years to assign its date, for Robert de Sutton was abbot 1262—73. Mr. J. H. Parker, in describing this church

---

* Taylor's 'Words and Places,' p. 159.
† Bridges, vol. ii. p. 572, quoting Reg. Kirketon, 128: also MS. Lansd. 1027, p. 119.

in 1861, from its architecture only, fixed its date at 'about 1260.' This is an excellent instance of how near the study of architecture enables the student to approximate to the date of ancient buildings.

The old chapel was dedicated to S. BOTOLPH, and it is reasonable to suppose that the present one has the same dedication. Among the provisions for remunerating the vicar of Peterborough was this, that he was to enjoy all the oblations in S. Botolph's chapel. Bridges to this says,

Of this chapel there are no remains, nor is the situation of it now known. It is mentioned, however, in a deed of *William*, vicar of *Burgh*, for the exchange of land lying between *Westwoode* and the chapel of St. *Botolph*, in the time of Abbot *Andreas*, who died about the year 1200.

There can be little doubt that the old chapel of Longthorpe is here referred to. Although used for 6 centuries as a chapel to Peterborough, there is reason for supposing that it was not consecrated till the 17th cent. A small brass is kept in the S. aisle which was formerly in the chancel. This appears from notes taken in the year 1731,* 'at yᵉ entrance into yᵉ chancel, fixed to yᵉ Pavement this inscription' is on a brass plate about a foot square.

Cum refectum et Deo (cœmeterij gratia) sacratum hoc fuit sacellum Anno. Dom. 1683 hoc primum Auxilij autimanu posuit saxum Gulielmus filius natu maximus Georgij Leafield Armigeri sub quo eodem saxo a dedicatione ipse primus corpore tenui sepultus erat Decemb. 21 Anno. Dom. 1685 Etatis 8°.

If this may be trusted, some repairs were effected in 1683, the object being to have the chapel consecrated in order that the inhabitants might have right of burial. These repairs possibly included re-flooring the church; at any rate a 'first stone' was laid in the chancel by a little boy, William eldest son of Mr. Geo. Leafield, then in his 6th year; who was himself, 2 years later, the first to be buried in the newly consecrated building. If the word 'autimanu' is copied correctly by Clement, for it is not now legible, its meaning will be clearly 'with his own hand;' but it is a barbarous compound, half Latin, and half Greek.

---

* Frit. Mus. Add. MSS. 11,425. The brass now is too much worn to be entirely deciphered: it is in simple Italic characters; but by the help of the copy, itself manifestly not quite reliable (for instance the words 'Deo' and 'primum' are both omitted), its general purport at least can be gathered.

The inventory of church goods here given proves that 130 years before the above repairs the chapel was indeed in need of restoration. Its one bell was cracked. A broken handbell had been sold to defray the expense of glazing the windows, the insecurity of which had enabled robbers to steal some of the vestments and furniture of the altar. This was in 1552.

<blockquote>
The Inventory of all mane off vestiments ornaments iouills[1] and bells belonging to the chapell there........
ffirste a chalis wth a paten pcell gilt in ye handis of the said Mr. Villars[2]
Itm iij verry olde vestements of bawdekyn[3]
Itm an olde crackyd bell
Itm where there was at the last inventory ij olde albes and ij latten candelsticks the same hath byn sith that tyme stolne by reason the chapell windoes were unglasyd
Itm a broken handbell solde for xxij^d towade the glasing of the windoes
</blockquote>

The list of incumbents, though brief, is perfect. The registers are of course only kept here since 1850, and are in no way remarkable.

INCUMBENTS.

1850   Thos. W. Were, A.B., r.
1854   Rob. Shapland C. Blacker, A.B., r.[4]
1860   Arth. Joh. Skrimshire, M.D.

The CHURCH is entirely of one period, in the early English style, of date 1262—73. Mr. Paley has some excellent remarks on it.

<blockquote>
Its plan is as simple as its construction; a nave and two aisles, with a spacious and tolerably lofty chancel. Built of coarse rubble, without a buttress or a string-course in any part of it, and having everywhere, except at the east and the west ends, its original windows of two plain but effective lancet lights, this church affords an instructive instance of what may be done in church building where means are very limited. It would easily hold three hundred people, and it might easily be built for six or seven hundred pounds.
</blockquote>

Upon entering the first thing that is noticed is the ample space. The nave is of three bays, and the piers are exceedingly light, being positively less than 15 inches in diameter. They stand on square bases. There is no chancel arch, nor marks of any screen. The windows are double lancets, trefoiled; except at the N.W. and S.W. of the chancel, where are single low side windows, and at the east and west ends. At the east is a poor insertion of three lights, transomed, all of one height, cinquefoiled in the heads. At the west the original pair

---

1. Jewels (?)   2. An inhabitant.   3. Baudekin, baldachin, or baldakin, a rich cloth, 'gold warp and silver woof,' so called from Baldacio or Babylon.
4. Now rect. of Marholm.

of lancets has been enlarged. The early windows have a broad splay. At the east end are two brackets. To the north is a square aumbry, which had a thick door; to the south a trefoiled piscina with stone shelf and oblong bason. There were altars also in each aisle; the brackets remain; that in the N. aisle being a very fine one. Many of the tall lancets are blocked in the lower parts. There are N. and S. doors. The seats do not extend west of these doors, and the great space thus left vacant adds much to the dignity of the interior. The open seats may be with great likelihood assigned to the restoration in 1683. The font is peculiar and not worthy of imitation. It is an alabaster mortar let into stone. It stands by the S.W. pier. Out of this same pier below there extends a twisted iron bar.

A small pencil plan of this church was made by Kerrich* in 1820. From it there seems to have been a symmetrical design: a quadrant of a circle touching one aisle wall, with the extremities of its arc in the centres of the east and west walls, would have its centre in the other aisle wall. These measurements are there given: length of chancel, 25 ft. $0\frac{1}{2}$ in., of nave, 47 ft. $3\frac{1}{2}$ in.; breadth of chancel, 25 ft. 4 in., of nave and aisles, 44 ft. 9 in. It is thus seen that each arch is upwards of 15 ft. in span, while the thin circular supporting piers are not so many inches. This is one reason for the light appearance of the interior. The bases and capitals are moulded well. The hoodmould over the arches comes down to a simple point, without a finial of any sort. The roof is concealed by a ceiling. Externally both nave and aisles are covered by one roof: inside the aisles the arrangement of the timbers for this purpose is peculiar. The stone brackets towards the nave are not indications that the roof has been heightened, but, as Mr. Paley has pointed out, they supported a wall-plate for the aisle roof to rest upon.

The modern belfry is no improvement upon the original. A western bellcot has been partly destroyed, and a wooden erection raised upon it. The apertures for the

---

* Brit. Mus. Add. MSS. 6738.

bells are now glazed. It is believed there is but one BELL: the combination of timbers above the present ceiling, itself only to be reached through a ricketty trap door by a lofty insecure ladder, renders it difficult to ascertain the fact for certain.

As there have been burials here for not more than 180 years, it will not be expected that there are many MONUMENTS of interest. Besides the brass already given there is another very similar one, to the 2 children of 'Matthew Booth, Writing M^{tr} and Dorothy his Wife,' dated 1709 and 1713. The earliest stone seems to be one in the nave, now displaced, 1692. It has only initials. In the S. aisle are two marble tablets. One is to Mrs. Frances St. John, spinster, daughter of sir Francis St. John, of Thorpe, 1704, which has this verse, above a coat of arms on a lozenge:

"All that e'er graced a Soul from Heaven she drew,
"And took back with her as an Angel's Due."

She was aged 82 years. The other is without date, in Latin, to John and Mary Bernard, concluding with this line:

Piorum reliquiis ut parcas, enixe rogo.*

In 1731, as appears by Clement's notes, there were two achievements in the S. aisle: one was 'St. John... impaling Gold,' for Mary, wife of sir Francis St. John, bart., and daughter of sir Nat. Gold, kt.: the other was 'St. John...with an escutcheon of pretence, Wakeringe ...impaling Foorth,' for Fr. St. John, esq.

The parish possesses a fine specimen of ancient domestic architecture. An engraving of it is given in Parker's Domestic Architecture, vol. i. 153. It is of the same date as the church. It is said by Mr. Parker to be an ordinary fortified house of the period, probably of a square plan with corner towers, one of which remains. The lower story is vaulted. The windows have shouldered heads. The pyramidal roof is modern, but it rests on the inner edge of the wall, as did the ancient one.

In the village there is the base of a wayside cross.

* 'I earnestly entreat you to spare the remains of the pious.' Compare this with the inscription at Marholm, given on page 9; and with the following excellent rhyme on a brass, dated 1656, in the north aisle of the church of Fornham All Saints, Suffolk: 'Let noe man steale away this brasse but hee whoe knowes himselfe unworthie memorye.'

Peterborough S. Mark.

The view of this church from the Lincoln road is striking and very effective. The tower and spire, placed in an unusual position, have been wisely brought close to the road: the whole height is thus visible, not shortened by the line of nave roof abutting on it, while the nave itself looks longer from the last bay being not used for the lower stage of the tower. The difference in the height of the nave and chancel is a pleasing feature in the composition. There are two main blots in the design. The chief is the spire itself, which is thin and meagre in comparison with the tower: the parapet at its foot is cut off at the corners, so as to form an irregular octagon, and this perhaps brings the defect into more prominent notice. The treatment also of the dormer windows in the roof, which form a quasi clerestory, is unsatisfactory. With these exceptions there is here a good example of an inexpensive district church. The grounds in which it stands are prettily laid out; there is no churchyard for burials. Mr. Ellis was the architect.

INCUMBENTS.
1856   Chas. Campe, r.[1]
1860   Sam. W. Merry, A.M.

The CHURCH consists of chancel with aisles, nave with aisles and S. porch, N.E. tower and spire, with vestry beneath. The whole is built in the flowing decorated style, though it would be difficult to find in ancient examples precedents for some of the forms of tracery here adopted. There are three windows in the nave roof on each side, each with a gable. The gables of nave and chancel are surmounted with crosses. Above the S. porch is a text, with the date of building the church, 1856. The nave is of five bays; the piers are octagonal, and the arches, which are rather broad, are plain. The side windows are all low, they are mostly of two lights

---

1. Now inc. of Christ Chapel, S. John's Wood.

PETERBOROUGH S. MARK.

with tracery; single lights are in the chancel aisles, and west of the nave aisles, and in each aisle is one window of three lights. The east has five and the west window four lights: the last mentioned is filled with stained glass, 'the blazon of episcopacy,' and contains the coats of arms of the 28 sees of the country. All the windows are partly glazed with tinted glass. Near the S. door is the font; it is octagonal, the faces carved, and stands on a stem with flowers carved on its edges, having four thin marble shafts. The nave roof is plain but of good pitch. The wall pieces are supported on rather large stone corbels, richly carved beneath: they are all different; two have angels, the rest foliage, animals, or fruit; one in the chancel has grapes and ears of corn, and one in the nave, perhaps the prettiest of all, has passion-flowers. The chancel roof is divided into squares, and is polygonal. Between the chancel and its aisles, and between these aisles and the nave aisles, are low indescribable arches. In the N. chancel aisle is placed the organ. The aisles do not extend so far east as the chancel does. In the S. wall of the chancel is an arcade with five doubly trefoiled lights: these have stained glass in patterns. The chancel arch, above which overlooking the chancel roof is a very small window, is supported on stone corbels terminating in heads. There are two steps to the chancel and one to the sanctuary. At the south of the chancel steps is the reading-desk, facing north and west; at the north is the pulpit (somewhat high), a wooden one on a stone stem. Besides the S. porch there is a W. door, an entrance for the organ in the N. chancel aisle, another for the vestry, and another for the tower. The belfry, which contains one BELL, has on each side two acute windows, separate, doubly trefoiled; the spire has near its base four gabled lights similar to those in the arcade S. of the chancel; and nearer the summit are eight small openings. There are low open seats throughout, and the church was built to hold 660 worshippers. The internal dimensions are these: length of chancel, 33 ft. 8 in., of nave, 76 ft. 6 in. Breadth of nave or chancel, 25 ft., of the aisles, 10 ft. 8 in.

Opposite the church is a building which claims notice, being strictly ecclesiastical. It is a tythe barn in excellent order, of best 13th cent. work. On the east side are two large porches. The roof is supported by massive timbers, whose arrangement resembles a wooden nave and aisles. Another large barn, called the Sacristan's barn, of cruciform shape, was demolished for the railway works.

Peterborough S. Mary.

The design of the church includes a N. aisle with W. tower and spire, yet to be built. The architect was Mr. Christian. Though incomplete it is in many respects admirable. There is a warmth imparted to the interior by a judicious use of colouring, and by laying red and white bricks in alternate rows: there is a simple dignity about the east end partly due to the elevation of the altar, partly to the stained windows round the apse, and partly to the colouring.

There is no burial ground attached to the church. The patronage was in earl Fitzwilliam's hands. It is now in process of transfer to the dean and chapter by exchange. There has been but one appointment.

INCUMBENT.

1856 Will. Rob. Thomas, A.M.

The CHURCH has a nave, with S. aisle, short apsidal chancel, S. door without porch, small vestry E. of the aisle, with a door near. The main entrance is gabled, far above the height of the aisle walls, and at the ridge of the gable is a small bellcot. The nave roof is continued over the aisle, at an angle without the intervention of clerestory, or parapet; this makes the aisle wall very low; and the great expanse of roof would be unsightly

PETERBOROUGH S. MARY.

were it not broken into by the gable of the S. door and the pyramidal top of the bellcot, and by a corresponding gable further east. This latter is for a larger window than the aisle walls would admit. The church is built of rough gray stones of two tints, with Ketton stone for the dressings. The nave is divided from its aisle by an arcade of 5 bays; the piers are circular, having large square capitals and carved foliage beneath. These are of stone, but the arches are of brick, red and white. To the top of the capitals is not more than 6 feet. The arch to the west window, and that to the chancel, have also bricks alternately red and white; the former a double row. The chancel arch is nearly as broad as the nave itself. The inner order is of stone; its edge has leaves and flowers running to the top. Round the whole is a text. Texts also are painted the whole length of the nave under the roof on both sides. The roofs are plain, the wooden rafters, which are slight, being visible; there are small hammerbeams, the wall pieces being supported on carved stone corbels; in the chancel the ribs radiate to the centre from the apse, and the divisions thus made are enriched with a little colour. The chancel is ascended by three steps; there is one more to the sanctuary, and a footpace beyond. The prayer-desk is at the S. of the chancel arch; at the N. is the pulpit, a circular one of stone, with good carving. A wooden lettern stands in the nave for the lessons. The seats are all open. Their arrangement, for saving of space, is excellent. They have wooden floors, but the rest of the church is tiled. The windows are of various designs. At the west are three large lancets of unequal height under one arch: two windows on the N. and one on the S. have three trefoiled lancets, the centre light being doubly trefoiled. Others are, in the S. aisle, square-headed, with shouldered cusps, of two and three lights; on the N. side of the nave, under the constructional arches left for the N. aisle, are two windows, each of two doubly trefoiled lights, with geometrical figures in the head. In the apse are six short lancets, twice trefoiled, all of which have stained glass. Though presented at different times they are of one character, and are very pleasing. Each light has one scene, and an explanatory text. From N. to S. the subjects are these: 1. Jairus' Daughter: 2. Good Samaritan: 3. Noli me tangere: 4. Crucifixion: 5. Ascension: 6. Last Supper. The last one is a memorial to the late earl Fitzwilliam, described beneath as the 'founder of the parish.' Two windows in the body of the church have stained glass. One has for subject Christ blessing children: the other has two lights, in one the Bridegroom coming, in the other, Christ preaching of the lilies of the field. A small organ is placed at the west. Near the S. door is a circular font. Round the edge is a text. It stands on six polished marble shafts. Externally a cross surmounts the roof between chancel and nave. Round the arch of the S. door are these words: 'Enter into His gates with thanksgiving, and into His courts with praise.'

Amongst the sacramental PLATE are two chalices of queen Anne's reign. One has the sacred monogram with a flaming heart beneath, and this inscription, 'Deo servatori sacrum.' These, with both patens, are of silver. The larger paten is handsome, and has this inscription:

Deo in Ecclesia Beatæ Mariæ Virginis, Petriburg. Pentecoste, A.D. 1858.

The style of the building is foreign, rather than English, and may perhaps be called Continental first pointed. Since its consecration many improvements and many additions have been made: and we hope before very long to see the completion of the whole, by the erection of the north aisle and spire.

PETERBOROUGH CATHEDRAL

Peterborough Cathedral.

The limits and scope of these notes admit only of the merest outline of the cathedral history. Learned and laborious antiquaries, as well as competent architects, have given us works, the simple enumeration of which would here exhaust nearly all our space. This sketch is therefore attempted not to supply a known want, but because a book on the churches of the neighbourhood, would be incomplete without a notice of the most noble and most glorious of them all. The notes on the cathedral will be arranged upon the same plan as those on the churches. It is unnecessary to subjoin a list of authorities for the admitted historical facts.

The present church is the third that has occupied the same spot. In the year 656,* the first was founded by Peada, king of the Mercians, brother to Kyneburgha, the foundress of Castor. He died before the work was finished. The first abbot who had charge of the house, being a man of eminence and wealth, the monastery was soon in a flourishing state. It was entirely destroyed by the Danes in 870, during the abbacy of Hedda the 7th abbot, who was himself with his monks slain in the attack.† For a century this desolation remained. The second church, founded by king Edgar, was ready in the year 971. Abp. Dunstan attended the king when he visited the restored church. This building was greatly injured by fire in another attack of the Danes, 1069; but its final destruction was due to an accident in 1116. The chroniclers give a curious story in connection with this accident. The next year was commenced the fabric which now exists. It took in all 120 years to build, and was consecrated 4 Oct., 1237. The western tower, spires and porch, the lantern, and the new building, were not

---

* Some of these dates are still matter of controversy.
† For a notice of the stone usually thought to commemorate this slaughter, see p. 11.

then erected. All the conventual buildings had been destroyed with the church, otherwise possibly less time would have sufficed. The building proceeded from east to west. Four abbots were engaged on the work; John de Sais, Martin, Waterville, and Benedict. This is exclusive of the west front. The nave was thus formed by gradual advances to the west: for any thing that appears to the contrary these steps may have been fitful and irregular. But happily a unity of design is adhered to throughout, although at the time of the erection of the most westerly bays the style of architecture mostly in use was becoming lighter; a fact which transpires in the various details of this part of the church, as in the bases of the piers, the heads in the wall arcades, and elsewhere. Two very able works on the architectural history of the cathedral have been published by Mr. Paley and Mr. Poole. No student of the fabric can do without them. One or two of the many positions established by their researches are most interesting. The nave was meant to terminate with two towers three bays from the present west front. It is not certain if both or either of these towers were actually built. But indications that they were at least contemplated are manifest. Mr. Paley says,*

> The third pillar from the west end on each side is considerably larger and wider than any others; and it also projects further into the aisles. The arch also, springing from it westward, is of a much greater span. The opposite vaulting shafts, in the aisle walls, are brought forward, beyond the line of the rest, to meet the pillars in question, so that the arch across the aisles is, in this part, very much contracted, and, instead of being a mere groin-rib, like the rest, is a strong moulded arch, of considerable depth in the soffit. What appears, at first sight, still more strange, the wall of the aisles opposite to the wider nave-arch just mentioned, is brought forward at least a foot internally, but again retires to the old level at the last bay; so that in this particular part the whole thickness of the aisle-wall is considerably greater .... The transformation of the base of these two immense towers into a compartment of the aisle, so similar to all the rest that its real nature has never been hitherto suspected, is highly ingenious.

That they were really erected is highly probable from some inferences drawn from the chronicles. This has been pointed out by Mr. Poole, who says,†

> Although these towers are never mentioned in any of the chronicles, I think their existence, and even something of their history, may be collected from the various ways in which the central tower is designated. Candidus, who lived and

---

* Remarks on the Architecture of Peterborough Cathedral, pp. 21, 23.
† Paper on the Abbey Church of Peterborough, amongst those of the Arch. Soc. Northants., 1855.

wrote while they were in existence, calls the central tower *magistra turris*, the chief tower, plainly inferring the existence of others. Swapham, who most likely remembered them, and witnessed their destruction, still gives to the central tower a distinctive name, *turris chori*, the tower of the choir, as distinguished from the western towers. Abbot John, who had most likely never seen these western towers, simply calls the central tower, *turris*, the tower.

The grand west front was therefore a subsequent design. There are some marked peculiarities about it which will be noticed hereafter. At its completion the church was consecrated. There were further additions made before long. In the 13th cent., of early English work, were the Lady chapel and the N.W. tower. The former was built by prior Parys, and consecrated 1290; he was himself buried at its entrance, where this inscription was visible in Gunton's day,

Hic jacet Willielmus Parys quondam Prior Burgi, cujus animæ misereatur Deus. Amen. Pater noster. Ave Maria.

It was east of the present N. transept, and the position of its gable is visible externally. This was entirely destroyed 1643. The latter was built by abbot Richard, while he was sacrist; it was erected for the bells, two of which were given by himself, and called *Les Londreis* from him, and a third given by abbot de Caleto dedicated to S. Oswald. This tower is therefore probably of date 1260. All the windows of the nave aisles are of this period.

Of 14th cent. work are the central tower now standing, the tracery of the apse windows and the lovely hanging tracery in the arches below, the raising of the aisle walls, and other details. Early in this century, and of purest decorated work, is the bishop's spire, as the S.W. spire has been named from its being adjacent to the palace. The N.W. spire is very poor in comparison with this, and is at least a century (Mr. Poole thinks a century and a half) later, nor is it of equal height.*

---

* It is strange that in all the measurements of the cathedral these spires are represented as the same height. On the cards hung up within the building they are given at 156 feet. Mr. Vallcott in his 'Memorials of Peterborough' (who condenses most of the history of the cathedral within moderate limits) on page 6 has transposed the spires: on page 9 he gives their height at 150, but this is probably a misprint, for on page 12 they are said to be 156 feet high. The same height is given by Mr. Craddock. In MS. Lansd. 993, bp. Kennett has preserved a note from Mr. Richardson 'giving accurate dimensions,' varying considerably from other lists, in which they are stated at 153 feet. But the S.W. spire is manifestly some feet loftier than the other. This is easily noticed at a distance due west, as on the Thorpe road: or still better due east, where at one spot the top of the bishop's spire is visible above the transept roof, and the top of the N.W. spire entirely below it.

It is perpendicular in character, but has very little merit, and suffers much by comparison with its 'fairer sister.' Other works of the 15th century are the parvise under the central arch, now the library (or possibly this may be late in the 14th century), the clerestory windows and those in the west front, and the new building. The last was built by abbot Kirton. His successor in the abbacy, John Chambers, was made first bishop. He acknowledged the supremacy of the king in 1534. The signatures of the monks to this acknowledgment may be seen in the Record office; they are here given, chiefly because many of the surnames are those of neighbouring villages.

Johns Abbas—Johes Walpooll Prior—Johes Alnewyk—Willm Castr—Willm Grystewe—Robte Burne—Robt[s] Kyrktun—Wyllm Meltun—Wyllm Thorntor Antoni[s] Morrys—Willm[s] Clyffe—Johes Ov[r]tun (Orton)—Ricard[s] Glyntor Rogerus Birde—Johes Pufferett[s] (Pontefract)—Wyllms Kyrkton—Robtus Stow—Willms Hertford[s]—Ricard[s] Grantham—Ricardus Alpyng—Robt[s] London—Hufridus Naturas—Johes Ryall—Ricard[s] Nottyngh[a]m—Xpoferus Lincoln[s]—Robertus Covetre—Johes Mortun—per me Edwardum Bardney—Johannes Holbeche—Willms Ramsey—Xpofer[s] Croyland—Griffinus Gloucest[r].—Henrycus Suttun—Johnes Burrowe—Ambrosi[s] Caster—Willm[s] Wysbyche—Galfrid[s] Lyne—Johns Croylade—Jhoes Lezygh[a]m—Willm[s] Exeter—Thomas Keteryng—Stephan[s] Harlton

In the following year queen Katherine of Arragon, who died at Kimbolton castle, was here interred. In 1541, the church was converted into a cathedral, the abbot being made the first bishop. Nothing of importance in the history of the church occurred for the next century, if we except the ejection of bp. Pole by queen Elizabeth, and the interment of another queen, Mary of Scots, in 1587. Her body here remained only till 1613, when it was removed to Westminster by her son's order. But the year 1643, was a sad one for the cathedral. A contemporary account of the destruction effected by Cromwell's soldiers, written by precentor Standish, is given at the end of Patrick's edition of Gunton. All the ancient records, a very few excepted, were burnt; the altar and the elaborate screen were levelled to the ground; the painting on the roof was defaced; the brasses and monuments were demolished; the stained glass windows were broken; the cloisters, which had an unrivalled series of such windows, were completely destroyed. The minster was assigned to the townspeople as a general workshop, and for public worship. This was done at the suggestion of Oliver Saint John, who gives this account of his embassy to Holland and its results for him :

> As to my Embassy into *Holland* with Mr. Strickland, I had no Advantage by it. The Plate, Furniture, Beds & other Things claimed formerly by Ambassadors were by us returned to the Wardrobe. The States at our Farewell as a Gratuity promised to return to each of us here in *England* a thousand Pounds in Gold, which I refused. All the reward of that Embassy was, that whereas the Minster of *Peterborough*, being an ancient & goodly Fabrick, was propounded to be sold & demolished. I begg'd it to be granted to the Citizens of *Peterborough*, who at that present & ever since have made use of it.

After all the mischief so recently done, the inhabitants with difficulty put the minster into some sort of repair. The Lady chapel was demolished to supply materials for this purpose, and the boards from the roof of this chapel were used as backs to the stalls in the choir, where they continued until the choir was reseated by dean Lockier. A wooden spire at one time surmounted the present N.W. spire. In the latter part of the 18th century dean Tarrant had the church repaved, and what fragments of the ancient glass could be found were by him collected and placed in two windows above the altar. A wooden octagon formerly on the lantern tower was removed by dean Kipling, and the present unsightly corner turrets erected. But the state of the fabric got gradually worse till the time of dean Monk. By him the whole was once more placed in decent repair. A brass plate under the present organ-screen commemorates his work. At the time the choir was fitted up, in 1830, it was esteemed a marvel of beauty. In Miss Martineau's History of the Peace, a work essentially political, it was thought of such national importance as to deserve this notice :*

> A new choir, of great beauty, was erected in Peterborough Cathedral during this period, and the church was made once more what it was before it was devastated by the Puritans. The expense was defrayed by a subscription within the diocese, and the work was superintended by the Dean, Dr. Monk, who had become Bishop of Gloucester before it was finished.

Nor would it be fair for us to compare the work of nearly 40 years ago, with what would be done now, however much we may regret that the re-arrangement of our

---

* History of England during the Thirty Years' Peace, ii. 185.

cathedral should have taken place in the infancy instead of in the maturity of the revival of architectural study. The ceiling of the choir has been painted in the time of the present dean.

The above traces in outline the chronology of the cathedral, apart from descriptive notice.

At the time of the dissolution there were at least 18 separate altars in connection with the church. They were all doubtless served by members of the foundation, but had not separate endowments as the chantries in parish churches. Besides the altars in the choir and Lady chapel, there were two, to SS. John and James in the N. transept aisle, three to SS. Oswald, Benedict, and Kyneburgha* in the S. transept aisle, one in the roodloft, one in the 'Ostrie' chapel (the chapel of the guest-house at the gate), one in the body of the church (a bracket in one of the pillars on the N. side marks its position), and others in the Trinity chapel, the infirmary chapel, the abbot's gallery chapel, and the 'other chapel.' It is not known where Trinity chapel was: that at Low, a cell of the abbey towards the north bank, was dedicated to the Holy Trinity, but Low chapel is mentioned by name as distinct. The abbot's gallery chapel was certainly that over the porch. Mr. Poole, in discussing the objects of this porch and chamber, has adopted the view of Browne Willis, that it was a consistory court, whose position would most fitly be at the great west door. He adds, 'I venture, then, to call this a Galilee.' In point of fact this name has been attached to it for centuries. The word was corrupted into 'gallery;' the great west court yard was called the 'gallery court;' and the portico itself was the burial place of minor canons, who left in their wills that their bodies should be buried 'with their fellows, in the gallery.' An inventory of all the furniture was made in 1539, but is too lengthy to be here given. Britton has copied it from Gunton, in whose book it occupies nearly six large pages.† It is altogether similar

---

* The connect'on of these three altars with the history of the place is obvious. The arm of S. Oswald was the great relic of the house; S. Benedict was the founder of the rule under which they lived; S. Kyneburgha was the sister of the founder of the monastery.
† Gunton's History, pp. 58—63.

to those already given, except in its magnitude. There seem to have been 313 albs, of various colours, 31 complete suits of vestments for Holy Communion, 169 copes, for festivals and processions. Many of these are called simply by their material; some by the embroidery on them, as 'the Kydds,' 'the Squirrels,' 'the Daysies,' 'the Popinjays;' some by names of their donors, as it seems from 'the Meltons,' 'the Overtons,' 'the Godfreys,' and others. Amongst the ornaments in the choir are these:

Imprimis. The high altar plated with Silver, well gilt, with one image of Christs passion, and a little shrine of Copper, enameled, for the Sacrament.

Item two pair of Organs, and two desks of Latten, seven Basins hanging, with four Candlesticks, and Banners of Silk above the Quire, joyning to the Tomb where Q. *Katharine* lieth buried.

Item at the upper end of the Church, three Altars, and upon every Altar a Table of the Passion of Christ, Gilt, with three stained Fronts.

Of these desks of Latten, one is probably the eagle lettern still remaining, given it is said by abbot Ramsey. It formerly stood on four small lions. The three altars, in the last paragraph, must have been one at the end of the apse, and one in each aisle. The high altar, it is needless to observe, was some distance west of its present position.

The REGISTERS begin in 1615. As might be expected they are comparatively scanty. But, with the exception of the necessary irregularities during the commonwealth, they are complete. The first book has this title in old English letters, excellently written:

𝕽egistrum 𝕰cclesiæ cathis de 𝕭urgo S⁽ᵗⁱ⁾ 𝕻etri in quo habentur omnia

𝕭aptismata   a folio : 3º :
𝕸atrimonia   a folio : 120º :
& funera   a folio : 140º :

𝕬b 𝕬nno 𝕯ni 1615.

The second book commences in 1756: the third in 1784, and was the book prepared with the impressed stamps under the act 26 George II. The remaining books are recent. A few entries from the register of the parish church refer more properly to the cathedral, and two are here given; they have been indeed copied into the cathedral book.

1587. The Queene of Scots was most sumptuously buried in the Cathedral. Church of Peterborough the first day of August who was for her deserts beheaded at Fotheringay about St. Paules day before.
Anthony More one of the children of the Queen's Maties kitchen wch followed at the funerall aforesaid of Queen of Scots was buryed the iij day.

From the cathedral register proper these may be quoted as of general interest:

1624. 29 Dec. M^{rs}. Elizabeth Beale ...... and lyeth buried in the chappell next to the Little Orgaines in this Cathedrall Church.
1642. Dr. John Pocklington late Prebendarie of this Cathedrall Church departed this life ye 14th of November, and was buried the 16, in the Monks churchyard, at ye east end of Abbot Hedda^s grave otherwise called ye Munks Stone.*
1646. William, the sonne of William Parker was baptiz'd the eight day of January in ye Cathedrall Church of Peterburgh according to ye directory, Mr Richerson, Minister of Botlebridge Preached, and Mr Hammerson, minister of Overton Baptiz'd it.
1648. Anthonie the sonne of Mr Willyam Parker was Baptiz'd the 28° of Aprill in his one house, after the new way by Mr Richeson Minister of Bottlebridge haveing neither Godfathers nor Godmothers.
1660. 7 Nov. Hellen Austin.... Baptized....in ye Cathedral Church being the first that was christned in ye ffont their; after ye setting it up; The said ffont being puld downe, and ye lead taken out of it; by Cromwells Souldyers.
1661. 10 Dec. Old Thrift on of the Almeshouse, of ye Minster was buryed.
1673. 29 Dec. Mr Gregory one of ye Petticannons met wth an untimely death.
1679. 24 May. John Lovin Free Mason, was buried.
1681. Two Persons Prisoners died out of ye Jayle wthin 10 dayes of one Another.
1682. 26 Mar. George Ellis a Scholar of ye Free-Schoole was buried.
1685. 21 Nov. Mr Laurence Parker who had outlived all his children was buried.
1689. 2 June. Wid: Woodward an Almswoman was buryed and contrary to ye Act of Parliament for woollen.
1702. 18 Nov. Goodwife Tunny an Almswoman was buryed in Monks Churchyard.
1702. (buried) John Mews of Wisbeach Oyl-Miller.
1711. 7 July. John Sherwood a Negro 3 foot high & Margaret Steward 2 foot & a half high marry'd.
1718. 27 May. William Harvey a Norfolk Gentleman who died in ye Jayl was buried in Monks Churchyard.
1720. 27 Nov. Robert Gibbs, one of Choristers, Son of Robert Gibbs one of ye Virgers bury'd.

---

* In the preamble to his will he says, 'Into thy hands .... Let my body be buried in the Monks ch. yard near the monument of those Monks martyrs whose monument is well known. Let there be laid on my grave a large stone with a cross cut upon it.' He had been fellow of Pembroke, Camb., rect. of Yelden, Beds., vic. of Waresley, Hunts., canon of Windsor, 1639, and chaplain to king Charles I. Two of his books, 'Altare Christianum,' and 'Sunday no Sabbath,' were ordered to be burnt by the long parliament. This was done by the common hangman at both universities and at London, 10 Mar., 1640, about which time they deprived him of his preferments, and had proceeded to further punishment, but he died almost broken-hearted. His tombstone had this simple inscription,

Johannes Pocklington
S. S. Theologiæ Doctor obijt
Novemb. 14. Anno. Dom. 1642.

See Clement's Church notes, Add. MSS. 11,425.

1725. 3 Mar. (buried) Jonathin Lammin a Debtor at Pix's.
1743. 30 Aug. William the Son of William & (Elizabeth) Ann Paley.*

Several people are described as 'woolcombers.' In 1778, a person is called a 'widowman.' In 1678, Luke Herbert, aged about 24, and being at the point of death, was baptized, 'he earnestly then desiring it, it being unknown before' that he was unbaptized.

The account books in the possession of the church are of great value. Besides the entries of a more private nature there are very many of general interest. A few are here quoted in English.

1548.	Wm. Glazier for 9 lbs. of Soder	3	0
	19 Nov. Mr. Wm. Murrey for going to Convocation 4	0	0
	To Rob. Hawkeman for taking down the roof of the new hall and setting up the great gate next the town................	2	10
	To Chr. Smith for the bell clapper at the cross altar		1
	To the said Chr. for girdles bought for the revestry		1
	For mending the lock on the deadman's door		2
	For a runlet of mamsey for the church	31	6
	For a new rope for the clock		13
	For a bow bought for the church and strings		7
	For 12 arrows and 6 bolts for the driving of daws out of the church		
1583.	The clocksmith of Barrowden for correction for the clock this year	0	8
1588.	To Wm. Lacy Gentⁿ for holding the court of Pye Pouder 40^s & for parchment 6^s 8^d	46	8
1590.	To the Lord Abp. of Canterbury for his Metropolitan Visitation this year as well for the Parish Church as for the Cathedral 4	0	0
1593.	The great column near the choir repaired with iron and timber 47	4	9
1600.	In expences in repairing and for cleansing out the river called the old Ea 74	3	4
1629.	For white lights spent in the church this winter	28	10
	To Morris Knowles for selling 3 trees in the Park 3^s for carriage 2 load of faggotts & one load of hard wood to the Deanery..	3	0
	To Mansfield making a new wheel for the sermon bell & for nails for the same	13	8
	For the making of a turning stile in the monks churchyard & the iron pin for the same		18

No accounts from this year till the restoration, except one in 1643, are to be found.

1661.	To Tho. Mansfield 4 days boarding up the windows that are unglazed	5	4
	24 Dec. For laurel to dress up the Church at Christmas	2	7
1662.	22 Jan. P^d Rob. Willowes for 2 windows on the south side at 6^d per foot	5 2	0
	1 Feb. P^d more (at 3 several times) 37	15	6
	13 May. P^d to old Mansfield 3 days mending the great gates of the body of the church being broken by the great wind Feb. 18.	4	6
	To Joh. Darby for killing 2 dozen of Daws.................	4	0

---

* The celebrated divine, author of 'Evidences of Christianity,' 'Horæ Paulinæ,' &c. He held many valuable preferments and was u'timately subdn. of Linc. and archdn. of Carlisle, in which latter cathedral he was buried. His father was minor canon of Peterborough.

Year	Description	£	s	d
1662.	The voluntary present to his majesty *	200	0	0
1664.	22 Oct. Given to the Train Band by Mr. Gunton's order at the training in the Town		10	0
1665.	7 June. Given the ringers for ringing the Great Bells at the overthrow of the Dutch fleet		5	0
	For one spruce dale (deal) for old Scarlett's picture		2	0
	Mr. Lilley for making a new pillory	1	10	0
	To the painter for Old Scarlett's picture drawing	1	10	0
	For 5½ yds. of canvass		7	2
	For frankincense to burn in the church			6
1667.	To Orlando Bagley for building a Cabin for Coltman in time of the sickness	1	0	0
	To Mr. Gibbs apothecary....for cordials for Coltman's family.		10	0
1669.	To Joh. Lovin for 4 new buttresses where the Ladies Chappel stood & making all that handsome, for stopping a great cleft in the North Isle & other work about the Minster as appears by his bill	20	0	0
	To the carrier for the carriage of Tho. Ball Chorister up & down from London to be cured of the King's Evil, and his charges by the way	1	4	0
1670.	To my Lord Fitzwilliam's keeper for half a Buck his fee		6	0
1675.	To several persons undone by fire at Northampton		1	0
1676.	To a seaman that was wrack'd coming from Barbadoes			6
	To 4 persons whose ship was taken by a French Caper		1	0
	To a Soldier that had lost his arm by the Turks			6
1678.	To Joh. Deacon a poor man in the Minster towards his charge in carrying his daughter to be touch'd of the Evil		10	0
1680.	For work done about the Poor Man's Box		1	9
1688.	Pd for cleaning the body of the minster & burning perfumes after the Prisoners had been		13	6
	Pd afterwards for washing the body of the Church's pavement all over		3	0
1689.	To 2 men watching the Deanery after the fire		2	0
1695.	Pd for a Bass for the Litany Desk		5	0
1700.	Pd for Coffee, Pipes &c. at the Chapter House		5	2
1745.	Pd Geo. Gibbs for making the Gamekeeper's green coat		6	0
	Pd the ringers on 25 Apr. on the news of the defeat of the Rebels		10	0
1747.	Pd Mr. Clifton for copying old Scarlett's picture	2	12	6
1752.	Pd Mr. Goodman for powder and shot to destroy the Daws at the Minster		10	2
1769.	4 Jul. Pd Thos. Crow for the Buck	1	1	0
1772.	Pd for Gunton's History with Manuscript Notes	21	0	0
1773.	22 May. Pd 2 labourers for work in the Almshouse Yard &c. at the time of the flood		5	0

The sacramental PLATE is very valuable. It is entirely of silver gilt. The alms-dish is the oldest, but is without date. Two massive flagons are thus inscribed ' Paulus Pyndar miles D.D.D. anno salutis 1639 Deo in Ecclesia sua Petriburgensi.' There are 4 chalices, one very large, presented ' Deo in Ecclesia sua Petriburgensi 1638,' the others uninscribed. One paten has an inscription identical with the last, a second has a similar one but no date, and a third none at all. Most have the coat of arms of

---

* The bp. also gave 400l. In Kennett's Register, p. 544, this is said to be ' for his pious care in restoring and protecting of them in their several Orders, Dignities, and Rights.'

the deanery. The whole set was mended and regilt in 1776, at a cost of 25*l*. 4*s*. 6*d*.

In the library is a book of benefactions, containing numerous gifts to the cathedral. Sometimes sums of money were given for special ends, as 'glazing the low east window,' 'towards beautifying the choir.' The library has been augmented by gifts of single volumes from clergy and gentry in the neighbourhood; bp. Patrick left a large number; in 1714 dn. Kennett and Mr. Sparke gave several volumes 'for the use of the school;' the largest accession was at the death of bp. Kennett. At one time the books were kept in the new building. In Botfield's Notes on Cathedral Libraries, 1849, is a notice of the rare and valuable works in this collection.

ABBOTS.

	656 Saxulphus, r.[1]	1128	Hen. de Augeli, deprived.[10]
	673 Cuthbaldus.	1133	‡Martin de Vecti, d.[11]
bef.	716 Egbaldus.	1155	Will. de Waterville, deprived.[12]
	Pusa.	1177	Benedict, d.[13]
bef.	793 Beonna.	1194	‡Andrew, m.d.
bef.	806 Celredus.	1200	Acharius, d.[14]
bef.	833 ‡Hedda, d.[2]	1214	Rob. de Lindesay, m.d.[15]
	971 Adulphus, r.[3]	1222	‡Alex. Holderness, m.d.
	992 Kenulphus, r.[4]	1226	Martin de Ramsey, m.d.
	1006 Elsinus, d.[5]	1233	Walter de S. Edmunds, m.d.[16]
	1055 Arwinus, r.	1246	‡Will. de Hotot, m.r.[17]
	1057 ‡Leofricus, m.d.[6]	1249	‡Joh. de Caleto, d.[18]
	1066 Brando, m.d.	1262	Rob. de Sutton, m.d.[19]
	1069 Thoroldus, d.[7]	1274	‡Will. de London, m.d.
	1099 Godricus, deprived.	1295	‡Will. de Woodford, m.d.
	1103 Matthias, d.[8]	1299	‡Godf. de Croyland, m.d.[20]
	1107 Ernulphus, r.[9]	1321	‡Adam de Boothby, m.d.
	1114 ‡Joh. de Sais.	1338	‡Hen. de Morcot, d.

‡ Buried at Peterborough. Those who had been monks of the house are marked, m.
1. Made abp. of Lichfield.
2. Murdered by the Danes, 870. No monastic establishment for a century.
3. Chanc. to king Edgar. Made abp. of York.
4. Made bp. of Winchester.
5. The great collector of relics. He brought here the famous arm of S. Oswald. He bought the body of Florentinus from a bankrupt abbey in Normandy.
6. Relative to king Edward. Held also abbeys of Burton, Coventry, Crowland, and Thorney.
7. A Norman; made bp. of Beavois in France; but expelled in 4 days and returned here.
8. Brother to Godfrey, chief justice, who was drowned in the wreck of the White Ship.
9. Prior of Canterbury; made bp. of Rochester.
10. Also abbot of Anjou; forced to surrender this and retire to his other abbey.
11. Prior of S. Neots. He entertained king Stephen here.
12. Chaplain to king Henry II.
13. Prior of Canterbury. He sold the chalices for king R'chard's ransom.
14. Prior of S. Albans.
15. He attended the 4th Lateran council, 1215.
16. Went thrice to Rome during his abbacy.
17. Resigned, but buried here before the altar of S. Benedict.
18. Prior of Winchester, went circuits as a judge, built infirmary, and gave great bell.
19. Took arms against king Henry III. Died abroad and buried in a monastery near Bononia. His heart was interred here before S. Oswald's altar.
20. Entertained king Edward I. and contributed largely towards his Scottish expenses.

1353 Rob. Ramsey, d.	1438 Ric. Ashton, r.[22]
1361 Hen. de Overton, d.	1471 ‡Will. Ramsey, m.d
1391 Nicolas, d.	1496 ‡Rob. Kirton, m.d.
1396 ‡Will. Genge, d.[21]	1528 ‡Joh. Chambers, d.
1408 ‡Joh. Deeping, d.	

BISHOPS.

1541 ‡Joh. Chambers, S.T.B., d.[1]	1638 ‡Joh. Towers, S.T.P., d.[9]
1556 ‡David Pole, L.L.D., deprived.[2]	1660 Ben. Laney, S.T.P., r.[10]
1560 Edm. Scambler, S.T.B., r.[3]	1663 Jos. Henshaw, S.T.P., d.[11]
1584 ‡Ric. Howland, S.T.P., d.[4]	1679 Will. Lloyd, S.T.P., r.[12]
1600 ‡Tho. Dove, S.T.P., d.[5]	1685 Tho. White, S.T.P., deprived.[13]
1630 Will. Peirse, S.T.P., r.[6]	1691 ‡Ric. Cumberland, S.T.P., d.[14]
1632 Augustine Lindsay, S.T.P., r.[7]	1718 ‡White Kennett, S.T.P., d.[15]
1634 ‡Fr. Dee, S.T.P., d.[8]	

21. The first mitred abbot.
22. During his abbacy the charter was granted for holding a fair on S. Matthew's day at the bridge. This is still held on the same holyday, old style.
‡ Buried at Peterborough.
1. King's chaplain, surrendered monastery, and had pension of 266*l*. 13*s*. 4*d*. and 100 loads of wood. By will he gave a pix and two silver candlesticks to the church, 20*l*. to the fabric, 20*l*. to the bridge, and 20*l*. to the poor. His funeral was costly; see Strype, iii. 286, under 5 March, 1555; he was buried 'with a godly Herse, adorned with Arms and Pensills, two white Branches, and Eight dozen of staves: wth an Herald of Arms, and five Banners: and an hundred in black Gowns and Coats, and a great many poor men in Gowns.'
2. Deprived by Elizabeth, suffered to live quietly in London, within 8 miles of his house. Had been fell. of All Souls' and dn. of Arches. Willis says 'probably' buried at S. Paul's cathedral.
3. Chaplain to abp. Parker, vic. of Rye, Suss., canon of Westminster, preb. of York. He greatly impoverished the see: made bp. of Norwich, and there buried. He was called Pseudo-episcopus by the Roman Catholics not because of his views, as some say, but because there was another bi-hop, Pole, alive.
4. Fell. of Peterhouse, and master of Magdalene and S. John's, Camb., rect. of Stathern and Sibson, Leic. Died at Castor.
5. Rect. of Framlingham and Saxted, Suff., and Heydon, Ess., also vic. of Saffron Walden, Ess., and dn. of Norwich. His monument was 'comely,' but destroyed with the rest in 1643. Amongst the lines on the epitaph were these:
Hic illa est senio argentata Columba
Davidis, cœlos hinc petit ille suos.
6. Rect. of Grafton Regis, vic. of Northall, and S. Christopher-juxta-le-Stocks; can. of Ch. Ch. Oxf., dn. of Peterborough; bp. of Bath and Wells, 1632. Afterwards deprived, but restored 1660. Buried at Walthamstow.
7. Fell. of Clare, preb. of Lincoln, had livings of Sedgfield, and Houghton-le-Spring, Dur., and Wickford, Ess.; dn. of Lichfield, 1628; bp. of Hereford, 1633, and there buried. Published edition of Theophylact.
8. Rect. of Allhallows, Lombard St., chanc. of Sarum, dn. of Chichester, 1630. Left 100*l*. to repair the cathedral. He gave parsonage of Pagham, Suss., for foundation of 2 scholarships and 2 fellowships at S. John's, Camb., for boys from the king's school of his name or kindred.
9. Fell. and master of Pembroke, Camb., chaplain to king Charles I., preb. of Winchester and Westminster, rect. of Buriton, Hants., vic. of Soham, Camb., dn. of Peterborough, 1630. He protested with 11 others against exclusion of bishops from parliament, and was confined in the tower about 4 months. Retired to king at Oxford. Deprived of his preferments. After his death in 1648, the see was vacant 12 years. Buried at Ely.
10. Fell. and master of Pembroke, Camb., chaplain to king Charles I., preb. of Winchester and Westminster, dn. of Rochester. Deprived of mastership, but restored. He, with the bp. of Gloucester, said the Litany at the coronation of Charles II. Made bp. of Lincoln, and ultimately of Ely. Buried at Lambeth, 1675.
11. Rect. of East Lavant and Shedham, Suss., vic. of S. Bartholomew the Less, London, preacher at Charterhouse, preb. of Peterborough, dn. of Chichester, chaplain to duke of Buckingham. Buried at East Lavant, Suss.
12. Bp. of Llandaff; made bp. of Norwich, 1685, of which deprived as a nonjuror. Buried at Hammersmith, 1710, being the last survivor of the seven nonjuring bishops.
13. Rect. of S. Andrew, Holborn, and of Botsford, Leic., archdn. of Nottingham, vic. of Newark. One of the seven bishops sent to the tower. Also one of the seven nonjurors. In 1697, he attended sir John Fenwick to the scaffold. Bequeathed books to the corporation of Newark, and money to the poor of Peterborough. Buried at S. Gregory's, now part of S. Paul's cathedral.
14. Fell. of Magdalene, Camb., rect. of Bampton, Oxf., vic. of All Saints, Stamford. A very learned man. A life is prefixed. Wrote, amongst other works, De legibus Naturæ disquisitio philosophica, against Hobbes.
15. Vic. of Ambrosden, Oxf., rect. of Shottesbrook, Berks., Aldgate, S. Mary Aldermary, archdn. of Huntingdon, dn. of Peterborough. A most industrious writer. His works are upwards of 50 in number, many being most laborious.

1728 ‡Rob. Clavering, S.T.P., d.¹⁶
1747 Joh. Thomas, S.T.P., r.¹⁷
1757 Ric. Terrick, S.T.P., r.¹⁸
1764 Rob. Lamb, L.L.D., r.¹⁹
1769 ‡Joh. Hinchcliffe, S.T.P., d.²⁰

1794 ‡Spencer Madan, S.T.P., d.²¹
1813 Joh. Parsons, S.T.P., d.²²
1819 ‡Herb. Marsh, S.T.P., d.²³
1839 ‡Geo. Davys, S.T.P., d.²⁴
1864 Fr. Jeune, D.C.L.²⁵

DEANS.

1541 Fr. Abree, S.T.B.¹
1543 Gerard Carleton, S.T.B., d.²
1549 Jas. Curthop, A.M., d.³
1557 Joh. Boxall, L.L.D., deprived.⁴
1560 ‡Will. Latymer, S.T.P., d.⁵
1585 Ric. Fletcher, S.T.P., r.⁶
1590 Tho. Nevill, S.T.P., r.⁷

1597 Joh. Palmer, S.T.P., d.⁸
1608 Ric. Clayton, S.T.P., d.⁹
1612 Geo. Meriton, S.T.P., r.¹⁰
1616 Hen. Beaumont, S.T.P., r.¹¹
1622 Will. Peirse, S.T.P., made bp.
1630 ‡Joh. Towers, S.T.P., made bp.
1638 Tho. Jackson, S.T.P., d.¹²

---

16. Fell. of University, rect. of Mersh Gibbon, Bucks., can. of Ch. Ch., prof. of Hebrew, 1705, bp. of Llandaff.
17. Fell. of All Souls', can. of S. Paul's, dn. of Peterborough, and Lincoln, bp. of S. Asaph, 1748, of Sarum, 1757, and of Winchester, 1761, and there buried.
18. Fell. of Clare, can. of Windsor, vic. of Twickenham, bp. of London, 1764.
19. Fell. of Christ's, Camb., rect. of Hatfield, Herts., and of Peakirk, dn. of Peterborough.
20. Fell. of Trinity, Camb., head master of Westminster, vic. of Greenwich, master of Trinity, dn. of Durham.
21. Fell. of Trinity, Camb., rect. of W. Halton and Haxey, Linc., and of Ashley, Berks., chaplain to king, preb. of Peterborough, bp. of Bristol, 1793. Translator of Grotius. He was first cousin to the poet Cowper.
22. Fell. of Wadham, rect. of All Saints, Colchester, master of Balliol, dn. of Bristol. Buried at Oxford; in his college chapel is a monument to him, and in the hall a portrait.
23. Fell. of S. John's, Camb., Margaret prof. of divinity. Author of many controversial works, Horæ Pelasgicæ, lectures, &c.
24. Fell. of Christ's, Camb., rect. of Willoughby, Notts., and Allhallows, London Wall, dn. of Chester, 1831.
25. Formerly head master of Birmingham, dn. of Jersey, master of Pembroke, Oxford, and dn. of Lincoln.
‡ Buried at Peterborough.
1. His real name was Leycester, a Cluniac monk; prior of S. Andrew, Northampton, which he had surrendered 1538, also vic. of Moulton.
2. Fell. of Queens', Camb., rect. of Stanway, Ess., canon of Westminster, 1640.
3. One of the original canons of Ch. Ch. Oxf., 1549, where he is buried.
4. Fell. of New, Oxf., preb. of S. Paul's and of Sarum, dn. of Norwich and of Windsor, registrar of the Garter, secretary of state to queen Mary. In 1560, he was deprived of his three deaneries by queen Elizabeth, and committed to the tower.
5. Inc. of Stackpole, dioc. S. Asaph, canon and archdn. of Westminster. He had been master of the dissolved college of S. Laurence, Pountney, London, and rect. of S. Mary, Achurch. He was the dean who saved the church when it was begged of the queen by a 'great peer.'
6. Fell. of Corpus, Camb., preb. of S. Paul's, and Lincoln, chaplain to the queen. Ministered at Rye, Suss., where his son John, the dramatist, was born. Rect. of Alderkirk, Linc., and of Barnack, 1586. He attended the queen of Scots at her execution, and his works refer only to her. Made bp. of Bristol, 1589, of Worcester, 1593, and of London, 1594. At Bristol he so squandered the resources of the see that it was vacant for 10 years. Died suddenly, while smoking; buried at S. Paul's cathedral.
7. Fell. of Pembroke, Camb., master of Magdalene, then of Trinity, where the court he built retains his name. Rect. of Dunnington, and Teversham, Camb., and of Churton. In 1587, canon of Ely. Britton says, rect. of Barnack, but his name does not occur in Bridges' list. Chaplain to queen Elizabeth and king James. Made dn. of Canterbury and there buried.
8. Preb. of Lichfield, archdn. of Ely, and master of Magdalene, Camb. When an undergraduate he acted king Richard III. before queen Elizabeth, and 'had his head so possest with a *Princelike humor*, that ever after *he did* what then he *acted*, in his Prodigal expences, so that (the *cost of a Sovereign* ill befitting the *Purse of a Subject*), he died *Poor* in *Prison*, notwithstanding his great *preferment*.' Fuller's Worthies, ii. 277.
9. Archdn. of Lincoln, master of Magdalene and S. John's, Camb. The latter he held till his death, and he is buried in the chapel of the college.
10. Rect. of Hadley, Suff., and dn. of Bocking, Ess. Made dn. of York, and there buried.
11. Fell. of All Souls'. Made dn. of Windsor, and there buried.
12. Vic. of Newcastle-on-Tyne, and of Witney, Oxf. Chaplain to king and preb. of Winchester. President of Corpus, Oxf., buried in the college chapel. His works are published in 3 vols. with a life.

1640 Joh. Cosin, S.T.P., r.[13]
1660 Ed. Rainbow, S.T.P., r.[14]
1664 ‡Jas. Duport, S.T.P., d.[15]
1679 Simon Patrick, S.T.P., r.[16]
1689 Ric. Kidder, S.T.P., r.[17]
1691 Sam. Freeman, S.T.P., d.[18]
1707 †Wh. Kennett, S.T.P., made bp.
1718 Ric. Reynolds, L L.D., r.[19]
1721 Will. Gee, S.T.P., r.[20]
1722 Joh. Mandeville, S.T.P., d.[21]
1724 ‡Fr. Lockier, S.T.P., d.[22]

1740 Joh. Thomas, S.T.P., ultimately bp.
1744 Rob. Lamb, L.L.D., made bp.
1764 Ch. Tarrant, S.T.P., d.[23]
1791 Ch. Manners Sutton, S.T.P.,r.[24]
1792 ‡Peter Peckard, S.T.P., d.[25]
1798 T. Kipling, S.T.P., d.[26]
1822 Jas. Hen. Monk, S.T.P., r.[27]
1830 Tho. Turton, S.T.P., r.[28]
1842 Geo. Butler, S.T.P., d.[29]
1853 Aug. Page Saunders, S.T.P.[30]

It is not proposed here to enter upon all the details of the architecture. Careful descriptions of this branch of the subject are plentiful and easily accessible. But a very few notes will not be out of place. It does not appear to have been pointed out that the choir and nave have not the same central line. The choir diverges slightly but perceptibly to the north; this can be noticed at the west door by looking along the line of roof.

---

13. Rect. of Brancepeth and preb. of Durham, archdn. of East Riding, and master of Peterhouse. He received the early part of his education at the king's school, Peterborough, and entered at Peterhouse at the age of 15. He was the first of the clergy whose benefices were sequestered by parliament. Was in exile 17 years. At the restoration he was made bp. of Durham. He died in 1671.

14. This dean also was at the king's school, from which he was removed to Westminster. Fell. and master of Magdalene, Camb. Deprived in 1650, for refusing to sign a protestation against the king. Presented to livings of Little Chesterford, Ess., and of Benefield, Northants. Restored to his mastership, 1660, and made chaplain to the king. Made bp. of Carlisle; buried at Dalston, Cumb. His life is published.

15. Prof. of Greek, and master of Magdalene, Camb., and canon of Lincoln. A long epitaph in Latin is on his mont in the cathedral. The writer of these notes has a special respect for the memory of dean Duport. He bequeathed an annual sum of 2*l.* payable to the second master of the king's school. All memory of this bequest had passed away, and it had become merged in another payment, until discovered and reclaimed by the present second master.

16. Vic. of Battersea, rect. of S. Paul, Covent Garden, and preb. of Westminster. Made bp. of Chichester, 1679, and of Ely, 1691, where he died and was buried, 1707.

17. See under Stanground, of which parish he was vicar.

18. Rect. of S. Anne, Aldersgate, and of S. Paul, Covent Garden, vic. of Stanton Barry, Bucks. Buried at Ecton. Description of his monument, and the epitaph, is given in Bridges, ii. 145.

19. Rect. of S. Peter, Northampton, Connington, Camb., and Denton, Hunts. Preb. and chanc. of Peterborough. Made bp. of Bangor, 1721, and of Lincoln, 1723, where he died and was buried, 1743.

20. Can. of Westminster, and rect. of S. Margaret, dn. of Lincoln, 1722.

21. Archdn. and chanc. of Lincoln, can. of Windsor. Buried at S. Mary Magd., Old Fish St.

22. Rect. of Hansworth. An intimate friend of Dryden and of Pope. See Malone's life of Dryden.

23. At his death he was subdn. and preb. of Sarum, preb. of Rochester, rect. of Bloomsbury, vic. of Wrotham, Kent, and chap. to the king. He had besides been preb. of Bristol, 1751, rect. of N. Tidworth, Wilts., 1757, of S. Mary-le-Strand, 1759, vic. of Staines, 1760, dn. of Carlisle, 1763, vic. of Lamberhurst, Suss., 1776.

24. Rect. of Averham, Notts., and Whitwell, Derb., bp. of Norwich, 1792, dn. of Windsor, 1794, abp. of Canterbury, 1805. Died 1828, buried at Addington, Suss. Memoir of him in Gent. Mag. 98, ii, 173.

25. See under Fletton, of which parish he was rector.

26. Fell. of S. John's, Camb. Editor of Theodori Bezæ Codex Cantabrigiensis. Died at Holme, York.

27. See under Peakirk, of which parish he was rector.

28. Fell. of S. Cath., Lucasian prof. of mathematics, reg. prof. of divinity, 1826 ; rect. of Gimingham, Norf., 1826, dn. of Westminster, 1842, bp. of Ely. 1845. List of publns may be found in Gent. Mag. iii, 16,388. Bequeathed nearly the whole of his property to charitable uses.

29. Fell. of Sidney, Sussex, head master of Harrow, 1805, rect. of Gayton, Northants., 1814, chanc. of Peterborough, 1836. Memoir by Dr. Vaughan is given in Gent. Mag. N.S., 39. 662. Buried at Gayton.

30. F.R.S., formerly student and tutor of Ch. Ch. Oxf., vic. of Tanworth, War., head master of Charterhouse.

The west front has 30 figures remaining in their niches. The northern of the 3 arches either fell down or was in imminent risk of doing so in the 17th cent. We find the bishop gave 100*l*. towards its restoration. In 1675 there was a great piece of work done in the N.W. tower. Its present state looks dangerous from below. The stones in the arch have some sad gaps. It is tied up by iron bands, and further protected within by a great number of wooden pegs, not of recent construction. When last observed it leant forward 14½ inches. The centre arch is the narrowest, and the acute angle at the top consequently the least, but the angles of the gables above have been wisely made equal. This inequality of the arches has been variously accounted for.* The portico is paved with gravestones, mostly not in their original position. Some are stones from which the brasses have been wrenched and then re-used, one is an incised cross formerly filled with some coloured composition. Of the numerous windows of stained glass with which the church was once enriched, fragments now remain only sufficient to fill the two eastern windows of the choir. These fragments were collected by dean Kipling. They are very beautiful. No scenes of course can be now made out, but the faces when examined closely, are singularly good. They were not from the cloisters, but from the church itself, and formed portions of a window or series of windows representing the life of S. Peter.† The date of the choir roof is not ascertained. On the shields are the instruments of the passion, some coats of arms, and a rood.

---

* None of the accounts seem quite satisfactory. The following suggestion is offered with diffidence. The gable above the centre arch is a *real* gable, it is the honest termination of the nave roof; whereas the other two gables have only lesser roofs built on purpose for the gables. Therefore, however far the extremities of the front should extend, the two central piers must be built so as to fit the existing nave roof: moreover, as they had to support a heavy arch of stone, they would have to be more massive than the nave piers, which supported only a roof of timber, and the width of the opening would be necessarily less than between two opposite piers of the nave. These two piers being then fixed, the outer piers might be as distant as was wished. A practical architect could tell whether the necessary contraction of the centre arch to support the stonework is too great to be consistent with the above theory. In the roof itself this view is confirmed. The walls that support the nave roof are distant 37ft. 8in. The end of the nave roof is 50 ft. from the west front interior. But at about half this distance the stone walls cease, and then the distance between the timbers begins to widen, and at the front itself they are 39 ft. 4 in. distant. And this looks as if the architect made the arch as wide as he could consistently with its double object, supporting both the nave roof continued and the new stone arch.

† This is apparent from the few words which can still be made out, all of them fragments of texts referring to the patron saint. A few of the texts have been reversed. Amongst them are these: Pasce oves—d(omi)ne non erit—es xpus (Christus)—no(n) sapis ea que—esse ducitis—B(ea)tus es Simon Barjona—d(omi)ne bonum) est nos esse.

There were at one time ten BELLS. Five of these were sold in 1831. The whole peal had been rehung in 1709, on the old timbers, and this was probably the origin of the insecurity which caused the sale of half the number.* They were sold to Dobson, of Downham, Norfolk, and with the metal a peal was cast which now hangs in the church of Witham-on-the-Hill, Linc. The following are the existing inscriptions.

1. TE DECET HYMNUS. RICH. REYNOLDS, L.L.D., PRŒB: HENRY PENN, FUSORE, 1709.

2. PSALLAM DEO MEO QUAMDIU SUM. THO. BALL PRŒB: 1709.

3. MAGNIFICATE DOMINUM MECUM. JOHN EVANS PRŒB: HEN. PENN, FUSORE, 1709.

4. HERBERT MARSH, D.D., BISHOP OF PETERBOROUGH; THOS. TURTON, D.D., DEAN OF PETERBOROUGH; WM. STRONG, D.D, ARCHDEACON OF NORTHAMPTON; JOHN JAMES, D.D.; WM. MC DOUALL, M.A.; WM. TOURNAY, D.D.; JOSEPH STEPHEN PRATT, L.L.B.; S. MADAN, D.D., AND THOS. HUGHES, PRŒBENDARIES, 1831.

5. PACEM TE POSCIMUS OMNES CONCORDIÆ RES PARVÆ CRESCVNT 1709 RIC^D CUMBERLAND, EP^o

The MONUMENTAL remains are mostly recent. Gunton gives several which in his day had survived the destruction of 1643, but even these with one exception are now lost, having apparently been obliterated when the nave was refloored by dean Tarrant.† At the entrance of the staircase to the N.W. tower is the only ancient inscription remaining. It is round a slab with an incised cross.

---

* This is suggested by a correspondent of the 'Peterborough Advertiser' in 1866, who also gives the inscriptions on the 5 removed thus:
  1. CANTEMUS DOMINO CANTICUM NOVUM, HENRY PENN, FUSORE, 1709.
  2. VENITE EXULTEMUS DOMINO, WILLIAM WARING, PRECENT., 1709.
  3. GLORIA DEO IN EXCELSIS, RICHARD CUMBERLAND, PRŒB., HENRY PENN, FUSORE, 1709.
  4. VOCE MEA AD DOMINUM, JOHN DALDERSTON, D.D., PRŒB., 1709.
  5. BENEDICTUM SIT NOMEN DNI., JOHN TAYLOR, A.M., PRŒB., 1709.

The old 9th bell was recast when the above were sold: its original legend was
TE DEUM LAUDAMUS, WHITE KENNETT, S.S.T.P., DECANO, HENRY PENN, FUSORE, 1709.

† Gunton omitted several very ancient ones, which are given in 'Notes and Queries,' viii, 215. One is in Norman French and runs thus:
VVS: KI: PAR: CI: PASSEZ:
PAR: LE: ALME: ESTRAVNGE:
DE: WATERVILLE: PRIEZ.

All cannot be deciphered, but the perfect inscription is given by Gunton thus :

CHRISTVS ROGERI CLYFF DIGNETVR MISERERI
IN BVRGO NATIQVE PRIORIS ET HIC TVMVLATI.

In the N. aisle of the choir is the matrix of a brass cross, but the inscription is gone. There are numerous tablets and slabs of the latter part of the 17th cent. and later. In the new building are many having simple initials and date. Three have mottoes in Greek. The tablet to dn. Cosin's wife, who died 'in festo annunciationis beatæ Mariæ virginis' 1642, was probably erected after the restoration. The cathedral dignitaries here buried have simple slabs : excepting bp. Cumberland, and dn. Duport. One slab, 1670, has this, 'Johannes Crimble Col: D: Johan: in Cant : Alumnus et organista Musis et musicæ devotissimus.' Here was buried John Calah, organist, 1798. The large monument on the south which has been cut down retains this prayer, ' Sanguis Jesu Christi purgat nos ab omnibus peccatis nostris.' This was erected by sir Humphrey Orme for himself in his lifetime. He survived his own monument, having lived to see its destruction by the puritans. The carving under the windows of the new building has great variety, and will well repay careful study. The large monument to Tho. Deacon, 1721, remains perfect. A remarkable instance of violated grammar occurs in the following.

G. B. 1721. Hic jacet Gowerus Barker Primo secundus Johannis et Saræ Barker Ecclesiæ hujus Minor Canonicus (!) Filius Qui novissimo Decembris Die Piam Exhalavit Animam anno Salut: 1718vo ætatis Decimo.

Besides the two queens there were buried at Peterborough two archbishops of York, Elfricus, who died at Southwell, 1051, and Kinsius, chaplain to Edward the Confessor, 1059. Both had been monks here. In 1226, the bishop of Durham, Ric. de Mansco, chancellor of England, died here. No memorials of either of these prelates have been preserved. The monastery possessed also the bodies of SS. Botulfus and Florentius.

The six effigies of abbots are of great interest. Attempts have been made to identify them from the conjectured date of the style of each : but as 4 of them are of the 13th cent. work, and one late in the 12th, and as 13 abbots ruled during that period, it may be pronounced impossible to name each one. Mr. Bloxam attempted to do so; but one that he assigned to Richard de London, 1295, has since been discovered to belong to Alexander, 1226. Gough had previously dated this same effigy at 1155. And this shews the difficulty of the attempt. The earliest seems to be the one behind the altar. The latest is certainly that near the spot where queen Mary was buried. It is of 16th cent. work, of clunch, and therefore more worn than the others, which are of dark marble. This last moreover has the mitre, rendering it probable that it is the tomb of abbot Kirton, or of the first bishop, Chambers. The other 4 are in the S. aisle of the choir. All are vested in alb and chasuble, four have the pastoral staff in the right hand. The raised coffin east of the S. aisle contains the body of the abbot. An oblong piece of lead inscribed 'ABBAS ALEXAN' was found in it when opened. At the west end of the nave is a picture with some verses beneath. This was removed in 1866, for exhibition at South Kensington, and it was hoped that the interior of the cathedral would see it no more, and that on its return some more suitable position would be found. It is doubtless a great curiosity, but is quite out of place in the house of God. Mr. Craddock unaccountably speaks in very high terms of its value in its present position, but this is the only exception. Mr. Walcott calls it 'a king of spades': the Rev. O. W. Davys says,[*]

Though we do not presume to doubt of the worthiness of the old man here represented, yet we cannot conceal our sentiments as to the unsuitableness of such a picture, and such an inscription, in such a situation.

In Murray's 'Eastern Cathedrals,' p. 71, is this passage;

The portrait is curious as an example of costume, but is scarcely a fitting ornament for the nave of a cathedral.

And the Rev. T. James, late hon. canon, speaks of it thus: [†]

Old Scarlett, who also "buried the town twice over," and whose portrait, now in the nave of the cathedral, would be better placed in the chapterhouse or elsewhere.

---

[*] Guide to Peterborough Cathedral, p. 72.
[†] Quarterly Review, CCI, Jan. 1857. 'History and Antiquities of Northamptonshire.'

It has not even the merit of being the original, but is a copy made in 1747. Several engravings of it have appeared. The one in Granger's 'Wonderful Museum,' p. 656, is dated 1804.

A number of memorial windows have lately been placed about the cathedral. They are of various degrees of merit. That to dean Butler, in the new building, is considered the happiest in execution.

Peakirk.

This village, distant six miles from Peterborough, has a station on the Boston Railway. The spelling seems to have been a difficulty as we find the following variations: PEGEKIRK, PEGEKIRKE, PEGECYRCAN, PEYCHURCH, PEICHIRCHE, PEICHIRCH, PEYKIRK, PEYKIRKA. The neighbourhood, perhaps not the parish only, was also known as Pegeland, or Payland. The etymology in each case is obvious.

The church is dedicated to S. PEGA. By her, about the year 716, was here founded a cell. She was sister of S. Guthlac of Crowland. From its connection with the abbey of Peterborough the parish is frequently mentioned in the chronicles. Under date 871 is this passage, after stating that Gored, king of the Mercians, had annexed, 'suo fisco applicavit,' the isle of Ely & other lands;

Idem fecit de terris S. Pege de Pegekyrk; quasdam sibi retinuit, quasdam militibus donavit........nil præter insulam et....mariscos monachis reliquit (chron Angl).

There was never a monastery proper here, though we read of the abbot of Peakirk: but he was really the rector of the church: the abbot of Peakirk *

was only the priest or curate of the church, who coming as a Monk from Burgh, affected to draw some others after him, and to turn his Manse into a cell, and by degrees into a separate independent house, till the abbey of Peterb. by degrees recovered their Right and dissolved the other's Pretensions.

* MS. Lansd. 1029.

The abbey did not recover its right without recourse to law. In 1048, Wulgatus, abbot of Peakirk, was ejected from his seat, and all his manors were taken from him, 'per judicium curiæ regis Hardcnuti,' the abbot of Burgh having established his claim. To make amends to the dispossessed Wulgatus, he was appointed at the next vacancy to the abbacy of Crowland. The parish is included in the district stated by Ingulf in 1013 to have been entirely destroyed by king Swane landing with a great fleet and a most cruel army. The rectory, in 1288, was valued at 16*l.* 13*s.* 8*d.* after deducting a pension to the abbot of 15*s.* and a portion of 1*l.* 6*s.* 8*d.* These amounts are subsequently assigned as due to the sacrist and subsacrist. In 1535 the deductions were 10*s.* 7*d.* for archdeacon's fees, and 15*s.* 7*d.* for the sacrist, the net value being, then 18*l.* 3*s.* 10*d.* and the tenths 36*s.* 4¾*d.*

The REGISTER begins in 1560. From 1560 to 1613 the entries have been copied from an older book by 'Nicholas Tytley clericus.' The second book begins 1642. The office of register during the commonwealth superseded the ordinary parochial arrangements: a copy of the appointment in the case of Peakirk is here preserved.

I John Cleypoole of Northborrow in ye Countie of Northton, Esqr one of the Justices of the Peace for the Liberty of Peterborough and County of Northampton, Doe by vertue of an Act of Parliam^t Dated the 24th of august 1653: approove of the election of Hamond Utting, Clerk, of Peakirk to be parish Register for Peakirk and Glinton, And doe authorize him to keepe the Register booke for the said Townes, for all Marriages, Births, and Burialls according to the purport and tenner of the said Act, And for the due execution of the said place I have given him his oath as by the same Act is appointed, witness my hand the 11th day of Aprill, 1654.

John Cleypoole.

This Cleypoole married the favourite daughter of Cromwell. The above appointment was not a good one, as we find by the following memorandum:

Mr. Utting being Curate and Regester in the time of the late warrs and usurpation, no Notes could be found, so that this Regester is defective.

There are no entries from the register itself of sufficient interest to be reproduced here. For two years, 1654—55, the births of children, not their baptisms, were registered.

A few memoranda of accounts are preserved. These were of the last century. The destruction of moles and rats formed an important item. The amounts paid vary.

In 1767 they were unusually troublesome: 1*l*. 11*s*. 6*d*. being paid at one time. In 5 payments in 1773, 3*l*. 7*s*. 6*d*. was disbursed. There is also a survey of the rectory in 1759. Two extracts from the books may be given:

1704. A bill of the folley Bridg Repairing 12 0 1
1768. 15 Jan. The flood came down.

In 6 Edw. VI. was taken the inventory of church goods, Wyll^m Barneby being curate. Besides the list given here, was one line 'church and chancel covered with lead,' but this was struck through with the pen.

Ffirst in ye steple ij small bells—It on handbell—It on chales of sylv^r—It on vestment of Red damaske—It on cope of blew......It on olde vestyment—It ij albes—It iij alter clothes—It iij towells—It ij small latyn candelstykes—It ij cruetts of leed—It on cryssmatory of latyn—It on surples & on Rochett—It a byble & a pafrayes of Erassimus—It a cross of cop^r—It ij corporal casses of Grene Sylke—It on olde cope solde to Thom^s ffoo for o iij^s iiij^d.

Bequests to the church are mostly small sums for repairs or for the poor. Such were Timothy Warren's, 1611, who left 10*s*. to the poor, and 13*s*. 4*d*. to the repairs of the church: rect. Will. Greenhill's, 1651, who gave 'unto every poor householder in Glinton and Peakirke xij^d': and rect. Timothy Morton's, 1703, who left 5*l*. to the poor. The will of Rob. Angell, 1566, who desired his body to be buried in Peakirk churchyard, is interesting. He left

to Peterborough abbey, 6^d: to the repairs of Peakirk, 20^d: to all that come to my buryall meat and drynke and to the povertie penny bread. Item I give to the povertye of Peekirke and Glinton fortie shillinges to be given unto them the next four yeares after my decease: unto the repairinge of St Pees image ii strike of barley and xx^d in money.

In 1712 Ann Ireland left 100*l*. for supporting in a school 5 poor girls from Peakirk and 10 from Glinton. The endowment is now in land: the annual receipts in 1786 were 6*l*. 1*s*. 4*d*.

The parish has figured in the law courts. In Dyer's Reports, p. 340, under 18 Eliz. Easter Term, is this passage.

The Parson of *Peykirke* and *Elmeton* (sic) juxta *Peterborough*, of which the Abbot of *P*. was patron, and also owner of the manor of *Elm.*, being a hamlet of that parish, at this day demanded tithe of hay and corn out of the demesnes of *El.* manor, of which the present Dean and Chapter of *P*. are both patrons and owners; whereas within time whereof memory runneth not to the contrary before the dissolution of the abbey, no such tithes, but only other tithes, as *of wool and lambs*, &c., were paid by the farmers by lease, or at will, being lay persons.

PEAKIRK.

RECTORS.

	Amicius.
1226	Ric. de Stavenesby.
1231	Will. de Burgo.
	Albred. de Fiscampo, d.[1]
1275	Phil. de Stanton, r.
1282	Galf. de Houghton.[2]
	†Griffinus, d.[3]
1311	Rob. de Croyland.
1318	Joh. de Elm.
1320	Joh. de Deping.
1327	Tho. de Luvedon.[4]
	Steph. Othebothe.
1373	Steph. de Whittowell.
1394	Tho. Newton, d.
1404	Ric. Wolte.
1420	Joh. Ederston.
1429	Joh. Burgoyn.[5]
	Rob. Palyngton.
1450	Tho. Hervy, r.
1451	Will. Pytteman.
1458	Joh. Dykelun, r.[6]
1473	†Will. Date, d.[7]
1481	Ric. Lincoln, S.T.P., r.[8]
1487	Joh. Whelpdale, L.L.D., r.
1488	Laur. Squier, d.
1493	Tho. Rydley.
1500	Joh. Gayton.

	Tho. Stevyus.
1516	Will. Pratt.
1526	Joh. Tully.
	Nic. Smyth, d.
1544	Ric. White, d.[9]
1565	Will. Woodcrofte.
	‡Nic. Tytley, d.
1619	†Will. Warde, d.[10]
1637	Will. Greenhill, S.T.P., d.[11]
1660	‡Laur. Wiltshire, A.M., d.
1682	Joh. Whitchall, A.M.
1682	Joh. Workman, A.M., d.[12]
1685	Dav. Llewellyn, A.M., d.[13]
1685	Nat. Spinkes, A.M., r.[14]
1687	‡Tim. Morton, A.M., d.
1703	‡Ric. Cumberland, A.M., d.[15]
1737	White Kennett, A.M., d.[16]
1740	‡Fred. Williams, A.M., d.[13]
1747	Rob. Lamb, L.L.D., made bp.
1763	Will. Brown, A.M., d.[13]
1798	Fred. Wollaston, L.L.D.[17]
1801	‡Ben. Barnard, A.M., d.[13]
1816	Jos. Parsons, A.M., d.[18]
1829	Jas. Hen. Monk, S.T.P., r.[19]
1850	Joh. James, S.T.P., r.[20]
1865	Ed. James, A.M.

† Buried at Peakirk.
1. Now called Fecamp, in Normandy.
2. Also rect. of Ingham.
3. He was specially permitted by the sacristan 'humanitatis causa' to be buried in the church of Peakirk, and the usual mortuary, a bay palfrey, was paid.
4. Archdn. of Chichester.
5. Seems to have vacated rectory of Barnack.
6. Exchanged with his successor for Welburn, dioc. Lincoln.
7. Also rect. of Colyngham.
8. Exchanged with his successor for Rayley, dioc. Lond.
9. Monk of abbey; first preb. of the 6th stall.
10. Probably vic. of Norton, 1615—42.
11. Presented by the king 'hac vice patroni per lapsum temporis sive per pravitatem Simoniæ legitime et de jure vacantem.' In his will, dated 10th Feb., 1651, he desires his body 'to be decently interred next to ye vestry in the chancell of the church of Peikirke wthout any Sermon or Solemnity.'
12. Fell. of All Souls', vic. of Hamilton, Rutl., and preb. of Peterborough. Buried in Peterborough cathedral.
13. Preb. of Peterborough.
14. Presented by abp. Sancroft during the vacancy of the see. His father was rect. of Castor, see p. 12, who had come with bp. Patrick from New England. Nat. Spinkes was of Trin. and Jesus Colleges, Camb., chaplain to sir Ric. Edgcomb and to duke of Lauderdale, lecturer at S. Stephen's, Walbrook, 1683, rect. of Peakirk and Glinton, 1685, preb. of Sarum and rect. of S. Mary, Salisbury, 1687. He seems to have resigned Peakirk at this time, but of his other preferments he was deprived in 1690, as a nonjuror. He was consecrated bp. by bp. Hickes, titular bp. of Thetford. The later nonjuring bps. had no titles. The last of them, bp. Gordon, died in 1799. At the funeral of Kettlewell, the celebrated divine, at Allhallows, Barking, in 1695, when the deprived bp. Ken officiated, Spinkes was a pallbearer. His works are controversial. He engaged in a prolonged pamphlet war with Collier. He wrote in 1712 'The Sick Man Visited.' He also assisted in publishing Grabe's LXX., Newcourt's Repertorium, and Walker's Sufferings of the Clergy. He is said in Chalmers to have been 'low of stature, venerable in aspect, and exalted in character.' He died in 1727, and was buried in the parish of S. Faith by S. Paul's, London.
15. Preb. of Peterborough and Lincoln, archdn. of Northampton. His son was bp. of Clonfert.
16. Preb. of Peterborough; buried in the cathedral.
17. Vic. of Wisbech, and preb. of Peterborough.
18. Rect. of Holwell, Beds., and preb. of Peterborough. Buried in Peterborough cathedral.
19. Fell. of Trin., Camb., reg. prof. of Greek, dn. of Peterborough, rect. of Fiskerton,

The CHURCH is small but of the very greatest interest. It consists of chancel with N. vestry and chantry, nave with aisles, S. porch, and N. door. At the W. is a triple bellcot. There are three bays to the nave; those on the N. are Norman, they have round arches with plain label and round piers, but the capitals are square with the corners indented and fluted beneath; those on the S. side are early English with pointed arches, round piers and capitals with the nailhead ornament. The bases here are exposed but those on the N. side are hidden. The clerestory windows, 2 on the N. and 4 on the S. side, are lancets with trefoils. The chancel arch is intermediate between the two arcades. Its piers are semicircular, and as lofty as the top of the arches of the S. arcade. It has a lofty pointed arch, and the foliage under the capitals is transitional. The marks where the rood screen stood are visible. The arch between the N. chantry and chancel is also pointed on transitional piers, but they are no higher than those in the N. arcade of the nave. The chancel has perpendicular windows, 2 on the S. side have 3 lights each, that at the E. end has 5 lights. The roof now is flat: originally it was high-pitched, and 5 corbels that supported the wallpieces remain, all but one have well carved heads. There are two seats in the chancel ranged stallwise. The sanctuary is raised on two steps. An aumbry remains N., with marks of 3 bolts, and a plain piscina with pointed arch and round bason opposite. On each side of the altar in the N. and S. walls are two square tablets, set diagonally in the stone. They are of alabaster incised with the sacred monogram, surmounted by a crown in one case and a crown of thorns in the other. These incisions are filled with a coloured composition, and have a most pleasing effect. The vestry is divided from the chantry by a stone wall of ancient date. Here is the stem of a 14th cent. lettern, set in a heavy stone socket. It retains fragments of paint in some of the crevices. The

---

ean. of Westminster, bp. of Gloucester and Bristol. Wrote Life of Bentley, and published many Greek works. Buried in Westminster abbey.
  20. Preb. of Peterborough and inc. of Glinton. Formerly fell. of S. John's, Oxf., head master of Oundle, vic. of Maxey and Peterborough.

design is a beautiful one, and has been
taste copied in a new lettern at Glinton
has a broad perpendicular window (mend(
from some domestic building) of 3 lights
the heads. In it are some fragments of
glass. At the east end are two brackets
perpendicular date divides this chantry
The roof to the N. aisle slopes more than
aisle. Here is one short 3-light window
without tracery; at W. end is a lancet.
also a lancet at W. end; at the E. and in
decorated windows of 3 lights, squa1
in the S. wall is enriched externally with
The font, a large octagonal one, is at the
aisle. The interior door of the S. porcl
date and very good. The door itself has
The ornaments in the tympanum above
large fans. There are two shafts, the eas
been renewed. The outer door is early
round piers and a pointed arch.

From these details it is not hard to for
history of the fabric. The Norman chu1
with nave with N. aisle and S. door an(
door simply, it was moved to the S. whe
added; if a porch, the present interi(
exterior door of that porch in situ. The
about the W. window of the nave, which
This may show that the front was buil
aisle, and that the piers of the S. arcade w
the site of the old wall, as at first inten
south. Or these may have been two s1
one may be blocked up by the buttress.
S. porch was added when these changes v
in the 13th cent. Both aisles were muc
decorated period, the N. aisle being nea
another century the chantry was built, a1
later the E. and S. sides of the chancel.

In 1477, *John Wysbeche*, Abbot of Croyland, rebuilt the
Paylond, as it was commonly called, which had lain in ruir

And he proceeds to identify the chapel

one still standing a short distance E. of the church shortly to be noticed. This could not be the case as that building is certainly of geometric date. It is very likely the chancel of the church that is alluded to above. A bequest to the image of S. Pega has been already quoted: in the E. wall is a very curious quatrefoil opening, N. of the E. window, well seen in the photographic view, which is thought to have been for the periodic exhibition of a relic.

But independently of the architectural interest of this church, it has two features yet to be mentioned of striking and unusual merit. These are the stained glass windows, and the oak fittings. The low open seats are of oak throughout; so are the desk and pulpit. The latter has some excellent carving, but would be better suited to a larger church. All the windows in the body of the church are filled with stained glass. They have all been presented. Among the scriptural subjects depicted (beginning at the E. window of the S. aisle) are these: the Saviour knocking at the door, Moses smiting the rock, baptism of the Saviour, woman of Samaria, disciples at Emmaus. Most are memorials, inscribed beneath. One in the S. aisle has this legend:

In Memoriam. Herbert. Marsh. S.T.P. Qui. hujus. Dioeceseos. per. biginti. annos. Episcopus. Obiit. Maii. 1º. A.D. 1839. Hoc. qualecunque. inane. Munus. Grato. Dicat. Animo. John. James.

The chancel windows have quarries. The flooring throughout has been much raised. The aumbry and piscina in the S. aisle prove this from being so near the present floor.

The bellcot has apertures for three BELLS, which is unusual. Only two are occupied. The inscriptions are thus given by Mr. Paley:

    1. THANKS BE TO GOD.
    2. THOMAS NORRIS MADE ME. 1677.

The MONUMENTAL remains are scanty. A floorstone

in the chancel to Wm. Grazier, 1796, and his wife, remains. Here are two tablets to rectors. One describes rect. Barnard as 'no less distinguished by the Urbanity of his Manners than by the Integrity of his life.' The other is as follows:

> Hic sui quicquid mortale fuit reponi voluit Richardus Ric. F. Cumberland, A.M. Eccles. Petri de Burgo Lincolniensisq : Præb : Hujusque Ecclesiæ Triginta plus annos Pastor dignissimus. Vir pietate erga Deum, liberalitate erga pauperes, Humanitate ergo omnes, Spectatissimus. Obiit Decembris die 24 AD 1737 suæq : Ætatis 63. Monumentum hoc Ipsius Elizæque conjugis dilectissimæ memoria factum, mœrens posuit Filius Denison Cumberland.

In the S. aisle is a tablet, 1859, to C. H. Webster. Externally the ground on the S. side is much raised by burials. The oldest noticed in a cursory review was this, 'Heare. lyeth. y^e. Body. of. Rebekah. Bateman. deceased. March. y^e. 8th. 1627.' There is an altar tomb at the E. end to rect. Morton, 1703. Hen. Tompson, who died 1721, aged 107, is said to have 'retained a great and uncommon strength of memory to his last.'

The little desecrated chapel called the hermitage has some good work. Its date is about 1270. An early cross is on the W. gable. In the S. wall is a fine double piscina, and the E. window is very good. The vestry and chantry in the church both belong to the owner of this hermitage, and he is charged with the repairs. The dimensions of the chapel, which has nave and chancel, are about 30 feet by 10 feet.

There is no other church in England dedicated to the foundress of this parish. But there was one at Rome. After she had left her relics (including S. Bartholomew's whip and S. Guthlac's psaltery) in the hands of the abbot of Crowland, and spent two years at her cell 'in lugubri lamentatione,' she went to Rome, and there died and was buried 'in ecclesia, quæ ibidem in honore ejus a fidelibus condita est.' It is not now known where this church stood.

GLINTON.

Glinton.

Adjoining Peakirk, and until recently part of the parish, though now divided, Glinton is one of the numerous instances in which the daughter has aimed higher than the mother; the ambitious spire of the chapelry being in singular contrast with the modest bellcot of the mother church. There has never been any change in the word as pronounced, and no form of the name occurs except that now used and GLYNTON. No etymology appears to have been suggested.

The CHURCH is dedicated to S. BENEDICT. He was the great ascetic, and several large Benedictine houses flourished in this neighbourhood. Although never in holy orders, he was abbot of Monte Cassino, which is the cradle of his order, and is still existing. He died in the year 543. In England but 16 churches have this dedication; and of these some may be perhaps to Bennet, bp. of Wearmouth.* There is a tradition of a dedication to S. Thomas of Canterbury, and this receives an apparent confirmation from the time of the feast, the second week in July; but the evidence of old wills that give the former dedication is conclusive.

The REGISTERS are scanty and of no special interest. They are in good order. From 1567 to middle of the 18th cent. there is but one book. The writing in it is clear and very distinct. In 1688 commence the usual entries about burying in woollen. At the beginning of the last century, about 1730, the only entries have been clearly made by an illiterate parish clerk. There is preserved here a confession of murder committed in the parish, for which the murderer, John Wyldbore, suffered death. It is thought to be somewhat upwards of 150 years old.† A few sentences may be extracted.

---

* The name Benedict is always shortened into Benet, as at Corpus Christi, Cambridge; at Huntingdon, now destroyed; and at these four London churches, S. Benet, Gracechurch St. (on the eve of destruction); S. Benet, Paul's Wharf; S. Benet, Fink; S. Benet, Sherehog.
† I have been unable to obtain the exact date, or any details of this crime.

Good people, I am very glad to see so many spectators of my death which I am now about to suffer for giving Death to one of my fellow creatures. I say I am glad to see so many witnesses of my death becaus I hope you will be all witnesses of my Sincere and hearty Repentence.......... should I number my sinnes, and the severall times I have fallen into them, the day would faile me, and I must die to day................I was never well but in drink. It was this sinne against myself which made me comitt this most notorious sin of murder—murder in the plane sense of it against my poore neighbour God grant I have not murder'd him body and soule............I shall say no more when I have desir'd you all to pray for me, and to continue your prayers as long as you shall think there is any of life in me............

The inventory of church furniture is as follows:

Ffirst in ye stepyll iij bells—Itm on sans bell—Itm ij hand bells—Itm ij chalysys of silver pcell gylt—Itm on vestement of gren silke—Itm on hold[1] vestement—Itm on hold cope of blewe worsted—Itm ij haubes[2] ij amyses—Itm iij corprasses & iij cases to them—Itm on crose of latyn—Itm on crysmatary of latyn—Itm ij auter clothes—Itm vi towylls—Itm a bybyll—Itm ij lytyll kandyllsteks of latyn—Itm on holy water stoke of brase—Itm ij surpless—Itm ij waytts of led stolne.

The chief bequest has already been specified under Peakirk. In 1538 Rob. Clark left his body

to be buryed in the churchyard of Seynt Benedict of Glynton. to the hie auter of Glynton dim. a seme of barley. to our lady light iiij^d. to the Roode light iiij^d wytness John Curtes & Sir John Ayre curatt of Glynton.

In 1541 John Herke left to the sacrament 2^d and 2^d to the mother church of Peterborough. In 1547 John Payne bequeaths

my soule to the merciful handes and custodye of our Saviour Jhesu and my bodie to be buried in the churchyarde of Glynton—to the hie aulter in the said church of Glynton iiij^d.

And in 1544 a will commences thus:

I John Parker of Glynton in the parishe of Peakirke in the countie of Northton husbandman .... commend my soule into the handes of our moste mercifull Lord God the father the son and the hollye ghost thre persons and one God and my bodye to be buried in the churchyard of Glynton.

The CHURCH is very fine though not large.* It has a chancel with a north chantry for a lady chapel, nave with aisles and clerestory, S. porch, N. door, W. tower and spire. It was not all built at one time, but is mostly of the latter half of the 14th cent. Parts are of earlier date, as certainly the S.W. chancel window, which has two cinquefoiled lights with a quatrefoil above, and probably the arch to the N. chantry and the chancel arch. The former is supported on semicircular piers; that to the east has a capital of early English design, that to the west is ambiguous. The E. window is of 3

---

1. One old vestment. 2. Albs.

* Glinton was amongst the places visited by the Archæological Institute, in 1861, but in the report it is confused with Northborough.

lights, later, apparently of 15th cent. work, as is the E. window of the chantry.* Under the S.E. chancel window is a plain bench for sedilia, and a remarkable drain for the piscina. It is much higher than the bench, very shallow, and has a projecting edge. The roof in the chancel, which is of high pitch, is new. In the chantry is a fine decorated piscina under a pointed canopy, having straight sides and excellent tracery beneath. The arch to the aisle rests on corbels like inverted cones. The two windows on the N. side have been restored: one has a slightly cusped quatrefoil in the head, the other, a very elegant one, is doubly trefoiled. The piers in the nave have embattled octagonal piers, supporting good pointed arches. The tower arch is similar to those of the nave. Against the tower is to be seen the weather-mould of the original decorated roof, removed to erect the present perpendicular clerestory, which has on each side three windows, each of three cinquefoiled lights. The labels of the tower arch, chancel arch, and extreme nave arches, have all an unfinished appearance: but the intermediate ones of the nave have small well carved heads. Large corbels remain to support the wallpieces of the roof. Some are grotesque, especially at the W. end. Those over the chancel arch have shields, one with crosskeys, one with a plain Latin cross. At the W. end of each aisle is a small thin lancet. The aisles are not of the same width. Measuring from the inside wall to the middle of the nave piers, the width of the N. aisle is 12ft. 7in., that of the S. aisle only 7ft. 10in. The E. window of the S. aisle has plain intersecting tracery, but good decorated mouldings. On each side is a bracket, and in the S. wall a good piscina. The passages in the aisles are against the walls. There are low open seats throughout. Those in the chancel are arranged as stalls returned against a low screen. All have well executed poppyheads of oak, of various designs.

---

* Bridges, ii. 578, says 'within this church was a chapel of the Blessed Virgin, and in the twenty-second year of *Hen.* VI. the high altar, a chalice, and the font, were consecrated by *Richard Ashton* Abbat of *Peterburgh*.' This would be 1443; but this seems too late a date for even the east window; and the decorated piscina in the chantry shews there was an altar there long before this time.

The pulpit, on the N. side, is beautifully carved; it stands on a stone stem. Opposite is the prayer desk; and between them a noble lettern with one revolving desk, its front carved in panels and its sides pierced; it is set in a stone socket, copied, as has been mentioned, from an original fragment remaining at Peakirk. A massive square Norman font stands by the S. door. The stem has been restored. The bason is richly carved: two faces have circular designs, two stars and zigzag. At each corner is a partial shaft. All the parapets are embattled. The S. door has a niche above. The outer door of the porch rests on round piers: a large series of dogtooth ornaments is a striking feature. The 'needle-spire' is unusually fine. Its sides are curved. The spire lights, of which there are two tiers, are very pointed. The W. window, of two lights, is a very good one. The chancel buttresses are fine; the gurgoyles very large. The N. door has curious short buttresses. There is an entrance to the N. chantry in the E. wall.

Except that the spire lights are not wired the arrangements in the belfry are very good. There are six BELLS, the 2 smallest being hung above the others. The 6th is a very large one. All are inscribed.

1. PEACE AND GOOD NEIGHBOURHOOD. THOMAS OSBORN FECIT 1799.
2. ✠ THE LORD TO PRAISE MY VOICE I'LL RAISE. T. OSBORN FOUNDER 1799.
3. GIVE NO OFFENCE TO THE CHURCH. THOMAS OSBORN FOUNDER DOWNHAM NORFOLK. 1799.
4. OUR VOICES SHALL WITH JOYFUL SOUND MAKE HILLS AND VALLEYS ECCHO ROUND.
5. EDMUND AND GEORGE WEBSTER CHURCHWARDENS THO^s OSBORN FOUNDER DOWNHAM NORFOLK 1799.
6. JOHN SCOTT DID PAY FOR ME ONE HUNDRED POUNDS AND ODD MONEY. THOMAS OSBORN FOUNDER, 1798.

Some of the MONUMENTS are as early as the 13th cent. In the churchyard are several stone coffin lids of this

PASTON.

date, on one the incised crosses are tolerably perfect. Under the tower is a defaced effigy of a man; and in the churchyard one of a woman. They seem to be of the same period, and are in all probability intended to represent man and wife. The head-dress of the woman is the well-known wimple. The man has a horn suspended by a strap, something tucked beneath it, possibly some arrows, and a staff or longbow on his left side. Mr. Paley suggests that the persons these effigies commemorate may have rebuilt the geometric parts of the church, the dates being coincident. Some floor slabs to members of the Arnold and Wing families are in the chantry. In the chancel is a tablet to one of the former name, 1792; and on the S. side is a slab of black marble in a framework of clunch, with this inscription nearly illegible:

D O M JOANNA Vidua JOHANNIS WILDBORE Generosi haud hinc Sepulta jacet Obijt Martii xxviii Anno Dom. MDCXCVI.

The excellent restoration of this church was effected in 1855. There is a fabric fund of £75 a year: this was mortgaged for a period and is now paid off. Many things, as service books, altar cloth, alms-dishes, were gifts. The woodwork was done at Stamford.

Morton, speaking of this church, says:

The spire of the Chapell of Glinton, for a Chapell, is, certainly the finest in England, tis so tall, and yet so very slender and neat.

Paston.

The high road to Lincoln passes through this parish, but the main part of the village and the church lie at some distance to the East, where the spire surrounded by trees is a most pleasing object. The name has remained unchanged since first mentioned: it is the *town* of some person in all probability, but the key to the etymology is now lost. The suffix TON is common in this neighbourhood: of 25 names of places described in this volume, no less than 12 have this ending. In Norfolk is a place of the same name. The ADVOWSON has been in the monastery and bishop, although for single turns other patrons have presented.

The church is dedicated to ALL SAINTS. In the taxation of 1291 the church was valued at 6*l*., deducting pensions and portions; no mean deduction, for the abbey had a pension of 13*s*. 4*d*. and a portion of 13*l*. 6*s*. 8*d*. In the king's books the gross value was 14*l*. 11*s*. 8*d*., the archdeacon's fees 8*s*. 7*d*. and the pension as above. The tenths amounted to 26*s*. 9½*d*.

The REGISTER commences in 1653, but a few entries of earlier years have been copied down at the beginning of the book. It goes down in the first volume to 1703. There are no entries from 17 Mar. 1662, to 1 Apr. 1669. The following extracts are given in order, without reference to their subject, as found in the register.

Edward Dickenson Rector of Paston began this new Register. Robert Brockwell Register chosen by the Parish according to an Act in Barbon's Parliament.

When I came to Paston wch was in October 1653 the Parish had no Register Book the old one being written full, and the former Minister writt the Baptisms Burialls and Marriages in many loose papers which after I had been at Paston about eight yeares Robert Brockwell delivered unto me wch I have here registred just in the same order as they were found in the said loose papers.

1648. 29 Aug. James a stranger died on his travell from St Neots and was buryed.
1657. Dec. Collected in the Parish church of Paston for the fire at Ashford (Asfordby?) in ye County of Leicester the sum of six shillings and nine pence & for the same fire in the Chappell of Werrington ye sum of six shillings.
    Collected for the towne of Blunham, Beds. in Paston 4*s*. 7*d*., in Werrington 5*s*. 2*d*. For Soulbay, Suff., 4*s*. 2*d*., in Gunthorpe, 3*s*. 9*d*. in Walton, 7*s*., in Werrington, 8*s*. 11*d*., in all 1*l*. 3*s*. 10*d*.
1661. 21 Feb. A stranger unknowne by name a woman dyed at Werrington.
1689. Margaret Eaton ye wife of Edward Eaton came to Gunthorpe by a pass September ye 11th & died September ye 12 & buried September ye 13th.
1706. Lavin of Werr. clam me * and Widdow Lampkin married a little before Xtmas by a Dissenting Teacher.
1762. (after a lady's death) NB. Rec^d. for a Mortuary on her Death 10*s*.
1764. 28 Feb. Mary Smeaton hang'd herself.

There is an unusual amount of Scripture names to be found here. Of others not very common are these: Avis, Cornelius, Custance, Hercules, Marmaduke. In 1678 W^m. Henson is Register. The parish chest has a number of indentures of the last century, and a vast collection of marriage licenses, very uninteresting. In the rectory

---

* 'Unknown to me;' a phrase of the comic dramatists.

is preserved a volume of accounts not often met with. The writing is in excellent order; but as the book is not bound, many leaves have gradually disappeared at each end. It is the book of Easter dues and offerings, and from the years 1608 to 1632 is quite perfect. It contains 116 leaves; but with the difference of variations in the dates, and the amounts, all are alike. The year's accounts are divided according to the districts: Paston, Waulton, Gunthorpe, Werington. These extracts, that follow, taken in no order, give all the different items.

The Easter book of paston parrish made in the yeare of oure Lorde god one howesand six hundreth & eightyne as ffolloweth this xxvijth of march 1618

    Off paston
    The manor house of peverills A waxshott[1] .... j^d ob
    Offering .... j^d
(1617) Richard poole A wax (shot) .... ij^d ob
    Offering .... j^d v^d
    A mayneport[2] .... ij^d
    Caulfes Runs on viii
    foles
    Sheepeskins
Tythe Lambs in Waulton (1611)
    Henrye Hawelye three tythe Lambes .... iij
    Mr Styles vij tythe Lambes .... vij
    William Spaulding too tythe Lambes .... ij
    Runs on fore[3]
    Jefferye Beale Runs on vij
    Ihon Inkerson one tythe Lambe .... j
      Sum xiij
    Robert Manbye Runs on vj

Receaved for this yere 1630 for the Easter booke Thirty and seven shillings. nd for the youths offerings seven shillings and eyght pens In All ffortye ffoure iillings and eyght pens 2 : 4 : 8 :

The inventory taken 6 Edw. VI. does not say much for he care then bestowed on the church.

Ffirst in ye steple iij belles—Item a sanctt belle—Item a chaliece of sylv^r w^t the ten—Item a nold vestim^t w^t a naube—Item a nold surples—All things ells re stollen away out of the said churche ffour or fvye yeres past sence whyche me nothyng hath ben provided.

The most important benefactor has been Edmund fountsteven. His will is dated 9 Feb., 1635, and he ied 4 March following. It provides that his body should e buried in the chancel at the feet of his dearly beloved ther, and that his monument shall cost less than 30*l*.

---

1. Or warscot, *ceragium*, according to Spelman, 'a tax anciently paid thrice a year towards a charge of candles in churches.'
2. Derived from 'in manu portatum,' according to Cowel, 'a small tribute, usually of bread, ich in some places the parishioners give to the rector of their church in lieu of certain hes.'
3. This means that W. Spaulding had 24 lambs, paid 2 as the tenths, and left 4 to be koned in next year's account.

He leaves 5*l.* to the repairs of the church, 10*l.* to the repairs of the chancel, 10*l.* to the poor, and land for the erection of an almshouse on the green. It has also this clause:

Item my will is that a licensed Minister dwelling wthin the soake of Peterborough not being advanced to a Benefice of thirty pounds a year shall yearly for ever by the appointment of the Bishop of the Diocese for the time being preach one Sermon at Paston church aforesaid on that day of ye month in the year on wch it shall please God to call me to his mercy out of this miserable world. And my will is there shall be paid to the said Minister presently after the said Sermon fourty shillings of current English money. Provided allwaies that no Minister shall preach the said Sermon and receive the said 40ˢ two years together.

He founded also scholarships at S. John's college, Cambridge, for boys from the king's school, Peterborough, leaving by will 1000*l.* for that purpose, with which and other moneys the college purchased lands at Leifeild, in Rutland. In the abstract of charitable donations published in 1786 by order of parliament, the bequest to the parish is said to produce 18*l.* a year, 12*l.* being paid to the almshouses, 30*s.* for coals, 30*s.* for repairs, and 3*l.* for apprenticing poor children.* In 1538 T. Ryley left 6*s.* 8*d.* for

one honest vestyment for the hye aulter in the paryshe church of Paston...... to every pore house within the parysh of Paston one stryke of barley and half a stryke of malte. and to every one of my godchyldren xii^d.

In 1539 John Cowper 'of Thorppe in the parish of Paston' (probably Dogsthorp) left

to the Sacrament of Paston vi^d, to the bells 3 strike of barley.

In 1569 Joan Baudrie of Walton left 3*s.* 4*d.* to the repair of the church, and to the parson her 'oulde whiche. The same sum was left in 1609 by Alice Clement.

RECTORS.

1217 Hen. de Wirmington.	1278 Rog. de la Grave.
1233 Will de Burgo.¹	1282 Nic. de Lodington, d.²
1238 Hugo de Stamford.	1293 Will. de Covergrave.
1240 Bart. de Stamford.	1294 Tho. de Freston.
1263 Rob. de Fraxino.	1307 Will. de Barnwell.
1269 Will. de Freston.	1310 Robertus.
Will. de Langtoft, d.	Hen. de Barnwell.

---

* There was in the parish at one time a very singular belief that the Mountsteven her spoken of would reappear every hundred years.
1. Held also (but perhaps not altogether) rectories of Peakirk, Castor, and Barnack.
2. Buried in nave of Peterborough cathedral.

	*Rob. de Mythingesby, d.[3]	1558	Will Barnaby.
1349	Rob. de Harwedon.	1559	Tho. Williamson, r.
1361	Joh. de Stene.	1560	Geof. Cowper, d.
1369	Rog. de Wymundham.	1594	Ric. Newton.
1397	Joh. Warde.	1627	*Rob. Laxton, A.M., d.
1421	Tho. Rydell.	1653	Ed. Dickenson, deprived.[8]
1422	Tho. Philipp.	1662	Tho. Lany, S.T.B.[9]
1433	Joh. Kyng.	1660	*Miles Delacree, A.M., d.
	Will. Bowdon.	1690	*Geo. Gascoigne, A.M. d.
1438	Joh. Chichele.		Will. Wigmore, d.
1439	Ric. Raynhill, r.[4]	1707	*Benedict Ball, A.M., d.[10]
1446	Joh. Hamerton, r.	1714	Tho. Foster.
1460	Joh. Wryght.	1720	*Tho. Gibson, A.M., d.[11]
	Joh. Hydson, r.	1759	Ch. Weston, A.M.
1470	Will. Pykeryng.	1762	Job. Lloyd, A.B., r.[12]
1512	Tho. Ryley.	1771	Will. Disney, S.T.B.
	*Tho. Cheyne, d.[5]	1777	Will. Jones, A.M.
1548	Humfr. Naturas, r.[6]	1800	Hen. Joh. Wollaston, A.M.
1553	Joh. Browne.	1803	*Hen. Mat. Schutz, S.T.P., d.
	Hen. Chapman, r.	1811	Jos. Pratt, A.B., now A.M.
1557	*Joh. Flynte.[7]		

Of the memorials to these rectors not many remain. That to Rob. de Mythingesby was perfect, except that the brasses had been removed when Bridges visited it early in the 18th cent., and had this inscription : †

✠ Hic jacet Robertus de Mythinggisbi quondam rector istius Ecclesie cujus anime propicietur Deus.

The upper part of this slab, with the letters very plainly cut, is laid at the entrance to the chancel. Rect. Gascoigne is described on his monument as 'Pastor vigilantissimus,' and rect. Ball as 'Vir suavis et doctus.' In the east wall, externally, is a slab to rect. Gibson: and in the chancel one to dr. Schutz.

The CHURCH is of the usual plan. It has a chancel with S. priest's door and N. chantry, nave with aisles

---

* Buried at Paston. † Bridges, ii, 534.
3. This rector is witness in Libro Albo 15 Edw. ii. His epitaph is quoted below, from Bridges. His name is however not given in Bridges' list of rectors, which is in other cases complete.
4. Also rect. of Stanwick and Castor.
5. His will was made 1548. 'I sir Thomas Cheyne Clarke parson of Paston being hole niet and parfite of mynde......bequeth my soul to God Allmighty and my body to be buried the church of Allhallows in Paston..........to the high altar 3s 4d........to the bells 3s 4d ......to the poor men's box 5s.'
6. Had been monk of the abbey, and in 1534 signed the paper acknowledging the king's supremacy. See p. 48. Also rect. of West Deeping and Winteringham, Linc.
7. In his will, dated 3 Dec., 1558, are these bequests: ' I give to the poor to be delt at my burial 3s 4d........I gyve to Thomas Pykeryng my buckskyne doublet. Item I gyve to Thomas Heyffes the iis that he oweth to me to be dronke amongst his neighbours. Item I gve to the church of Paston xiid.'
8. Deprived under the Bartholomew act: but Calamy says he ultimately conformed.
9. Preb. of Peterborough.
10. Called also rect. of Conington near Grantham, but there is no such parish. There are more than one for which it may be intended. He and three children died of fever, 'exigno erum intervallo.'
11. Also rect. of Polebrook, and preb. of Peterborough.
12 Buried at Orton Longueville.

and clerestory, S. porch and N. door, W. tower and spire. There is also a brick room built against the E. wall of the chantry for a vestry. The earliest parts of the existing church are the chancel with its aisle, and the lower part of the tower. Two stones of Norman date have been used in the building: one is to be seen in the E. wall of the chancel, nearly hidden by a tombstone, and the other, which has a scalloped ornamentation, in the E. wall of the S. aisle. The chantry does not extend so far east as the chancel. It is divided from it by two early English arches and a low wall, room for a passage being left. East of these two is a third arch, similar but unconnected. Beneath it is the door to the vestry, occupying probably the site of an original one. Of the altar appointments three sedilia only can be seen, other features being concealed by wainscot. These have shafts and the notchhead. They are later than the arches before mentioned, as was the E. window, now a simple wreck, the mullions having lost their tracery and being bisected by transoms of wood. Their date may be about 1320, the same as that of the spire. This being on a tower of perhaps 60 years greater age, may have replaced a low pyramidal covering. This spire is of very great beauty, whether we regard its effect as a whole, or the separate details. In the lowest stage are lancets on the N. and S. sides, the former blocked, and a broad one (manufactured out of a two-light window by destroying the mullion) at the west. In the next stage the belfry window has a large quatrefoil in a circle. The alteration in the masonry above is very noticeable. The buttresses were added with the spire, they are placed at the angles, which is always indicative of later work. The staircase turret, at the S.E., is a graceful addition. It stands out in bold relief, and its pyramidal top combines well with the outline of the spire. The spire is without parapet: a broach. The ballflower cornice runs continuously round the turret as well as the spire. This ornament also appears on the lower spire windows on the S. and E. sides. At the foot of the spire are two-light geometrical windows, not pierced in the head but with paneled tracery. Above are single lights, all on the cardinal faces, and all gabled. There is early decorated work also in the N. aisle. But the nave arcade, and the entire S. aisle, are perpendicular. The nave has four bays, the piers being octangular and the arches very well proportioned. The S. aisle and the clerestory have windows of three lights each. All the perpendicular work is about the same date, the middle of the 15th cent. This includes the nave roof and the chancel screen. This latter is lofty. There are no traces of stairs whereby the roodloft could be reached, but the screen certainly spread out into a loft, for on the W. side can be seen the marks of the groining which supported it. The chancel roof is flat. The windows in the S. side are much later than the wall in which they are placed. At the S.W. corner is a low side window, square, filled up with masonry. The E. end of the chantry is railed off and is now used as a baptistery. The font is octagonal. The dimensions given by Bridges are 96 ft. by 45 ft. 4 in. The tower is 12 ft. 4 in. by 7 ft. 9 in., and Mr. Paley gives the height of the spire at 98 ft.

We have some slight mention of stained glass formerly existing; but not a fragment now remains. In 1731,* there was to be seen

at upper end of south aisle in ye window a man kneeling, and over his head in Saxon letters, Ora........Thomæ Sutton.

And a few years earlier Bridges observed,

In the windows of the North ile are several imperfect portraits of mitred abbats, saints, and of our Saviour on the cross.

In the belfry are three BELLS, all inscribed. The latest is without date: but the name of the rector on it fixes it between 1762 and 1771. The first has fleur-de-lys between the words. The second has a foundry mark consisting of a shield with three bells, the lower one crowned.

1. ✠ OMNIA FIANT AD GLORIAM DEI 1607
2. PRAISE THE LORD 1601
3. JOSEPH EAYRE FECIT JOHN LYDE RECTOR THOMAS HENSON CHURCHWARDEN.

---

* Clement's notes, Brit. Mus. Add. MSS. 11,425.

With two exceptions the MONUMENTS are unimportant. There is a handsome incised cross in the chancel floor with inscription round the edge in black letter, but the name of the parish is obliterated. It is as follows:

☩ hic : jacet : dns : rogerus : hatwmile : quondam : rector : ecclesie : . . . . cujus : anime : propicietur : deus : amen.

And under a canopy in the S. wall of the chancel is a figure in a praying posture, recently restored, with this inscription:

Edmvnd Movntststeven Of Peterborovgh, within ye libertie of Nassabvrgh in ye Covnty of Northampto Esq. where he lived 45 years, plvs minvs a Ivstice of peace & qvorvm, and where he died so in ye yeare of his age 73 & in ye yeare of ovr Lord 1635 March 4 stylo Angliæ. He bestowed his whole Estate in piovs & charitable vses. He gave a thovsand povndes towards ye fovnding of two followships and two scholarships in St Iohn's College Cambridge of wch College himself was sometimes a stvdent. These to be chosen into that College ovt of Peterborovgh Schole. He bvilto and endowed ye Almeshovse on Paston Greene. He gave lovingly and liberally to ye Poor of this Parish & towards ye repare of this Chvrch & Chancell. He gave an hvndred povnds towards ye repare of ye Cathedral Chvrch of St Pavl, in London. His debts discharged & legacies payd the remainder He devised to good vses. He was a learned & religiovs Gent, a bovntifvll hovsekeeper to ye vtmost of his abilitie, & very Beneficial to very many Poore. His workes praise him in ye Gates.

In memoria æterna erit ivstvs.
Ivstitia eivs manet in secvlvm.
Sibi, in præmivm.
Tibi, in exemplvm.

Besides the memorials already mentioned to former rectors the chancel has a slab, 1839, to the Rev. J. Boak, rect. of Brockley, Somerset; and one to Harriot, wife of Lieut. Col. Desborough, 1802. The N. chantry was the burial place of the Stiles family, and they used to repair it. Mr. Paley has preserved some of the inscriptions. They are mostly 17th cent., and one is adorned, in the taste of the period, with a skull and cross-bones. In the N. aisle are tablets to Francis and John Low, 1788, the latter of whom was 'a Man diligent in his profession, sincere in his Friendship, Just in his dealings, and a good Neighbour.' In the S. aisle members of these families are commemorated; Fovargue (several), Whitwell, King, Newcomb, Hopkinson. On the Hopkinson stone is a greek hexameter (also in the S. choir aisle of the cathedral), quoted from the 6th book of the Iliad, thus

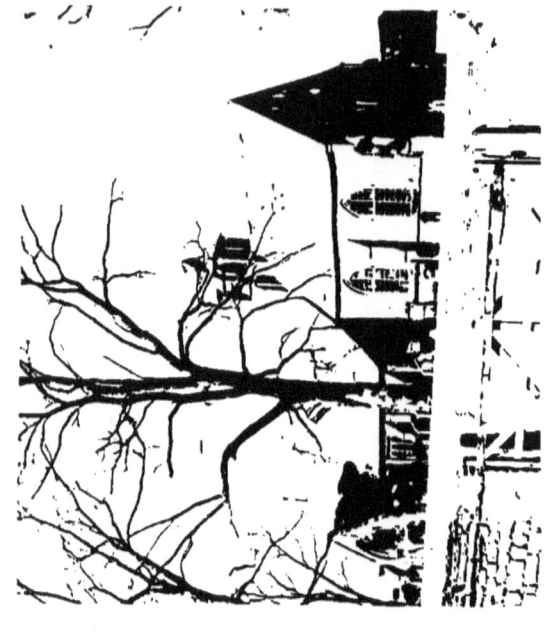

WERRINGTON.

translated by lord Derby: 'The race of man is as the race of leaves.' There is a large royal arms over the chancel arch of queen Anne's time: here too are the Pater noster and Credo.

The earliest tomb in the CHURCHYARD is dated 1724. At the E. end is a tablet to rect. Gibson, and one to his son, rect. of Marholm. There are numerous tombstones to Johnsons and Griffins. The S. porch has stone seats. There is a dial above the outer door dated 1756. A short avenue leads from this porch; and there is a marked seclusion about this churchyard although a public pathway runs through it. The S. side is skirted by lofty trees. In 1866 a beautiful little nest with six eggs was found built against the face of a tombstone.

Werrington.

This place is only a hamlet, and its church a chapel of ease to Paston. The main street lies along the ridge of a slight incline, running nearly due east and west. In Domesday book the name is spelt WIDERINTONE; from this it has passed through the forms WYTHERINGTON, WITHERINGTON, WIRINGTON, WERINGTON, to its present form. There is a place of the same name in Devon; it has the same root as Warrington. Both names signify a town or settlement of the Varini, a German clan,* 'who are placed by Tacitus in juxtaposition with the Angli.'

The church is dedicated to S. JOHN THE BAPTIST. Old wills speak also of the altar of the Blessed Virgin. The destroyed chantry to the N. of the chancel was therefore probably a Lady chapel.

The REGISTERS were always kept at Paston. The births and burials at Werrington were entered in a rough manner here, and transcribed (apparently once a year)

---

* Taylor's Words and Places, 129.

into the register of the parish church. These preliminary copies have only been preserved from 1709. There are overseers' books from 1796. Other parish documents include numerous indentures of apprenticeship; many certificates from churchwardens of families 'legally settled' in other parishes, some dating 1704; and a few certificates of bodies 'buried in sheep's wool,' 1716.

The goods of the church in 1552 were thus enumerated;

It. a chalyce of sylv^r pcell gylt w^t a patten—It. a pax of latyn—It. a vestm^t of chaungeable sylke w^t a albe—It. a vestm^t of darnax w^t a albe—It. a vestm^t of changeable darnax w^t a albe—It. a old vestm^t of Worstede—It. A grene vestm^t of worstede w^t a albe—It. one other w^t a albe of ye same—It. ix alt clo^s and ix towells—It. ij letle candlestyke of latyn sold to John Grene for x^d of the same towne—It. A pere of censars sold to ye said John for x^d —It. a chest—It. a surpless and a Rachett—Itm one Cross of Latten two hand bells and a sacring bell sold by the towne iiij^s viij^d —Itm a corporass case with a clothe of blewe worstede—Itm in the steple ij bells and a sanctus bell.

In the abstract of charitable donations, 1786, but one bequest to this place is mentioned. It is that of John Goodwinn, 1755, who left 100*l*. to poor widows, producing now 4*l*. a year. Small amounts were constantly left to the chapel. In 1528 a will has these clauses:

Ego Henricus Person capellanus de Weryngton ex parochia de Paston...... lego sacramento ibidem xii^d. Item lego S^{cto} Edmundo Regi de Weryngton predcta xvi^s ....Item lego campanis de Paston xx^d. Item lego ecclesiæ de Paston v^s.............

And in 1530 John Clerke left

To the hie aulter for tythes forgotten v^s to the faderless children of sent Katerine of Lincoln viii^d to the reparations of the bells of Paston iii^s iiii^d to Weryngton chapell x^s to the Reparations of the crosse at the Northgate iii^s iiii^d for an honest preste to synge for my soule by the space of a hole yere in Weryngton Chapell to have for his stipend v^{lb}.

In 1639 Frances Penny, of Dogsthorpe, widow, left 40*s*. to the cathedral, 40*s*. to Peterborough church, 40*s*. to Paston church, and 40*s*. to Werrington chapel.

The CHURCH has many points of interest, although in a bad state of repair, and although the external appearance is not promising.* Its plan is very simple; chancel and nave with aisles and S. porch. There is no spire or tower: between the nave and chancel stands a bellcot.

---

* Architectural students never take for granted that a church is not worth visiting because it looks poor or dilapidated from without. Last autumn I saw a church in Brecknockshire that looked far less promising even than Werrington; but within were to be seen a Lady chapel at the west end (like the Galilee at Durham) containing an original stone altar with a fine niche; a good chancel screen, supporting an elaborate rood loft with stairs, quite perfect; and on the west side of this screen two stone altars, a feature probably nearly unique. In a little desecrated chapel in Herefordshire, now used as a carpenter's workshop, I found two stone altars west of the screen, and the original high altar, with its crosses, unmutilated.

In general bellcots, as at Peakirk and Longthorpe, are at the W. end. The various parts are of different dates. The oldest portion of the fabric now standing is doubtless the arch to the chancel; not the narrow one, hardly more than 6 ft. across, visible from the west, but a much larger one, within which this has been formed: the outline c this earlier arch can be seen from the chancel, but al. details are obscured by the whitewash. The later arch is itself good Norman work; it has excellent capitals, with bold zigzag, recently picked out. The interior door of the porch, formerly the exterior door of the old church, is also of this date, the middle of the 12th cent. Fifty years later was the time the old church was enlarged by building aisles. The arches in the nave are of this period. There are three bays; all the arches are round-headed, those on the N. side being supported on plain circular piers, very elegant, the others on clustered shafts. At the W. end of the nave is an unequal triplet, part of the same alteration. Part of the W. wall seems Norman. The N. side of the church has suffered destruction at each end: at the W. one bay of the aisle is gone and the arch blocked up; at the E. a chantry, apparently coeval with the original church, has been destroyed. The arch that led from the chancel remains, it is Norman, and similar to the chancel arch. Beneath it has been inserted a square-headed decorated window of three lights. The whole of the chancel is decorated. The E. window is a good example of net-tracery, it is of four lights, very like the E. window of the grammar school at Peterborough, but a little earlier. It is however in an unsafe condition, and a piece of the mullion fell out not many months since. There are stone seats round the chancel. The piscina has a round head, with trefoiled tracery, and a wooden shelf. Opposite is the aumbry, which also retains its shelf; the door to it is modern. The S. windows of the chancel were evidently filled with net tracery: in the view can be distinctly seen the commencement of the meshes of the net. Why the tracery here was destroyed and the present hideous mullion and transom inserted, it is now idle to conjecture. The windows were not enlarged, so no additional light could be gained. In the case of the aisle windows there was at least this excuse, they were much enlarged. The alteration is however not the less to be deplored. The early English aisles very likely had a set of lancets. The present aisles are not original: and the windows are almost of any date, quite nondescript, and very ugly. The nave has a ceiling, very low. The chancel has a whitewashed roof, modern and plain. The arch between the N. aisle and the destroyed chantry has remains of decorated work. It is now converted into a window. The S. porch is of decorated date; it has an elegant outer arch. The font, near the S. door, is very striking. It has been figured in Mr. Paley's book on the churches of the neighbourhood. It is of the 12th cent., octagonal, standing on eight dwarf shafts, supported on an octagonal plinth, and a large step of the same shape. There is no priest's door. The low side window occupies the usual position S.W. of the chancel: it is now blocked. The state of the fabric throughout is unsatisfactory. But the shell is sound, and so it is not too much to hope that some day will see the whole put in thorough repair.

The bellcot contains two small BELLS. They are rung from the chancel. There is no access to them except by scaling the roof. The cot itself has been enclosed by woodwork, not unlike a pigeon-house. The nave roof is prolonged over the aisles in one extended slope. The aisle walls are thus very low.

No memorials of any interest remain. The old custom of strewing the church with grass is mentioned by Bridges (ii, 536), in these words:

On the feast Sunday it is a custom to strew the church with grass or hay, cut in the *Innhams*, a meadow, which on that account claims to be tithe-free.

The feast is on the first Sunday in July. This custom is now discontinued. The strewing churches with rushes was at one time very common. It is still practised at some few churches in the lake district, and till a comparatively recent period Norwich cathedral was once a year strewn with rushes. Bridges gives also the dimensions: length, 80 ft., breadth of nave and aisles, 38 ft. 6 in.

EYE.

Eye.

This is a large and long village though the parish itself is but small. It is perhaps the only one in this neighbourhood which exhibits a marked decrease in the population: there are 500 or 600 fewer inhabitants than in 1861. The name in old records was written EYA, or EEA. It has remained for centuries almost unchanged, being derived from EA the Anglo-Saxon for an island. The word is made into a termination for numbers of villages in the fen districts. Its diminutive, *eyot*, contracted into *ait*, is a well-known word.

The present chapel is dedicated to S. MATTHEW THE EVANGELIST. The consecration of the former one took place in 1543; and there is an entry in the register, here given, apparently a copy of the deed.

Notum fit universis quod die Martis ante Meridiem videlicet septimo die mensis Octobris festivo Scti Dionysii martyris anno a Virginis partu millesimo quingentesimo quadragesimo tertio Regniq nobilissimi Principis & Domini nostri Dni Henrici octavi Dei gratia Angl. Franc. & Hibern. Regis, ffidei Defensor^s & in terra Ecclie Anglicanæ & Hibernicæ sub Christo supremi Capitis Anno 35to Dedicata fuit Capella ista in honorem Dei & beati Mathei Evangelistæ per Reverendum in X^{to} patrem & Dominum Dnum Robertum divina permissione de Downe Episcopum ad id peragendum per Reverendum in Christo patrem & confratrem suum Dominum Johannem eadem permissione Petriburgensem episcopum primum, authoritate Regali legitime consecratum specialiter rogatum quoq & requisitum.

It has been too hastily inferred from this ascertained date of dedication that a new church was built at that time. Bridges speaks of the church existing in his time, which was destroyed 1845, as having been built in 1543. But it was certainly in its main features more than two centuries older. Mr. Paley says:

From an existing drawing of it, as well as from fragments preserved, it is clear that it was of the Geometric or early Decorated era. It had a bell-gable like the churches at Thorpe, Peakirk, and Werrington.

So that in all likelihood the example was set here which was afterwards followed at Longthorpe,* the chapel was

---
* See p. 30.

consecrated in order that the inhabitants might have right of burial, &c. And this view is confirmed by the register, which commences the same year. The chapel was always served by a monk from the abbey: and the chaplain was obliged every year to present his key at the altar in token of his holding it at the pleasure of the abbey.

The value of the tithe was not returned, as Eye was only a chapelry. In Bacon the curacy is said to be of the certified value of 16*l*. Chapels also existed at one time at Northam and Singlesholt; the latter was standing at the dissolution of the abbey. Both are now demolished.

The REGISTER commences in 1543, the date of the consecration. Its first volume, a thin parchment, is in very good order. From 1543 to 1601 all the entries are made by Malcolm Johnson, copied of course from an older book of paper. This book, after being lost for 40 years, was recovered by an inhabitant in 1711 and restored to the church. The second book, from 1665 to 1727, is still lost. A few entries from the older book are worth transcribing. The year of the king's reign is placed at the left of the page: a few events unconnected with the place are noted, as queen Mary's marriage.

1550. The vijth of february the first Bishopp of Peterborough called John Chambers departed.
1506. The laste of August Richard Darby the elder a wyse & upright man was buryed.
1625. The vijth of Aprill Saray Grawley of Well beinge droned in a well was buryed.
1646. 24 Apr. Margarett Cowley vidua senex paupercula.
1 June. John Hans above a hundred yeares old, pauper.
1648. 28 May. John Penn Curat morte obijt repentina.
1731. 16 Aug. (buried) Augustine Mac Duggle a Vagabond.

The last is from the present second book, which lasts from 1727 to 1797. The first volume is very imperfect towards its close. There are no baptisms in 1662, one only in 1663, none in 1664, and two in 1665. At the beginning of the last cent. the form of marriage entry, ' John—and Mary—were married together,' seems to shew the incumbent came from Suffolk.

When the inventory was taken in 1552 the chapel was well supplied for so small a place.

ffirst a chalice of sylv^r p gylt w^t a patin—It^m one vestement of blewe & white damask furnished, & one oth^r of fusthen furnisshed & an olde cope—It^m ij surplices & one paire of censors of latin & a shyppe of latin w^t a chrismatorye of latin—It^m an old altare clothe & a towell—It^m a pix of latin & a lavor of latin—It^m a chest w^t it ye poor mans boxe—It^m a coffer wherin ye regist^r book ys kept—It^m one holy wat^r stocke of brass—It^m ij bells in ye steple—It^m one handbell—It^m one old vestiment of redd sylke—It^m one vestiment of greene satten—It^m a crewott of pewter—It^m ij lytle candelsticks of lattin.

In 1786 the charitable donations were returned as 'None.' A bequest to the poor in 1629, quoted below, is therefore probably lost. In 1522, Will. Catell of Eye

left to the mother church of Lincoln iiii^d; to every gilde w^thin the Church of Peterborough xii^d; to our Lady chapell of Eye a bullock ii yere old.

It is possible that the dedication of the church may have been changed at the consecration in 1543. The following will, made very soon afterwards, in 1545, is that of Hen. Spaldynge, who left his body

to be buryed in the churche of Saynt Matthew the Evangelist in Eye. I bequeth unto the hie aulter of the same churche for forgotten tythes vi^d unto the churche of Peterborough iiii^d. Also I bequeth to the churche of Eye in whiche my bodye dooth lye 6^s. 8^d. Also I bequeth to the welth of the churche at tow reckenynge dayes in the yere by the space of seven yeres every reckenynge daye one stroke of malte. Allso I will that y^y cause at my buriall daye my seventh day and my thirtie day thre prestes to say thre Masses in the same churche for the welthe of my soule and all Crysten soules and of all thes thre dayes every daye ii strekes of corne to be taken and delte to the poore for my sowle.

Richard Butcher, in 1629, left

five pounds to be put out to the use of the poorest folke in the towne and the Rent every Christmas to be distributed as aforesaid.

It is almost impossible to make out a perfect list of incumbents, because they were licensed only, not instituted. The following very imperfect one has been compiled from various sources.

INCUMBENTS.

bef. 1522 Joh. Reynolds.	1648 Rich. Mason.
bef. 1552 Joh. Thomas.	bef. 1680 — Hargrave.[1]
Malc. Johnson.	1688 Joh. Hughes, A.M.[2]
Fr. Standish.	bef. 1711 Jos. Sparke, A.M., d.[3]
1631 *Hen. Gowin, d.	1740 Geo. Jefferys, A.M.[4]
1633 *Joh. Penn, d.	1769 Jas. Clarke.

* Buried at Eye.

1. His name occurs in the list of clergy in Kettlewell's life thought not to qualify themselves at the revolution. It is probable, therefore, that he was ejected from this preferment as a non-juror.
2. Minor canon of Peterborough cathedral.
3. Registrar of Peterborough: a learned antiquary: he edited "Historiæ Anglicanæ Scriptores." Buried in the cathedral.
4. Precentor of Peterborough cathedral, and second master of the king's school.

1794 Will. Drury Skeels, A.M.	1832 Jas. Henry Stone, A.M.
1800 Joh. Girdlestone, A.M.	1843 Rob. Bell, A.M., r.[6]
1810 Job. Wing, A.M., r.	1862 Geo. Thurnell, A.M.
1816 Tho. Mills, A.M., r.[5]	

The CHURCH was built in 1846. It is cruciform, with a W. tower and spire. It has neither aisles nor clerestory. There is a door at the N. end of the N. transept, and one under the tower. There is a very small vestry S. of the chancel. The chancel is very short, and this is the great defect in the church. It is little more than a sanctuary. It is all in the early English style. The nave has on each side four trefoiled lancets. At each end of the transepts are two-light windows with pointed quatrefoils at a little distance above: the walls here have lancets, as in the nave, in pairs. The E. window is a triplet, and has been recently filled with memorial stained glass. The subjects are seven scenes from our Lord's life: in the centre light are the Crucifixion, the Resurrection, and the Ascension. There are three steps to the sanctuary. The seats are low, but with doors. The pulpit and desk have been placed at the W. corner of the N. transept; and the seats E. of it in the nave have been turned so as to face west. There is a plain timber roof. At the W. end is a gallery, and in it a grinding organ, no longer used. The width of the chancel is 19 ft.; of the transepts, 20 ft.; of the nave, 29 ft.

The spire is a fine one, and is visible at a great distance. It is without parapet. At the base of the spire are two-light windows in the cardinal faces: near the summit are smaller lights. The belfry windows are also two-light, with a quatrefoil in the head. There are but two BELLS; the larger one being quite new.

1. HENRY PENN FUSORE 1712.
2. CAST BY JOHN WARNER & SONS LONDON 1865.

The designer of the church was Geo. Basevi; but his fatal accident at Ely cathedral occurred during the

---

5. Minor canon, and subsequently hon. canon of Peterborough cathedral. Also vic. of Bringhurst with Gt. Easton, rect. of Dembleby and Northborough. Buried in the cathedral yard.
6. Exchanged with his successor, the present incumbent, for vic. of Newbottle and Charlton.

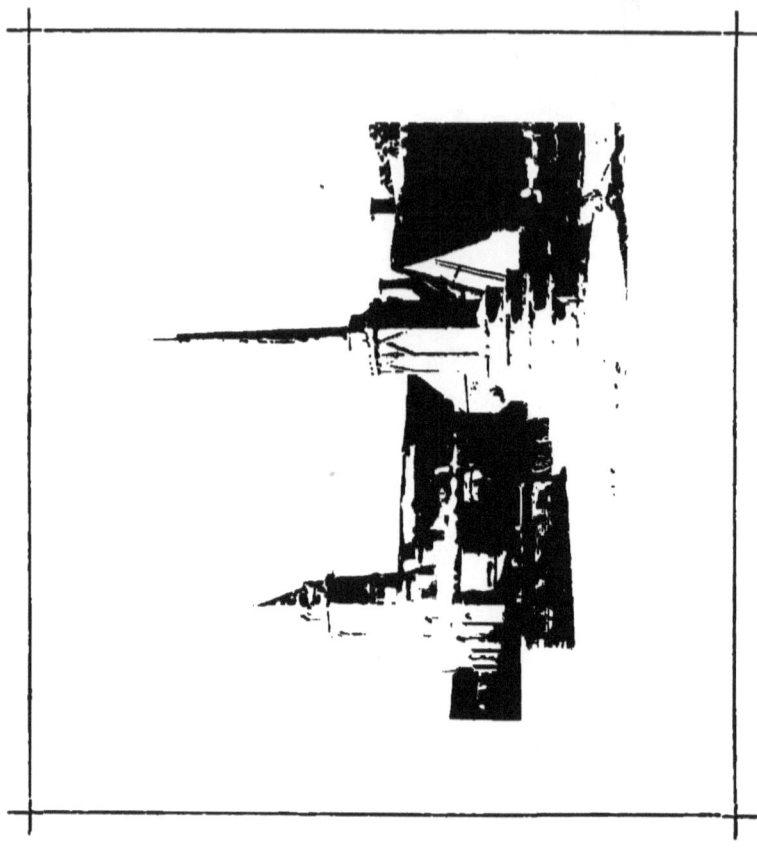

progress of the works, and they were concluded by F. T. Dollman.

The churchyard is small and greatly overcrowded. Many of the stones have been used for inscriptions on both sides. Many are used as flags for paving. There seem none remaining so early as the 17th cent.

Helpston.

This is a long and straggling village, seven miles from Peterborough. It is picturesque from the excellent stonework of nearly every building. The parish adjoins Barnack, and had a quarry of its own. The name only occurs as above, or as HELPESTON. A final E has sometime been added, but as it seems inaccurately, for there is no reason to doubt the etymology given by Bridges, HELPO'S TOWN.

The dedication is to S. BOTOLPH. He was born in Cornwall, in the 7th cent., and died about the year 680, having founded the town and monastery of Boston, where his name is perpetuated.* In 1254 the value was 10l., and the sacrist of the abbey had a portion of 1l. 6s. 8d. In the king's books the vicarage is worth 3l. 3s. 6d., the lord of the manor claiming yearly 3s. 2d., the tenths were 10s. 0½d.

The earlier REGISTERS are lost. The present ones commence in 1685. The first book ends in 1780; the second in 1800. They have not been very well kept, and the interesting entries are but few.

1715. 29 Nov. (Buried.) A poor stranger incerti laris.
1722. 15 July. Amy Levit, Felo de se, was buried wthout Christian Burial.
1791. The church was Wite Weshed in May (signed by Churchwarden and Clarcke).

---

* Dedications to S. Botolph were not unfrequent. There were 4 in London, 6 in Suff., 3 in Camb., 3 in Hunts. The church at Huntingdon is destroyed, so is that at Bottle-bridge, where the saint's name survives in corrupted form. See also p. 36.

1719—20. 19 Feb. (Buried.) A poor man, a stranger at Widow Bellars's.
1864. 25 May. John Clare. St. Giles, Northampton. 71 years.*

The following extracts from the churchwardens' books, which are preserved only from 1781, are curious.

1781.	21 May. P^d for Bear (beer) on the Perhambling day....	14s.	0d.
	P^d for Bread and Cees...............................	8s.	6d.
1782.	17 July. P^d eating and drinking for twenty seven Peopel	1l. 0s.	0d.
	My expencis	4s.	0d.
1789.	Paid God save the King	10s.	6d.
1790.	20 Sep. Postage of a Letter from the Treasury Chambers Whitehall		2d.
	9 Mar. A journey to Bainton † to make Complaint before the Magestrate against two Dilinquants for breaking the church windows	1s.	0d.
1791.	1 Dec. A Beesom for More		3d.
	2 Dec. 1 ^{yd} of greenbaize to wrap the surplice in	1s.	6d.
1826.	18 May. P^d Mr Rowe bill for fiddel strings	7s.	0d.

The inventory of church goods in 1552 is similar to those already given. Rob. Hare was vicar.

ffirst in the steple iij belles—Item in the same steple one little belle—Item tow handbelles—Item a chalice sylv^r pcell gylte—Item a crosse of coper & gylte—Item a crosse staff of cop & gylte—Item a holie water fatt of brasse—Item a basyn of lattyn—Item a crismatorie of lattyn—Item a pyx of lattyn—Item a vestmct of purple velvet—Item a cope of blewe sattyn brigs brothered w^t dyv^s flowers—Item one old vestment & one old cope—Item iij awbes & ij table clothes—Item iiij towels, one surples and one rachet—Item a byble & the paphrases & the holie Commyon boke—Item the pore mans chest w^t one other old chest—Item ij lytle candlesticks—Item ij corprasse case w^t ther corprasses in them.

There is also a line stating that the chancel, church, and aisles were covered with lead; but this is erased.

In the abstract of charitable donations, 1786, it is said that Bonner and two people unknown at unknown dates left money to the poor (Bonner to poor widows) producing 5s., 3l. 2s. 6d., and 10s. a year respectively. Bp. Kennett gives a great number of old wills of this parish. The first shews there stood a large cross in the churchyard. It is that of Rob. Hochyn, 1504, who leaves

corpus meum sepeliend. in cemeterio parochialis ecclie de Helpston, ante introitum porticus, prope magnam crucem. Item lego summo altari dicte ecclie pro decimis oblitis iij^s iiij^d campauis iij^s iiij^d.

There are interesting clauses in most of the wills. Such are these that follow.

1526. Ric. Russell—my body in ye paryshe churche of Helpston before the place accustomed to be left a kneeling place. to the hygh aulter for tythes for gotten xii^d to the bellis halfe a seme of malte. to the ryngers at the carrying of my corpse in the chyrche at the Masse time iiij^d.

---

* 'The peasant poet.' Within the last few days a coped stone has been placed over his grave.
† The next parish.

HELPSTON.   93

1545. John Worseleye, gent.........to our mother church of Peterb. iiij^d to the hyghe aulter in Helpeston churche iiij^d. to the reparations of the same churche xii^d.
1548. John Wynslowe......to the highe aulter of the churche of Helpston in discharginge my conscyence for oblyvyous tithes by me omytted by ignoraunce viij^d. to the reparations of the said churche xii^d to every poore housholde a streake of malte.
1552. Rob. Hechyn (or Hochyn)........I wyll my body to be buryed nye to the churche porche of Saynt Botulphe in Helpeston. Item I give for my mortuary as the law of this realme of England doth requyer. Item I give to the mother church workes of Peterborough vi^d. Item I geve to the church workes or Helpeston ii^s. Item I geve to the workes of the chauncell aforesaide in recompensing tythes and oblations ignorantly neglected viij^d.

In 1629, Hen. Wells, yeoman, left 10 groats to the church, and 6s. 8d. to the poor. In the following list there is some confusion among the earlier names between vicars and rectors. It does not appear when the rectory ceased to go with the church.

RECTORS AND VICARS.

1230	Galf. de Helpeston.	
1231	Walt. de Burg.	
1254	William.	
1274	Joh. de Helpeston, deprived.[1]	
1280	Will. de Cheyle.	
1296	Will. de Hegham.	
1298	Joh. de Hegham.[2]	
1322	Will. Wake.	
1358	Ric. de Treton.	
1364	Ric. de Wyttilbury.	
	Will. Bonde.	
1391	Tho. Allington.	
1412	Rob. Ballard.	
1445	Hug. Tapton.	
1457	Joh. Thorp.	
1465	Will. Basset.[3]	
1475	Rob. Melton.	
1507	Hen. Wylson.	
1540	Rob. Hare, deprived.	
1554	Tho. Diconson.	
bef. 1573	Ric. Swannock.	
1595	Tho. Crosier, A.B., d.	
1590	*Ric. Basset, d.	
1615	Abel Buddel.	
bef. 1663	——Vaughan.[4]	
bef. 1675	——Knowles.[4]	
1682	Tho. Ixem, d.	
1703	Sam. Bourn.	
1706	*Tho. Smith, d.	
1720	*Major Currer, A.B., d.	
1731	Will. Garforth, A.B.	
1734	Ric. Philpot, A.M.	
1735	Will. Paley, A.M., r.[5]	
1799	Joh. Jackson Serocold, A.B.	
1817	Ch. Mossop, A.B., r.[6]	
1853	Rob. C. Hubbersty, A.M., r.[7]	
1855	Joh. A. Legh Campbell, A.M.	

The CHURCH has specimens of all the styles of architecture. The plan is, chancel with priest's door S., nave with aisles and clerestory, S. porch, W. tower and spire, he aisles extending west as far as the tower. It has ecently received extensive repairs, and the stonework is

---

* Buried at Helpston.
1. Deprived for some irregularity in his orders.
2. Probably rect. of Twywell and Laxton.
3. Master of God's House at Cambridge, now Christ's college.
4. These names appear at the bp.'s visitations.
5. Minor canon of Peterborough, head master of Giggleswick, Yorks. His son was archdn. f Carlisle. He held the living 64 years, and resigned it a few months before his death. This ng incumbency has been exceeded at Hull, the late vicar (who is living) having resigned :is year the incumbency to which he was presented in 1797.
6. Now vic. of Etton.
7. Now inc. of Cartmel, Lanc.

now in excellent order; the tower was entirely rebuilt with the old materials. During the work, interesting discoveries were made which will shortly be noticed. Of Norman work is the lower part of the tower. Though within the church it was not open to the aisles, but the walls were solid. In the new work there are arches instead, built in the Norman style. The belfry arch is pointed, of transitional date. The best work of distinct 13th cent. date is the S. door. This had one shaft at each side, one now remaining, with stiff characteristic foliage. The door itself is dated 1708. The nave arches are peculiar. On each side are two broad ones, and one very narrow one by the chancel. The former are round-headed, except that to the N.W., the latter very pointed. Mr. Paley conjectures that the chancel arch of the original early English church stood where these narrow arches have been added. They and the whole chancel are of the geometric style, probably not later than 1270. The chancel now has three very lofty windows square-headed (the tracery was destroyed, according to a date outside, in 1609), of two lights: the E. window is of three lights similarly mutilated. Here are a piscina and three sedilia on a level, separated by their shafts, trefoiled in the heads. The piscina has two projecting basons, restored. On the N. side are three arches similar to the sedilia, most unusual. They were not stalls, being too high. One may have been an aumbry. The parish chest is attached to one by a chain. The stringcourse is good and similar on each side: on the S. it drops going over the door, and the same on the N. where is no door. There are two steps to the altar which have some very remarkable tiles.* They are arranged in circular pattern, with a border. Just by the altar step N., is a blocked door. There are stone seats along each wall of the chancel, having curious elbows. Two poppyheads much worn remain, one has a figure with a sword. From each aisle is a squint, or slanting aperture to allow people in the aisles to see

---

* Coloured engravings of these are given in Parker's Glossary. ii, pl. 206, 208, and their date is there assigned to the early part of the 13th cent.

the altar. The marks of the screens are very conspicuous. A small fragment of the screen itself is all that is left. Partly over the priest's door is a two-light window, later than the other, and much smaller, having cinquefoiled lights and a quatrefoil in the head, the horizontal stone above being also paneled in shallow quatrefoils. A low side window in the usual position has the iron stanchions remaining. The aisle windows are square headed of two lights, the cusps being inserted into the stone. On the S. side these have been restored, but on the N. the original cusps remain, and the spandrels have some early quarries. The gem of the church is the beautiful decorated window E. of the S. aisle. It is of two lights with segmental head. The string below has ballflowers the entire length of the wall, and it runs round a bracket at the S. end. There is a plain piscina with round bason. The bottom of the window is high, leaving an ample space for reredos. When the levels of this altar platform were lowered some time back, a stone coffin was found on a level with the floor; it had no lid and is now placed below. Both aisles have a stringcourse on each wall of the original roof: in the N. aisle can be seen that to the nave roof before it was heightened for the perpendicular clerestory. The W. window is 15th cent. work. There was an early door here, some trace of which remained before the late rebuilding of the tower. The N. aisle door is also blocked: and there was a door pierced W. of the S. aisle, to admit to the vestry; but the wall is now replaced. The S. porch is perpendicular. In it is the base of a holy-water stoup.

The tower, as rebuilt, is a very fine work. It is rigorously identical with the former, and but few stones have had to be restored. The square tower dies into an octagon, which is surmounted by a low spire. All the upper part is 14th cent. work. The belfry has windows of two lights of net tracery: this is at the top of the octagon. The spire, so short as to be almost a pyramid, has two-light windows in the non-cardinal faces. Beneath the embattled summit of the octagon is a string of ballflowers. The lowest stage has trefoiled openings.

There are four BELLS. One is quite new, in place of the third given below, which was broken in many pieces. The fourth was the sanctus bell and is very small: it was filled with lead and used as a clock weight: it used to be rung from outside the church and the mark made by the chafing of the rope from the S. belfry window is clearly to be seen in views taken before the tower was pulled down, but cannot be seen now.

1. OMNIA FIANT AD GLORIAM DEI. 1618.
2. GOD SAVE THE KING 1671.
3. ✠ GOD SAVE THE KING.
4. ✠ CUM VOCO VENITE. IW. WL. 1612.

The first bell has fleur-de-lys between the words.

There are two ancient MONUMENTS; one in the N. aisle had a rich floriated cross standing on a lion in brass, with two coats of arms: the metal has been long torn away. The inscription is partly hidden under pews, and a few words have been supplied (in the following) from Bridges and Mr. Paley: but neither of them give the whole inscription. One word only is doubtful.

✠ ICI : GIST : ROGER : DE : HEGHAM : DE : KY : ALME : DEV : DOYNT : REPOS : E : KY : PVR : SA : ALME : PRIERA : III : CCC : IOVRS : DE : PARDOVN : AVERA.*

In the S. aisle is a slab much worn, in black letter. It is to a rector of some church, and the name seems Nuscote, or Hinscote. In the chancel are tablets to Bellars, 1778, Sweeby, Wattkin, Clark, and rect. Smith, 1725, who is said to have been 'A Diligent and Painfull Minis^r of the L^{ds} Gospel, a faithfull friend, A disdainer of Worldly Greatness, A Most Passionate lover of Order and Regularity in Holy things, and the L^{ds} Day in Particular, of an Inviolate Attachment to his unweared Labours of Prayer and Preaching.' On a nave pillar is

---

* 'Here lies Roger de Hegham to whose soul may God give rest, and whoever shall pray for his soul shall have three hundred days' pardon.' This Roger de Hegham died between the years 1297—1310. The only doubt is the number of days: III CCC is a most unusual notation for 300. The following passage from an old life of Edward the Confessor, of about the date of this stone, will be sufficient authority for the word 'doynt:' 'E dist, Douint Deus les pruf voirs sont,' 'May God grant that the proofs be authentic.' Inscriptions with grants of indulgence are not common: one remains in this county at Brixworth, for 240 days, of date 1508. Bridges gives 'de ky alme,' the construction properly requiring 'a ky alme:' but the phrase 'donner de' was used, though not commonly.

+ haupaston:

S : botolph:

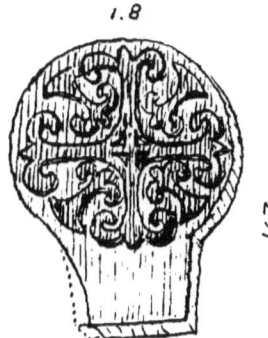
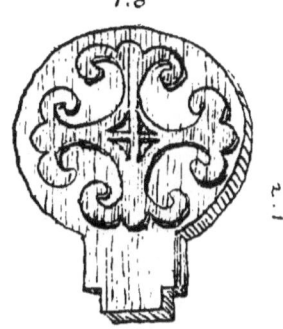

✠ Halpaston:  S: Botolph:

a tablet to Geo. Lawrence, 1769, who 'was a constant Attendant and lover of y̓ᵉ Church of England as by Law Establish'd.'

In the village there is a very beautiful CROSS. The head itself is unhappily gone; but the steps, base, and shaft remain perfect. It is contemporary with the spire.

Many features of interest were revealed by the pulling down of the tower. The foundations were found to be Saxon. For 5 ft. below the surface on the N., S., and W. sides of the tower is long and short work. Below this, at the N.W. corner is a concrete floor 2 in. thick, resting on the rock; but on the S. side the rock is 2 ft. below the termination of the Saxon work, and 7 ft. below the surface. These early foundations extended also westward into the churchyard. In the masonry of the tower itself, above the level of the aisle roof, were found numerous sepulchral slabs; in the W. wall below were found some Norman fragments; and 3 ft. above the floor in the N. wall there were four more stones found, earlier than any. Two of these were part of a very early headstone, and are figured in the accompanying sketch. A rude cross in a circular head, with entwined carving on the stem, forms the design. On a third stone is part of a similar cross. It will be seen that these are of Saxon date. Of Norman date were several stones of an old arch, worked up in the interior of the tower, and four short pillars belonging possibly to some old altar. Mr. Bloxam, of Rugby, visited the stones thus discovered, in September, 1865, and he pronounced * all the slabs to be of 13th cent. work. The Saxon ones above spoken of had not been brought to light at his visit. Seven of these, including the two excellent headstones, have been roughly sketched for this work. There were many more fragments, but all of the same period. Their dimensions are all given. The two smallest are very singular. One of these is rebuilt in the tower with its face visible: most of the bodystones have been again worked up for masonry in the rebuilding. The headstones have been preserved;

* In a letter to the Northampton Mercury, dated 28 Sep., 1865.

one is in the possession of the writer. The three headstones are all carved on both sides. Those at the top of the page represent front and back of the two 13th cent. stones. In every case the carving is in relief. The curious thing is that these should be found in a 14th cent. tower; only a century after their own date. Mr. Bloxam has a most ingenious suggestion on this head.

<small>Helpston is within three miles of the once celebrated quarries at Barnack. Could these sepulchral slabs and crosses have formed part of the stock-in-trade of some adventurous stone mason, the fashion for such articles having changed; and were they on that account worked up simply as materials ready at hand?</small>

All the bodystones are slightly coped. Most of them are very elegant, and would form excellent patterns for imitation.

This village is mentioned by Hone * as the residence of Ben Burr, a sort of prophet, who lived about 40 years ago, but his name does not appear in the registers. And the descendants of David Clapham, a noted proctor in the Arches, who died 1551, resided here.† Bridges gives the dimensions of the church as 76 ft. 9 in. by 41 ft. 6 in.

Whittlesey S. Mary.

The town of Whittlesey is the most important place within 10 miles of Peterborough. The population of the two parishes is about 8,000, and their extent upwards of 25,000 acres. A tradition of a market lingers about the place on Friday afternoons. The name as pronounced has never been altered; but its form has been often changed, having been written WITLESEY, WHITLESEY, WITTLESEY, WYTTLESEY, WHITTLESEA, and in other ways. The termination EY is *the island* so common about here. Of the former part of the word no reliable explanation has been given.

<small>* Every Day Book, i, 524.
† A Genealogy is given in MS. Harl. 1500, 42.</small>

WHITTLESEY S. MARY.

The ADVOWSON of S. Mary's church was originally with the abbot of Thorney, it afterwards was held by the Waldegraves, as lords of the manor, and when the manor was subdivided and in the hands of various persons, the advowson was held by them conjointly: Mr. Childers now holds both manor and advowson.* In the taxation of 1291 the value of the church was 16*l.*, and of the vicarage 6*l.* 13*s.* 4*d.* The bishop's procurations were 4*s.*, and for the vicarage 1*s.* 8*d.* In 1402 the value was 20*l.*, and the vicarage, as before, 10 marks. In the king's books the value was 19*l.* 13*s.* 9*d.*, and the tenths 39*s.* 4½*d.* The clear yearly value of the vicarage in 1786 was returned at 7*l.* 10*s.* But at bp. Green's visitation, in 1731, the living is called a donative curacy, and its value, 10*l.*, is said to have been 'augmented by lot' and so worth 38*l.* In the register is this note by Thos. Topping, referring to this augmentation.†

<small>About the year 1706 Symon Patrick Bishop of Ely wrote to me to give him a true account of the yearly value of St. Mary's and St. Andrew's Churches in Whittlesea, and wch I did thereupon the Bishop recommended to the Stewards of Queen Ann's bounty as proper objects for an augmentation: About the year 1713 the first Lotts were drawn and a lott of two hundred pounds fell to St. Mary's Church B^t I was never able to obtain either principal or interest while White Kennet Bishop of Peterborow undertook the mater, and in the month of October 1722 he secured ye 200*l*, and all the arrears of interest 76*l.* to the everlasting honor of that great good Bishop.</small>

The oldest REGISTER is dated 1560. For upwards of 100 years the registers are unbound; the detached leaves are much worn, and in most cases illegible. Very few pages are quite perfect. In some cases the damage seems to have been wilful, for the page dated 1611 is torn from top to bottom; and this has been done since 1827, for a

---

<small>* A curious piece of intriguing occurred with regard to the presentation in 1828. The two vicarages had been for many years held by one clerk. The payments to the vicar of S. Andrew's being made by the lords of the manor of S. Mary's, his living was of very insignificant value. The patron was the lord chancellor: and the custom had been for the lords of the manor to present to the living of S. Mary's upon a vacancy, and for the lord chancellor to present their vicar also to the vicarage of S. Andrew's. On the death of Mr. Pratt, in 1828, it occurred to Mr. Cook that this arrangement might with advantage be reversed. He accordingly succeeded (it is said through the influence of the late lord Palmerston) in obtaining the vicarage of S. Andrew's from the lord chancellor, before the lords of the manor had made their presentation, fully expecting that they would readily present him. This, however, they declined to do. He therefore instituted enquiries as to the tithes due to him from the said lords, and finding them to be greatly in excess of the sum paid, he commenced a lawsuit to recover them. This lasted some years, until the passing of some acts of parliament during the progress of the case facilitated his final victory. But he only lived a short time to enjoy the increased value of the living. It is now the more valuable of the two.

† A MS. letter on this subject, from Thos. Topping to bp. Kennett, is preserved in MS. Lansd. 1038. It encloses the new articles of the bp. of Ely, and asks for instructions about the queen's bounty. It is dated 'Whittlesea, Sunday noon, July 7, 1728.'</small>

MS. note by Edward Ground, the curate, of that date, is itself torn in half, and one half lost. The baptisms from 1560-94 are tolerably regular, but only a few entries can be made out. About 1562 the entries ceased to be made in Latin. The first legible burial register is 1590, after which it is continuous; except that a leaf of date 1606 is lost, and that there is only a small fragment between the dates 1654-64. There are no entries from 1647 to March 25th, 1650; but these are not lost, because the entries of the latter date follow immediately, on the same page, those of the former date. The parish registrar during the commonwealth was Will. Selby. The following extracts are of some interest.

1620. 14 May. Hellen Kent of the almes house.
1654. May. Sarah Vangalloway a Dutch-woman.
1707. 8 Apr. Stephen Bishop in ye Quaker's yard.
21 Aug. Christian Kermihil a hylander in Scotland.
1711. 30 Dec. Amy Payne 104 years old when she died And had her memory perfect to ye last.
1729. 10 May. Joⁿ Gates, the old Antinomian Whitesmith, Great Grandson of Francis Gates, who was Vicar of St. Mary's Church for 64 years or thereabouts.[1]
1733. 4 May. Mr. John Underwood.[2]
1738. 24 Jan. (married) Will. Webster An. Negus: who poison'd herself soon after.
1739. 4 Feb. a stranger without any name.
1740. 27 Dec. An. Hutchinson, Gent. That founded the Sermon on Good Friday. 30s. [This is still paid.]
1783. Oct. In the beginning of this month the nasty three penny Tax[3] took place, and as I expect from the great Number of poor and the Rebellious Humour of the Parishioners, to collect but few threepences I shall mark those that pay with V in the Baptisms and Burials. N.B. As people are most frequently openhearted on the day of Marriage, I expect most of my Parishioners will pay ye 3^d on that occasion I shall therefore mark those that do not pay with a V.

I squeezed 3^d from many a poor wretch ill able to give even so so much to Government I am affraid—I think I ought not to urge quite so hard.
1784. [The fees amounted to 1l. 0s. 9d., on which sum Rob. Addison, Curate, says:—] 'tis very much more than I expected or than I shall have

---

1. Mr. Topping in this entry is deceived by his handwriting extending from 1560 to 1622. This is no evidence of his being vicar all that time. See the Churches of Cambridgeshire, (Soc. Camd.) p. 15. An entry in the register at Cherry Hinton says that Tho. Moigne was vicar for 64 years. But he died before he was 70, and was made bp. of Kilmore 17 years after he resigned this living. The fact is that in 1597 an order was made by convocation that transcripts on parchment should be made of the registers previously written on paper, and that each page should be attested by the minister and churchwardens. This order of the synod was confirmed by the queen's injunction. See also p. 2, and the notices of other register books in this volume.

2. This entry is only noticeable for a very eccentric will and funeral of the deceased. See Hone's Year Book, 540; where is a notice from Gent. Mag. He was an enthusiastic admirer of Horace, and among other provisions of the will was this, that the six gentlemen who attended as mourners should sing the 20th ode of the 2nd book.

3. This duty of 3d. on each registry of births, deaths, and marriages, except those of paupers, was imposed by act of parliament, and began 2 Oct., 1783. It ceased 1 Oct., 1794. In the cathedral is a book prepared under this act, with a stamp impressed for every entry.

1794. 11 Feb. William Speechley (a Barber by Trade and an honest, industrious, faithful servant as ever was born—these are ye Men, who are a Loss to Society.)
   next year for as Poverty is admitted a plea it will be very frequently urged.
   (baptized) Matt^w. of James and Alice Loomes. By the mistake of ye Nurse this child was named Matthew instead of Martha, the name given her by her Parents.

There are also notices of occasional gifts to the church. Thus in 1712 Ann Bull, Widow, gave a brass branch with six candlesticks in it, which cost 2*l.* 7*s.* 0*d*. All memory of this has now passed away. Cole, in 1745, says 'I think there hangs a neat brass branch by Pulpit.' And in 1731, 6 June, is this notice:

On this day being Whit Sunday, there was given a Larg Silver Flagon, by an unknown hand, to be used at St. Mary's and St. Andrew's while one Minister officiates at both these Churches, But if ever there shall happen to be two Ministers, then this flagon shall belong to St. Mary's wholly and solely, and shall be used only at all Comunions in St. Mary's Church; But not at Comunions in St. Andrew's Church: This is the Will of the donour. Value £38.

Tho: Topping, Vic^r.

But afterwards found to be given by Frances Hurry.

Her burial is entered 17 Sep., 1732. This flagon was cumbrous and practically useless. It has recently been exchanged for more serviceable plate. In 1764, Mary Forster left 100*l.* for plate for the celebration. That given by her executors cost 100*l.* 1*s.* 8*d*.

The inventory of church goods for this parish was taken 27 July, 6 Edw. VI. It mentions a vicar who cannot be identified with any in the list that follows. The writing is very crabbed and indistinct.

Playt remanyng there this psent............iiii lb.
Ornaments. Itm a vestem of grene silke wth deacon & sbdeacon copleyt—a vestem of blewe worstede—a vestem of rede dornyx—a coope of Red velv^t—a coope of grene syllke—iij table clothes of lynnyng—a pyxe of copper—ij cruetts of pewther—a pare of sencers of copper—a stouppe of copper—a chrysmatorye of pewther—a surples wth flower—ij........ ....a holywayter paile of latten. Belles. Itm In the Steaple iij great bells a sanctus bell & ij handbells & a sacrey bell.
Memorand^m the ij candlesticks & i laver of latten mentyoned in the last Inventorie was sold to Symon Labyr (?) vicar there about a yere agoo by the churchwardens for the sum of iiij^s which was employed upon the repairing of their churche.

At Eastree, or Eastrea, in this parish, was a chapel dedicated to the Holy Trinity. The licence for its foundation is dated 1403. There was also a hospital of S. John the Baptist. And at Eldernell was a chapel to

Our Lady. This was consecrated in 1525 by the bishop of Down and Connor; but the chapel had existed before, perhaps only with a licence.* Cole has preserved a fragmentary account of a reputed miracle here wrought, which is worth recording.†

VICARS.

1338 Rad. de Witlesey.	1552 Nic. Wiltshey.
1345 Joh. de Ikleburgh.[1]	1555 Joh. Griffith, r.
1349 Rob. de Harwedon.	1561 Joh. Beawater.
1349 Joh. de Brampton.	1570 ‡Joh. Forster, r.
1350 Rob. de Crayton.	1590 ‡Fr. Gates, d.
Rob. de Ellesworth, r.	1622 *‡Will. Mason, d.
1383 Rob. de Newton, r.[2]	1666 *‡Ric. Mason, A.M., d.
1392 Ric. Beleby.[3]	bef. 1684 *‡Ric. Mason, A.M., d.
1406 ‡Tho. Pope.	1703 *‡Tho. Topping, A.M., d.
1457 Rob. Kyrton, A.M., d.[4]	1742 ‡Will. Beale, A.M., d.
1488 Ivo Hamserley d.	Geo. Moore, d.[5]
1495 Sim. Childerhouse.	1772 *‡Tho. Ch. C. Moore, d.
Edw. Hawtrey, d.	1816 *Joh. Pratt, d.
1517 Hen. Mores.	1828 Simeon Lloyd Pope, d.
1527 Tho. Wyllson.	1856 Will. Waller, A.M.[6]
1551 Nic. Leaves.	

The CHURCH consists of chancel and nave, both with aisles and clerestory, W. tower and spire, and S. porch.

---

* Cole's MS. vol. ix. In bp. West's register is a licence dated Somersham, 20 July, 1525, to the bp. of Down and Connor, to consecrate the chapel, and to remove chalices, &c., which 'had been abused, were old, deformed, or improper, as al-o to bless and reconsecrate others of the same sort; so that this Licence and consecration brought no prejudice to the Mother Church.' And a second Licence, dated 11 Jan. following, grants to the same 'Robert Blythe by Divine Permission Lord Bishop of Connor and Downe and Abbat of Thorney to dedicate and consecrate the chapel of our Lady of Aldernall and also of consecrating and blessing the Altars, Superaltars, Chalices, priestly Vestments, and other ecclesiastical ornaments, belonging as well to the said Chapel, as to the Monastery of Thorney and Church of Wittlesey, likewise to confirm in the Deanery of Wisbeche, and to give the first Tonsure to such Clercs and Scholars as desired it, and also to confer all holy and the lesser Orders to the Monks of Thorney, as shall be found fit for them, till such time as the Bishop should withdraw his licence.'

† It is unfortunately without date. The paper which Cole copied was torn: there was a rude picture at the top. The authorship of the account is attested thus: '¶ This myracle comprysed and wryten by a monke unworthy of Thorney Abbay dane Roger Lodynton in the honour and praysinge of our blessyd lady yᵉ moost mekest moder to our lorde Jhesu crystᵉ to whome be praysinge and honour. Amen.' It recounts how one Robert Whyt of Whittlesey S. Mary was bedridden; how he prayed to Our Lady of Eldernell; and how he got up on Monday before the feast of SS. Simon and Jude, and 'barebede and barefote........... wente thrugh thycke and thyn in that cold frosty mornynge........... space of thre myles.' The vicar of S. Mary's and many neighbours followed him to Eldernell with tapers burning in their hands. For some time he could not speak; at last, 'with grete payn and grete brayne he spake and sayd Lady helpe. The sayd Vycare, with all the neighbours sawe the teres of our blessyd [Ladye as] bygge as feches.' So the man turned to good health, the story finishes, 'and is a lyve.'

* Buried at Whittlesey.
‡ Also vicars of S. Andrew.
1. Presented by papal provision.
2. Exchanged with his successor for Haxey, Linc.
3. Perhaps also rect. of Castor. See p. 18.
4. Made abbot of Thorney, 1464, retaining this living.
5. Min. canon of Peterborough cathedral.
6. Formerly inc. of Dukinfield, Cheshire.

There are doors in each aisle and one under the tower, also a priest's door in the S. chancel aisle. It is in a most excellent state of repair, having been opened after restoration by Mr. Scott in 1862. The contrast between the present interior of the church and the appearance it presented ten years ago is most striking. The tower arch was blocked up with a wooden partition: the floor of the nave was encumbered with huge pews, some upwards of five feet in height: the pillars had in many cases been cut into for the purpose of holding the woodwork of these boxes, and round several pillars were rows of hat-pegs. Between the windows of the clerestory were painted in black and white the signs of the tribes of Judah: these were unedifying specimens of the art and taste of the last century. Two galleries occupied the aisles; and ugly skylights had been let into the aisle roofs. It is needless to say that galleries, pews, hat-pegs, 17th century frescoes, and boarding of the tower arch have now alike vanished. The nave is fitted with low open seats of admirable design; and the floor of the church now seats comfortably upwards of 800, more than were before uncomfortably accommodated in galleries and pews. The S. aisle was first restored. It is fitted with a pine roof, of very low pitch; supported on ungainly corbels. A very curious little window, which probably gave light to the rood-loft, and is not often met with, was wantonly destroyed. The rood stairs, with doors above and below, remain. They are lighted by two tiny windows; the lower of two, the upper of three disconnected lancets. The chancel deviates to the north.

The church was fortunate, at the time of its restoration, in securing the money, over £700, which had been subscribed as a memorial to the late sir Harry Smith. This money was entirely spent in the restoration of the chancel aisle. In the S. wall is a marble monument, with a bust; the roof is new, and four stained glass windows have been inserted. This aisle was formerly used as the parish schoolroom; and the propriety of this memorial consists in its being the very place where sir

Harry received his early education.* The vicars themselves, or their curates, taught in this school. In 1731, Mr. Topping, the vicar, is called, at the visitation, curate; and Mr. Beale, afterwards vicar, is called schoolmaster. The piscina remains. It has only been recovered to the use of the church within memory. Beneath the east end of this aisle is a crypt, which was formerly used as a charnel-house, but now holds the apparatus for warming the church.

The oldest existing part of the church is part of the N. aisle wall, and one pillar with three arches of the N. nave arcade. Two of the pillars here are round, and the mouldings of early English character, but the west one has been rebuilt in fac simile.† Another fragment of the 13th cent. was dug up from under the floor of the S. aisle. It consisted of a coffin lid of striking design and in good preservation. It is now placed on the cill of one of the west windows of this aisle. It is of unusual character for so early a date: for the head of the deceased is sunk in a hollow, and the hands raised in the attitude of prayer: but the stone from the breast to the feet is carved with conventional foliage, and it represents therefore a man entirely covered, except his head and toes. It cannot be clearly ascertained whether it commemorates a priest or not. When first discovered it was broken, but all its parts were perfect: and from a drawing made at the time it seems to have been broken only into five parts. It is now in seven or eight pieces, and many fragments are lost. But enough remains to shew the beauty of the work, which is not later than the middle of the 13th cent. The chancel arch itself is also 13th cent. work, so is part of the N. chancel wall. This

---

* Sir Henry George Wakelyn Smith was the son of a surgeon, at Whittlesey, and was born 1786. In 1805 he entered the army, and he served at the Peninsula and at Waterloo. He was made K.C.B. after the battle of Maharajpoor, in 1840, and he received the thanks of Parliament for his services in 1845. In 1846 he was made Major General, and commanded at the battle of Aliwal, in Sutlej, after which he was created Baronet of Aliwal. In 1847 he was appointed Governor of the Cape of Good Hope. He died in 1860.

† When the church was being repaired the clerk of the works, without the knowledge of the architect, had pronounced these pillars to be unsafe, and their restoration impossible, and had proceeded to destroy one of them. They had been much mutilated by being cut into for the mass of woodwork which enveloped them. Happily Mr. Scott himself came and saw the church before the second pillar had been pulled down, and he at once absolutely forbade its destruction. It was a bold decision, and one not altogether without risk: but by working night and day, the architect himself working with the rest, the defective parts were made good, and the pier was saved.

is seen from the N. chancel aisle, the stringcourse above the arch dividing the aisle and chancel being clearly early English work. This string is external work; so the roof of this chantry has been raised. Perhaps in few churches can the gradual extensions, to accommodate larger congregations, be traced so regularly as in this. A chancel with nave of three bays and N. aisle formed, we may conjecture, the original church.* There must have been a W. tower, as the N. aisle, which is early, extends further W. than the early nave arches. The next alteration was very likely the N. chantry. Then the S. chantry and aisle were added, the W. faces of both aisles at this time being flush with the W. side of the tower. Later still the old tower (if one existed) was removed and the two present W. nave arches erected, thus getting more space in the church; the S. arcade was rebuilt; the chancel itself was elongated; the clerestory throughout was added; and the tower and spire built. These various perpendicular alterations were done at different times. The enlargement of the chancel is marked by the second piscina there: the old chancel had a piscina and two sedilia, and when the altar was placed further east, another piscina had to be provided. This had escaped notice until the recent restoration. By a notice in the register it appears that the nave roof was erected 1704—8; and that 'over the school-house & to the first Arch Westward.........the roof was patched up in the year 1720.' In the same year a new dial was put up for the clock. The chancel roof is dated on a beam, 1744. The lower part of the rood screen remains. The chancel is fitted with returned stalls of modern date, but not part of the recent work. The pulpit and lettern are excellent. The font is octagonal of stone. It was erected in 1840, replacing one of wood. The decorated windows in the S. aisle are noticeable: two at the W. have net tracery, two at the E. flowing tracery. The S. porch has a plain stone groined roof.

---

* A Norman church existed, but this must have been entirely destroyed, as no traces whatever of Norman work remain. The church is mentioned in a privilegium of pope Alexander III. to Thorney abbey; and this instrument recites that the church was conferred upon the abbey on the day of its dedication by Hervey, 1st bishop of Ely. This would fix its erection between the years 1106—1131.

WHITTLESEY S. MARY.

The glory of this church is its tower and spire. They can be seen very distinctly due E. from the bridge at Peterborough. The tower has three stages, all richly ornamented.* The belfry windows are singular: there are on each face two large transomed windows, close to one another, of single lights, cinquefoiled below the transom, and double lights above. The parapet is embattled: at the corners are crocketed pinnacles with flying buttresses to the spire. The spire itself is crocketed, and has three rows of windows. The whole is 120 ft. high.

There are eight BELLS, which play tunes every three hours. Some of the sentiments upon them are peculiar.

1. THE LORD TO PRAISE MY VOICE I'LL RAISE 1803
2. OSBORN AND DOBSON FOUNDERS DOWNHAM NORFOLK. 1803.
3. PEACE AND GOOD NEIGHBOURHOOD. JOS: EAYRE FECIT.
4. DO JUSTICE LOVE MERCY AND WALK HUMBLY WITH THY GOD. 1758.
5. JOHN SUDBURY AND JOHN JOHNSON CHURCHWARDENS OF SAINT ANDREW'S. 1803.
6. THE FIVE OLD BELLS INTO SIX WAS RUN WITH ADDITIONAL METAL NEAR A TUN. 1758.
7. PROSPERITY TO THE ESTABLISH'D CHURCH OF ENGLAND AND NO ENCOURAGEMENT TO ENTHUSIASM. 1758.
8. THOMAS MOORE VICAR, EDWARD GROUND AND WILL^M, DAVY GROUND CHURCHWARDENS OF S^T, MARY'S 1803.

There is a fine stone groined roof under the belfry floor, having the symbols of the evangelists carved on the bosses.

The MONUMENTAL remains are numerous, but none of any great antiquity except the recumbent effigy

---

* Cole's criticism is of no great value, but may be here produced. 'This is a very handsome Church, with ye most beautiful Spire I ever beheld, placed on a square noble Tower adorned all about with fine curious work after ye Cathedral Fashion: The Tower is very lofty & ye Spire of Stone, exceedingly taper & elevated, is adorn'd with Leafwork in a most expensive manner. The Church is by no means answerable to ye Magnificence of its Tower & Spire, wch may vie with any in England for Beauty & Strength. All leaded & in good Repair. The Church was beautifying last year (1744) as I rode thro' ye Town.'

WHITTLESEY S. ANDREW.

already mentioned. Cole has copied *in extenso* the whole of the inscriptions as they existed in 1745.* The only monument remaining of the 16th cent. is that to Tho. Hake, 1590. It is on the N. chancel wall. It is very similar to the one in Peterborough cathedral to sir H. Orme.† At the top are these words; 'Celæstia sequor terrestria sperno.' There are others later to members of the same family. Other names are, Reade, Aveling, Underwood, Wiseman, Moore, Whitstones (B.D., rect. of Woodston), 1721.‡ In the sedilia are tablets to Geo. Burges, vic. of Halvergate and Moulton, Norf., his wife and daughter. Robert Blyth, last abbot of Thorney, and bp. of Connor, who consecrated Eldernell chapel, appointed by will, 19 Oct., 1547, his body to be buried in this church 'before the sacred sacrament of the altar.'

The churchyard, to use Cole's words, 'is as full of gravestones as ever it can hold.' A large piece has been added since that time, but it is now entirely closed. The last interment was on Christmas-day, 1855. The East Anglian peculiarity of describing a man who dies before his wife as 'husband of Sarah,' 'husband of Elizabeth,' is noticeable on a great number of gravestones.

Whittlesey S. Andrew.

This church belonged to the chapter of Ely, having been given to them together with two other churches, Impington and Pampisford both in this county, towards the charges of their library. Bishop Nigel, who made this gift, presided over the see from 1133 to 1169. This transaction is thus recorded:

Nigellus Episcopus dat in perpetuam Eleemosinam Scriptoriæ Ecclesiæ Eliensis, ad Libros ejusdem Ecclesiæ faciendos et emendandos, Ecclesiam de Wittleseye cum tota Decima Domini et Parochianorum et omnibus Rebus cidem Ecclesiæ pertinentibus. Et papa Honorius, et Prior et Conventus confirmant donum.

---

* A great number are also given in Clement's notes, Brit. Mus. Add. MSS. 11,425. These were copied in 1731.
† See page 61.
‡ On one stone are commemorated Elizabeth and Barbara Whitstones; of which Cole has this piece of gossip; 'This stone ye People have a Notion covered ye Bodies of two maiden sisters who built this Church. Mr. Whitstones, it seems, had it turned & ye present Inscription put on it: It had, as I am told, 2 figures on ye other side; But this I take to be an idle Conceit.'

The church at Ely had previously acquired lands in Whittlesey, the pope having enjoined the surrender of some estates of one Leofwin, as a penance for striking his mother. In 1290, the value of the church was given at 10*l*. and the tenths at 20*s*. In the king's books the vicarage is worth 4*l*. 13*s*. 4*d*. and the tenths 9*s*. 4*d*. The procurations, &c., were 2*s*. 6*d*., and for the vicarage 1*s*. 8*d*. In 1731 the value was 40*l*. In 1595, Mr. Gates was rated for his vicarages of both the Whittleseys to find jointly with the vicar of Elme-cum-Emneth, one pike furnished: and in 1609 in the same way to find three pair of curols furnished. The ADVOWSON was in the hands of the chapter of Ely, then in the king, and now in the lord chancellor.

There is one old REGISTER book, containing births, marriages, and burials from 1653 to 1687. There are also entries on to 1695; but the last 8 years were supplied by the new vicar from the books at Cambridge. Both churches were so long held by one incumbent that the registers of both parishes were kept for convenience at S. Mary's. A great many 'strangers' are entered among the burials. The names Cassandra and Melchior here found are not common. Among the burials we find these:

```
1667.  21 Jul.  A strange woman.
       30 Jul.  A stranger called John the Dyer.
1672.  27 Sep.  Marye filia populi.
1676.  21 Jul.  Maudlin Starkye Infant died in ye field.
1677.  25 Apr.  Old Bud.
1679.  26 June. Thomas Barnes Infant drownd.
1814.  14 May.  A stranger whose name was never ascertained. Died at a
                lodging house in House Gate Whittlesea. Appeared to be about
                50 years of age.
1815.  18 Aug.  A woman unknown who died *suddenly*, on the north bank,
                between Dog and Doublet and Peterboro' apparently between 50
                & 60 years (old).
```

There are also a few notes about collections under briefs. Some have no date.

Collected........towards the releife of great drayton in the Countye of Salop	19	1½
....towards the Tower of Hedon in the East ridinge of Yorkshire	6	10
....towards the releife of the Inhabitants of Oxford	8	0
....towards the releife of Thomas Welbye of Dublin	5	3

1667. 22 Mar. Memor^m. the daye & yeare above written ther was given to the Poore the sum of seventeene shillinges & seven pence being monye collected upon 2 Breifes for

	the Towne of Bridgnorthe which monye if ever deman- ded is to bee repayd out of the collection for the poore.		
1660. 23 Jan.	.... toward the releife of the distressed Inhabit- ants of Cotton end in Northamptonshire	9	9
	.... toward the releife of the distressed people of Sumersham	13	9
	towards the releife of Beccles	0 16	0

The inventory in 1552 is as follows.

Wyttlesey—Saynt Androwe—infra Insul^m. Eliens^m.

This is a true & p(er)fcte Inventorie Indented made & taken the xxvith day of Julye A^o Regis Edvardi vi^{ti} vi^{to} by us Richard Wilkes, Clarke, Henry Godewyk & Thomas Rudstow Esquyers—comyssion^{rs} amonge others assigned for to survey & viewe of all man^r of ornaments plate Jewells & bells belonging to ye p(ar)she churche there as hereafter followeth.

playt—ffirst one chalysse wth ye paten of sylv^r pcell gilt p(er) oz xii oz d wth c(er)tayne leade in the foot of the same.

Ornaments—Itm a blewe vestem^t of worstede wth an aulbe, a vestem^t of reed taffetay wth an aulbe, a coope of blewe satten—a table clothe of lynnyng— ij pylloes—ij corporas c(as)es—viij surplesses—x towels—iiij candlesticks of latten—a crosse of copper and gilt.

Belles—Itm in the steaple iiij great belles a Sanctus bell and two handbelles.

All whiche pcells above wryten be delyvered & comytted by us the said comission^{rs} unto ye sayff custody & kepyng of Roger Wilson & Richard Back- house pishoners their to be at all (times) forthcomyng to be answered except & reserved (?) a chalysse wth ye paten of sylv^r pcell gilt p(er) oz xii oz d—a coope of blewe satten—i table clothe—viij surplesses & ij handbelles delyvered to Thoms Pleynson & Richard Peirson churchwardens for the only mayntenance of devyne srvice in sayd p(ar)she church.

Rych^d Wyllkes	Henry godewyke	Thom^{as} Rudstow
Rye^d Backhouse	Rychard Pierson ⎫	
Rog Wylson	(illegible) ⎭	

In the abstract of charitable donations, 1786, the two parishes were returned together. Five benefactors are there given who left land, or rent-charge, for the poor; Nic. Davie, 1654; Ann Randall, and John Daw, 1716; Ric. Noble, 1722; Adam Kelfull, 1735. The total proceeds of these bequests amounted annually to 33l. 2s. Ric. Peirson, 1627, gave to the vicar of S. Andrew's and his successors, nine acres of 'Tythe Grasse, lying neere Northey Gravell.' He is described, in the register of his burial at S. Mary's, as 'Clarke and Minister of the Parishe:' but it does not seem that he was ever incum- bent. At bp. Green's visitation, 1756, it was reported that there were 'Lands given to the Repair of the Church, but not so applied. M^r: W^m: Beale, Curate Assistant resides personally, but not in the Vicarage House, that being too small for his family.' The vicarage house here spoken of was a poor little cottage, and was demolished a few years ago.

VICARS.

1349	Joh. de Thorndon.		Joh. Forster, r.
	Joh. Wodeham, r.	1590	‡Fr. Gates, d.
1403	Will. Smythe, r.	1622	*‡Will. Mason, d.
	‡Tho. Pope.	1660	*‡Ric. Mason, A.M., d.
	Rob. Lynton, d.	1683	*‡Ric. Mason, A.M., d.[1]
1419	Tho. Walsingham.	1703	‡Tho. Topping, A.M., d.
	Tho. Delf, r.	1742	‡Will. Beale, A.M., d.
1467	Geof. Mees, d.		Geo. Moore, d.[2]
1498	Joh. Mandevyle, d.	1772	*‡Tho. Ch. Cadwal. Moore, d.
1503	Geof. Bocher, d.	1815	Jas. Tobias Cook, A.M., d.[3]
1504	Hen. Haldure, d.	1849	Edm. Reynolds, A.M., d.
1535	Tho. Browne.	1861	Hen. Burgess, L.L.D.
1567	Ed. Harrison.		

The CHURCH consists of chancel with aisles, all gabled, nave with aisles and clerestory, N. door, S. porch, S. priest's door and W. tower. Like S. Mary's church this has been much altered, and contains portions of different styles. It is chiefly perpendicular. The nave, of four bays, is lofty, and has a good roof. The bosses are all carved, mostly with faces, and the wall pieces are supported on grotesque corbels. In the N. chantry a similar corbel remains, to be seen from the gallery: but the N. aisle roof has been much mutilated by the insertion of skylights for the galleries, and in other ways. The S. aisle roof and that to the chancel, were put up in 1842. The roof of the S. chantry is good and mostly original; but it was 'patched up,' as appears from the register of S. Mary's, in 1742. The earliest work in the church is an excellent two-light window in the S. aisle, W. of the S. porch. It is of early geometric date, about 1250. There is a trefoiled circle in the head, and the lights below are quite plain, without cusps. Of more advanced decorated work is the E. window of five lights, of rather nondescript character, but of pleasing design. The S. chantry is an entire work of the middle of the 14th cent. The E. window is of three lights, pointed, and the side windows are of two lights each, square headed, all of net tracery. The door in the

---

* Buried at Whittlesey.
‡ Also vicars of S. Mary.
1. Also vic. of Morborne, Hunts. The inscription on his monument in the S. chantry says 'He is buried in the Grave wth his Father and Granfather, who were Ministers of this Place before him.'
2. Min. canon of Peterborough cathedral.
3. Fell. of S. John's, Camb. Buried at S. John's, Hampstead.

S. wall here is evidently an insertion. The N. aisle and chantry are perpendicular. The junction with the chancel at the E. end is rather clumsy. The gable here is crocketed; and an enormous crocket occupies the summit instead of a cross. The nave and S. chantry have original crosses. If the chancel itself had a roof of more acute pitch, like the chantries, instead of a low pitch with battlements, the E. end would be very good, resembling the general arrangement of churches in Devonshire and Cornwall. There are two sedilia in the chancel, but not of one date. The rood staircase remains, N. of the chancel arch, and its door above is visible. The tower is entirely cut off from the church by a partition of wood and glass. The galleries and pews are monstrous. Mr. Paley's remark that 'the whole interior of this church urgently needs a thorough restoration' is unfortunately still true: it is happily no longer the case at S. Mary's. The tower has small square buttresses surrounding the corners, like those built in early English times; they are of five stages, the second stage being embattled. The west door is under a square head. The belfry windows are of two lights, transomed. The five windows on the N. side of the church are all of two lights, square headed; they seem to be 15th cent. imitations of the 14th cent. windows of the S. chantry. The W. window of this aisle is late and poor. The pinnacles at the ends of this aisle are triangular and rather heavy. They have very shallow paneling which indicates their late date. In Cole's time, 120 years ago, the nave and chancel were separated by a screen, over which were the royal arms. His notes of the church are meagre. He calls it 'a handsome and neat building.' The E. end of the N. aisle is used as a vestry: here is a piscina.

There are six BELLS, of which two are very large. The inscriptions have no great interest.

1. JOSEPH EAYRE S^T NEOTS FECIT 1759

2. THESE FIVE BELLS WAS CAST MAY THE 12 1759

3. WILLIAM BEALE RECTOR IOHN LOMES CHURCH-
WARDEN EAYRE FECIT 1769
I TO THE CHURCH THE LIVING CALL AND
TO THE GRAVE DO SUMMON ALL.

4, 5, 6. REV. J. T. COOK THOMAS JOHNSON WILLIAM
READ CHURCHWARDENS THOMAS MEARS
FOUNDER 1843.

The last three bells were taken in exchange for three old ones of about equal weight, no doubt part of the peal of five cast in 1759, of which two remain. The verses on the third bell are round the outside of the lip.

No MONUMENTS of early date or of special importance are preserved. Tablets to vicars Mason, Cook, and Reynolds remain. The former only was buried here. The lines on his monument, which are rather curious, have been quoted by Mr. Paley. In the N. aisle is a small copper plate in a wooden frame painted to represent marble, commemorating the wife of vicar Topping. It is about 10in. by 7in. in size. It is in poor Latin with several gross errors corrected. It concludes, ' obdormivit 24to Martii hora quasi 2da matutina AD $170\frac{7}{8}$.' There are memorials also to members of the families of Ground, Underwood, Stona, Moore, Read, and others. Cole has preserved the inscriptions.

One of the abbots of Thorney, Odo de Whittlesey, was born in this town. So was William, archdeacon of Huntingdon, bishop of Rochester, and lastly archbishop of Canterbury in 1368. Many French names are now naturalised here. There was even a congregation of the exiles, but it was of short duration only; doubtless it became merged in that of Thorney. Burns (Foreign Refugees, 48,) says, 'It appears by the records of the colloque held in London in 1646, that Le Sieur Du Perrier, Soy disant Pasteur, of Whittlesey, presented letters,' &c. In the 'East Anglian' iii, 40, there is a notice of seven tradesmen's tokens of the 17th cent. all bearing the name of this parish.

The churchyard, which is specially crowded on the S. side, is spacious. It contains no ancient stone.

THORNEY ABBEY.

Thorney.

Before the foundation of the monastery a hermitage had existed here from about the year 662, a few years only later than the original church at Medehamsted. It was at that time called ANCARIG, and shared the universal desolation caused by the Danes in 870. As at Medehamsted, a century passed by without any attempt at restoration. In 972 a monastery for Benedictine monks was founded by Ethelwold, bp. of Winchester, and a church built dedicated to S. Mary. The place had by this time acquired the name of THORNEY, the ISLAND OF THORNS, so called, 'propter spineta circumquaque succrescentia,' because of the thorns growing around it on all sides. This church remained standing barely 90 years, and was pulled down in 1085. The new church was finished in 1108, but not rededicated until 1128 by bp. Hervey of Ely. The nave and triforium arches now existing are part of the earlier portion of this building, built about 1090. The western front is later, and was doubtless the last to be completed, as was very common in building large churches. The following dates are translated from the annals of the monastery.*

973. In this year a privilege was granted to the monastery of Thorney by king Edgar, S. Ethelwold the bishop assenting.
1001. The body of S. Ivo was discovered.
1066. There was seen here a comet (cometa); and the same year earl (comes) William came and Harold was killed.
1096. The journey to Jerusalem began.
1098. In this year we men of Thorney entered into the new church on 12 Nov. Afterwards on 1 Dec. we translated the relics of the Saints, the presbytery, the two porches, and the tower only being completed; in the presence of our neighbours Aldwin abbot of Ramsey, Ingulf of Crowland, and Aldwald prior of Burgh, because Burgh was then without an abbot, and many others whose names I do not mention.
1105. The relics of S. Theodore, martyr, were received at Thorney, on 11 May from a pilgrim named Heverardus.
1108. The church of Thorney was completed and the last stone laid on S. Luke's day, and in the following year the towers and pinnacles of the front were finished.
1128. The dedication of the church at Thorney on 5 Nov.
1315. A great flood which inundated the whole district for three years.

* Brit. Mus. MS. Cott. Nero C. 7. This is an illuminated MS., and embraces the years 061—1421. Dugdale has quoted those relating to the abbey buildings, but, as will be seen from the above extracts, they are not exclusively such. The disputes between the neighbouring abbeys fill up large spaces in their chronicles. Once the cause of quarrel was that the abbot of Peterborough killed a hound belonging to the abbot of Thorney.

The whole of the domestic buildings having been completely destroyed, as also the choir and transepts and part of the nave of the church, it would be impossible to describe the gradual erection of the buildings from the difference in the architecture. But some of the works are mentioned in the Thorney register. Abbot Robert, who died 1236, had built a Lady chapel, in which he was buried; this chapel was afterwards destroyed and a new one of great magnificence erected. Abbot David, 1238—1255, was a great builder: amongst other works he built the great gateway* and the bakery. Abbot William of Yaxley, 1261—1293, added a roof to this bakery, which had before been thatched, and built a grand new refectory. His two successors built largely; the latter of them, William of Clapton, built a new chapterhouse, a large new hall and chapel for the abbot's house, and greatly adorned the Lady-chapel by inserting stained glass windows, the Jesse window over the altar being given by him. William of Yaxley was the first abbot summoned to parliament: the last abbot sat there in 1538.

In the Domesday valuation the sum total of the rents was 52*l.* 15*s.*, and the value of the fisheries in Whittlesey mere was put at 3*l.* There were also pensions in all the churches in the patronage of the abbey. In the Valor Ecclesiasticus, 1534, the goods are given at 411*l.* 12*s.* 11*d.*, and the tenths consequently 41*l.* 3*s.* 3¼*d.*† The abbey was dissolved by statute in 1539. In the document known as Edgar's charter the dreadful possibility of a suppression is evidently contemplated, and to a certain extent provided for, by a very solemn denunciation. It is better left untranslated.

<small>Si quis igitur hanc nostram donationem in alium quam constituimus transferre voluerit, privatus consortio Sancti Dei ecclesiæ, æternis baratri incendiis lugubris cum Juda proditore Christi, ejusque complicibus puniatur, si non satisfactione emendaverit congrua quod contra nostrum deliquit decretum.</small>

There is another in pope Alexander III's privilegium. The names of the pensioners at the dissolution with the several amounts are given in Dugdale. The difference

---

<small>* In a description of towns in Edward II's. time, 'Entrée de Thorneye' is named as something specially grand.
† According to Speed this is below the real value.</small>

between the sums granted to the abbot, 200*l.*, and to the prior, 9*l.* is striking. The least is 40*s.* to a lay brother, 'Robert Bayte beyng no preste.' The sum was 340*l.* 13*s.* 4*d.* Sixteen years afterwards this sum was reduced by deaths and other ways to 64*l.* 6*s.* 8*d.*

The church was originally dedicated to S. MARY. But it was, after the translation of the bones of S. Botolph hither, placed under the united invocation of SS. MARY and BOTOLPH, and is so spoken of in the charters.

The REGISTER commences in 1653, in which year Kenelme Booth was 'sworne & confirmed Register' by Fr. Underwood. The following extracts are interesting.

1660. 20 Aug. Peter Harrison a dutchman was buryed.
1666. Circa hoc tempus pestis plurimos corripuit, quorum nomina huic libello inserta non habes.
1669. 22 Oct. Thomas Loftes advena agri Eboracensis circa Richmond mortem obiit in Thorney et sepultus fuit.
1672. Abrahaimus } gemini { major } natu { filii Thomæ et Katharinæ Fowler
      Isaacus   { minor   baptizati fuerunt Junij 9º.
1701. 25 June. Was buryed a stranger woman y^t came from a towne 4 or 5 miles from Darby, being seized wth a feaver and frensye at Jo^n Reads, and could give no other account of herself shee dyed at Jo^n Reads coming in as a work-woman her name Mary Burgess.
1706. 18 Dec. Advena fortuito in fossa suffocatus fuit.
1714. 13 Dec. Gulielmus Shellit (vulgo deaf Will) sepultus est (affid: Judith Kirby)
1722. 13 Feb. Anna Clathery cum duobus Infantibus sepultæ sunt.

The first book extends from 1653 to 1724. The second to 1778. The Latin entries were not, with few exceptions, discontinued till 1735. The formula for baptism is 'sacrum lavacrum accepit;' for burying in woollen 'panno laneo convolutus.' The number of persons who met with violent deaths, as killed accidentally, drowned, &c., is remarkable. There is another book of exceptional character, and of great interest. It is a French register of baptisms dating 1654—1727. The French settlers came over from Holland to drain the fens. A petition of sir Will. Russell's is extant which states that he was seized of a great quantity of marsh and drowned grounds, late part of the possession of the monastery of Thorney; that various persons in North Holland were willing to come over and inhabit it and recover the lands upon conditions. They were not to be molested in their offices of religion. Accordingly they had a separate congregation which met at a tollgate towards Wisbech. An inscription in the church shews the congregation began in 1652: the first page of the register is therefore lost. This congregation lasted for 75 years, after which they conformed to the English church. The book is a small folio of paper, and contains 146 pages and 1710 entries of baptism. A dyke in the parish is called 'French drove' from these emigrants. Many names in Peterborough and around, especially towards Thorney, give ample evidence of a French origin.* The ministers were these:

1652—74.	Ezekiel Danois.	1689—1713.	Jaques Cairon.
1685—1712.	———Jembelin.	1715—1727.	Louis Charles le Sueur.

It seems from this that there were more than one pastor required for the work. The number of entries is added up at the foot of each page in these words: 'Il y en a jusque icy.' The mother is always described by her maiden name. Three examples are appended.

Aoust 30. 1663. Susanne Egar fille de Piere et Sara Vaudeberk esté baptizee. Ses tesmoings sont Jaques Egar et Susanne Vaudeberk.

Le 25ᵉ jour d'Aoust, 1689. Rebecca Bouchereau, fille du Sʳ Pierre Bouchereau, chirurgien et apoticaire demeurant au bourg d' Eye et d' Elizabeth Giraud; née le sixieme jour de ce mois, a esté batizée par le Sʳ Jembelin et a esté presentée par Monsieur Cairon, ministre du St. Evenigile, et par Mᵐᵉ Rebecca Holmes veuve du Sʳ Jacob le Houcq.

1691. Susanne Dornelle fille de Pierre dornelle et de Marie le fevre née le 14ᵉ jour davril 1689 et batizée le 29 due [du meme] mois ayant pour parrin Jean Hugle et pour marrine Esther le Leu n' avoit point été enregitrée par la negligence de son pere qui a prié qu'il ensoit fait mention sur le regitre en ce lieu.

A memorandum at the beginning of the English register mentions a gift to the church in these terms: '✠ Two pieces of Plate of yᵉ value of twelve pounds given to yᵉ Church of Thorney to be used at yᵉ Comunion by the Revⁿᵈ. Mʳ Thomas Brecknock late Minister there who died Janʸ 12ᵗʰ 170$\frac{9}{10}$. NB ✠ A cup & cover.'

The charitable donations to the parish, in the report made in 1786, were capable of being returned in a single word, 'none.' No accurate list of incumbents is possible.†

---

* In Burn's 'Foreign Refugees,' 99—101, is an account of this congregation. He gives a number of names from the register 'not uncommon in Thorney and its vicinity at the present time.' Amongst them occur: Tigardine, Provost, Gaches, Fovargue, Le Tall, Ainger, Le Fevre, Descamps, Deboo, Harley, Guerin, Massingarb. And on gravestones in the churchyard these names are still visible: Flahau, Leahair, Delenoy, Durance, Egar, Le Pla, Usill, Beharrell, Mango, Sigee. The list of ministers above given is from Burn.

† The condition of the patronage of the church is unsatisfactory to the last degree. The whole parish was made over so entirely to the Bedford family, that the church itself is their private property, and used by the inhabitants for divine service with their permission. The incumbency also was a donative, altogether exempt from episcopal visitation; and the parsonage house was let to the incumbent at a nominal rent to shew that it did not belong to him, but that the use of it was granted him. The value of the preferment is also dependent on the

ABBOTS.

972	Godeman.[1]
	Lefsius, r.[2]
1017	Lefsinus.
bef. 1031	Oswy, d.
1049	Lefwinus.
	Siwardus.
1068	Fulcard, deprived.
1085	*Gunterus, d.[3]
1113	Rob. I., d.
1151	Gilbert, d.
1154	*Walter I., d.
1158	Herbert, d.
1162	*Walter II., d.[4]
1172	Solomon.
1193	Rob. II., deprived.
1198	Ralph.[5]
1216	*Rob. III., d.[6]
1236	Rich. de Stanford, d.[7]
1237	David, d.
1255	Tho. de Castor, d.[8]
1261	Will. de Yaxley, d.
1293	Odo de Whittlesey, d.
1305	*Will. de Clopton, d.
1322	Reg. de Water-Newton, d.
1346	Will. de Haddon, D.C.L., d.
1365	Joh. de Deeping, L.L.B., d.
1396	*Nic. Islep, L.L.B., r.
1402	Tho. de Charwelton, d.[7]
1425	Alan Kirketon, L.L.B., d.
1437	Joh. Kirketon, L.L.B., d.
1450	Joh. Ramsey, L.L.B., d.
1457	Will. Ryall, r.
1464	Tho. de Wisbech.
1484	Joh. Murcott.
1485	Rich. Holbech.
1514	Rob. Moulton.
bef. 1523	John.
1525	Rob. Blyth, r.[9]

INCUMBENTS.

1660	Tho. Brecknock, d. 1709.
bef. 1730	Will. Wells.
1736	Jas. Ris, d. 1758.
	Will. Sandivers.
1761	Jas. Thompson.
	Joh. Hunt, A.M.[10]
	*Joh. Girdlestone, A.M., d.[11]
1821	Joshua Cautley, A.M.

The CHURCH consists of a small portion of the nave of the conventual church, together with modern transepts. There is no chancel. There is a doorway at the W. end, and one to each transept. The E. end of the church is in a line with the sides of the transepts, so that the ground plan is simply T. The nave is of five Norman bays, now filled up with masonry and pierced with three-light windows, but which originally opened into aisles. Above these aisles was a triforium passage, the arches to

mere caprice of the owner of the estate. Sometimes the parson was called 'curate,' sometimes 'incumbent curate,' sometimes 'chaplain of the donative.' Those who sign in the register 'curate' are supposed to have been in possession of the benefice, such as it was. Is it too much to hope that before long this important parish will be properly endowed by the noble possessor, and the above anomalous state of things put an end to? Much has been done in the way of improvement in the place of late years: there is room for one crowning improvement more, which would remove from the wealthy ducal house the slur of being in the enjoyment of very large revenues from church property in this parish, and yet supplying from them a stipend for the minister of the church grossly inadequate to the magnitude and importance of his charge.

* Buried at Thorney.
1. Monk of Winchester, and chaplain to the bp.
2. Made bp. of Worcester.
3. Archdn. of Sarum.
4. A vacancy of 7 years occurred after the death of this abbot.
5. Prior of Freston, Linc. Surnamed 'Simplex.'
6. Sacrist of S. Edmund's Bury.
7. Prior of Deeping.
8. Prior of Thorney.
9. Also bp. of Down and Connor. Buried at Whittlesey S. Mary. See pp. 87, 102, 107. He sat in the convocation concerning the king's divorce.
10. Also rect. of Benefield.
11. Also inc. of Eye, 1800—10.

which remain as clerestory windows. The clerestory itself is altogether removed. Each pier has a massive semi-circular shaft reaching to the present roof, where it is met now by a continuous moulding, projecting a great way, wholly incongruous. The piers are alternately circular, with this inner projection, and shafted. Each of these latter piers has two attached shafts where one of the former sort has a quadrant of a circle. The capitals of the triforium arcade appear a little later in character than those of the nave; but the whole is doubtless of one date, and is entirely in agreement with that given in the annals, 1000—1008. All the E. end is new and built in the plainest Norman style.* The shafts of the E. window are more in the early English style. This window is filled with stained glass, mostly blue and red; it is a copy of one at Canterbury, and the imitation of the old work in glass is very happy. Its subject is the life of Thomas-a-Becket. Perhaps this, with the reredos beneath, would be considered the most satisfactory part of the recent restoration. This reredos is of clunch, in five panels, the central one being the largest. The commandments, &c., occupy three of these. In the spandrels of the centre arch are two shields, coloured.† It is probable the original roof may have been a flat one, as at Peterborough; the present one is a whitewashed ceiling, of an elliptical shape. The internal arrangements are very poor. There is a cumbrous gallery in each transept, and one at the W. end. In this last is placed the organ (a very good one), divided into two parts so as not to interfere with the W. window. All the pews have doors, and there is a batch of 'free' sittings in the middle. The pulpit and desk occupy a most commanding position in the very centre facing west. In each of the eastern windows of the nave are three scenes of foreign

---

* The new portion was added at an unfavourable time, and does not happily adjoin the ancient work. The new work could not of course be carried out in Barnack stone, like the old abbey church, as the quarries have long been exhausted; but a stone surely might have been found more suited to the tone of the old work than that actually employed.

† There is an amusing simplicity about these two shields. Their fitness in a reredos might perhaps be questioned: no one will venture to question the innocence with which they are made part of one design. For the one is the ecclesiastical coat of the abbey of Thorney; the other the family coat of the house of Bedford. Why were they not joined with a label? An appropriate motto might have been found:
'Look here upon this picture and on this.'

glass, in black and white. They are chiefly from the time of our Lord's passion. There are also some coats of arms in coloured glass. That of the Bedford family is reversed. Two have France and England quarterly, one encircled in a garter, and one with a label of three points.

Considerable alterations were made in the year 1638. That date is over the W. door. It seems not unlikely that the ruins of the old church were then first put into decent order, so as to be fit for service. The stones with which the nave arches are now blocked up were part of the original building. The stones of the destroyed abbey would be in great request for building purposes, and have consequently almost entirely disappeared. Dugdale says that some were even removed as far as Cambridge, and were employed in building the chapel of Corpus Christi college.* This was done in 1579, and the church and domestic buildings alike were despoiled for this purpose. The easiest way of fitting up the remaining parts for worship would then be to use the existing nave arches for walls, destroying the upper story, as the aisles which formed a support to it would be removed. This is in fact what was done. The windows inserted under the nave arches are of clearly debased date. They are moreover exactly similar in detail to the great W. window, which is part of the work dated 1638. These windows are all cinquefoiled in each light, and have mullions to the top. These windows and the W. doorway were the work of Inigo Jones.

The W. front, although so much altered, is still a very fine specimen of Norman architecture. It is flanked by two square turrets. At the angles they are indented several times, but have neither chamfer nor shaft. They are surmounted by octagonal turrets, embattled. These latter were added apparently when the other alterations were made in 1638. They are distinctly of debased date: the four-leaved flowers in the chamfers, and the carved heads, as seen from the leads, are very poor. The front

---

* He refers to Masters' History of the College, p. 209, where we read: 'The Queen........ contributed towards this Work' (the building the chapel) ' about thirty Loads of Timber, by a Warrant under her Privy Signet, from the Estate of the dissolved Monastery of——lying in *Barton*, as did in like manner *Francis* Earl of *Bedford* 146 Tuns of Stone from that of *Thorney*, which were delivered at *Guy-Hirne* upon the Lord Keeper's Letter and the Earl's Warrant.'

however retains traces of a grand alteration in the 15th cent., while the abbey was flourishing. Between these side turrets, and occupying the whole space between them, is a noble window arch. The tracery of this window has long been destroyed. It is now partly blocked up, and partly occupied with the 1638 window of five lights with an embattled transom. It is remarkable that the internal shafts of this smaller window are Norman, and of the same date as the body of the church. But they may have been removed hither during the alterations: or may mark the extent of the original Norman west window before the enlarged Perpendicular one was inserted. Above the larger arch is a row of nine niches under a horizontal battlement: each niche retains its statue. They are apostles: each holds in his hand some symbol: but the central one is apparently the Saviour after resurrection. All have two holes in the chest, as if riveted to the wall behind. At the W. end of the nave, on each side, one original clerestory window remains, now filled up with masonry. Round the arch of that on the N. side and down each jamb is a double row of billets. In the N. turret is a capital newel staircase, giving access to the W. gallery, and to the one small BELL, which is uninscribed.

There is but one MONUMENT of any interest. This is a brass inscription inserted in the N. wall of the nave. It is worth giving entire.

M S Venerandi senis Ezechielis Danois Compendiensis Galli cœtus Gallici qui hic congregari cœpit A° Dⁿⁱ MDCLII Pastoris primi qui studio indefesso, doctrina et severitate morum, nulli secundus, ingens litteraturæ thesaurus, hic orbe(m) latuit. Deo, sibi, paucis aliis, notus eisque contentus testibus, per LIV annorum spatiu(m), ex quibus XXII hic Thorney Abbatiæ, sum(m)o cu(m) fructu Ministerio suo functus, tandem hic ubi laboris ibi et quietis locu(m) i(n)ve(n)it obijt 24 Febr. A° Dⁿⁱ MDCLXXIV Ætat.*

The churchyard is very limited to the S. side; on the E. it has been extended. There are several altar tombs. The S. entrance is by an arched gateway surmounted by a cross.

---

* Freely translated: 'Sacred to the memory of the Reverend Father Ezechiel Danois, of Compiegne in France, first pastor of the French congregation which began to assemble here A.D. 1652; who, second to none in unwearied study, in learning, and in strictness of morals, a great treasury of letters, lived here in obscurity. Known to God, himself, and but few else, and with the testimony of these content, for the space of 54 years he discharged the duties of his Ministry with the greatest profit, of which 22 years were spent here at Thorney Abbey; at length where his labour was there he found the place of his rest. He died 24 Feb. A.D. 1674. Aged——.' In Burn's 'Foreign Refugees,' p. 100, this epitaph is given. 'Quietus' on the monument is evidently an error for 'quietis.'

CROWLAND ABBEY, S.E.

Crowland.

As in the case of Peterborough, the materials for a history and description of this place are so plentiful, that a digest of them into a few pages becomes a matter of considerable difficulty. The name is now commonly spelt CROWLAND. In Domesday it appears as CRUILAND, or CRUILANDE. Afterwards the spelling got changed into CROILAND, CROYLAND, or CROYLANDE, and not till the very deed of suppression do we find W inserted for Y. Ingulf's etymology, 'the muddy land,' is well known.

The abbey church was dedicated to SS. BARTHOLOMEW and GUTHLAC. The latter saint was not adopted as patron from the first; but the coat of arms of the abbey exhibits the joint invocation, as it bears three knives and three scourges quarterly.* The accounts of Guthlac are very complete. He was born in 673 and died in 713. Brought up as a soldier he renounced, when 25 years old, the profession of arms, and devoted himself to a hermit's life. Bp. Hedda of Lichfield consecrated his oratory and ordained him priest. He had arrived at Crowland originally on S. Bartholomew's day. The origin of the foundation is thus accounted for. Ethelbald, next heir to the throne of Mercia, about 710, endeavoured to anticipate the decease of Ceolred the king in possession by seizing his crown. Obliged to fly he came to Guthlac, who encouraged him and foretold his ultimate success. Ethelbald promised, if this came true, to found a monastery on the spot. Guthlac did not survive to see it, but the king kept his word. A chantry at Marholm was dedicated to this saint.† So is the church at Market

---

* The apostle Bartholomew has a knife for a symbol in allusion to his traditional martyrdom by flaying. The convent on his feastday gave away knives to all comers. These are still occasionally found at Crowland. This custom was abolished 1476. The whip of the other patron saint was esteemed a valuable possession; and in their greatest distress the monks never forsook it. The statues of both remain in the west front, each with his symbol in his hand. The whip indeed might well be thought invaluable. Had it been only S. Guthlac's own it would have been highly treasured: but it had before him belonged, as they said, to the apostle himself. See also p. 70.

† Dugdale names several lives or accounts of the saint extant. In the Brit. Mus. (Cotton. Nero. C. 8) is a very beautiful MS., richly illuminated, containing his life. His future renown, according to this document, was predicted at his birth in these words, 'Stabilitote, quia futuræ gloriæ huic mundo natus est homo.' His character and person were alike beautiful: 'Erat enim forma præcipuus, corpore castus, facie decorus, mente devotus, aspectu dilectus, sapientia imbutus, vultu floridus, prudentia præditus, colloquio blandus, temperantia clarus, interna fortitudine robustus, censura justitiæ stabilis, longanimitate largus, patientia firmus, humilitate mansuetus, caritate sollicitus.'

Deeping, where this inscription was put on a window of painted glass: 'Orate pro anima R. Iwardby, quondam rectoris hujus loci, qui hanc fenestram fieri fecit ad laudem Dei, et Sancti Guthlaci, A.D. 1438.' At Swaffham, Norf., was a chapel, and at Hereford a priory, dedicated to this saint.

The value at the suppression of the estates was given at 1217*l*. 5*s*. 11¼*d*. by Speed. The same in the king's books. Other accounts make it a little less. If this amount is increased to represent its present worth, it will contrast almost ludicrously with the clear value of the living as given by Bacon in 1786, viz. 34*l*. 16*s*. 4*d*.

Lists of the more important documents, deeds, registers, &c., relating to the abbey are given in Dugdale. Cole has 180 pp. copied from one of these books. The present parochial REGISTER dates only from 1639. The books are all excellently bound. They contain but few entries worth transcribing. On the first page is recorded Oliver Cromwell's death in 1658, for whom the inhabitants must have had a special veneration.

1640.   Mr. Augustine Bracher Clarke.
1662.   16 Jul.   Elizabeth ye wife of John Ashbey.
        17 Jul.   John Ashbey himselfe.
1696.   9 Dec.   Elizabeth Burroughs who died felo-de-se was buried.
1713.   7 Sep.   A Poor Child its Father a Travelling Tinker.
1714.   13 Sep.   William Lord Russell.
        3 Nov.   A Stranger found dead in Postland.
1719.   27 Dec.   Richd Thorp of Peterborow alias Petty Canon Dick.

The living is now a rectory. How it became so called, or why this description was recognised, is not known. Small as its value is it has two patrons. The ADVOWSON is in the alternate presentation of the owners of the abbey farm and the Postland estates.

Amongst the sacramental PLATE is a large chalice with an open cross engraved. In it are the words 'Ecclesiæ Croylandiæ sacrum.' Above the cross is INRI. There are also two patens. The smaller is engraved as the chalice; the larger has 'Given by M^r. Luke Cowley 1724.' All have coats of arms with whips and knives.

Bequests to the monastery were very frequent.*

---

* A great number of donors of special gifts such as lights before the altar of the Lady-chapel, glass windows, vestments, are recorded in the continuation of the history of Crowland. Laurence Chateres, the cook, made a professional bequest: 40*l*. to find milk of almonds for the convent on fish days.

Legacies were left sometimes to the foundation, or for specific religious ends, and sometimes (as in the will of T. Ryley, 1538, mentioned on p. 78,) to individual monks. There are now three benefactions to administer. Bothway's charity, and Brown's charity are for the poor. A tablet in the church says of the latter that John Brown died 25 Oct., 1684, and gave 11½ acres to the parish. The distribution was to be on the feast of S. James, now altered to that of S. Thomas. Roger Walker, 10 Oct., 1612, left after his wife's death, a tenement in the Church St. called Crabtree Corner to four feoffees in trust, to let and apply the rents

the one half thereof (the outrents and charges of Repairs being yearly deducted) to be bestowed yearly towards ye Repair of ye Church in Croyland, and ye other half to ye poor People in Croyland, at ye Discretion of his said Feoffees the same to be given yearly at ye Feast of St Thomas the apostle only.

ABBOTS.

716 *Kenulphus, d.[1]	1236 Ric. Bardenay, m., d.[11]
Patricius.	1247 *Tho. Welles, m., d.
794 *Siwardus, d.	1254 Ralph de March, m., d.
856 Theodore, d.[2]	1281 Ric. de Croyland, m., r.
870 Godric I., d.	1303 Simon de Luffenham, r.
941 *Turketyl, d.[3]	1324 Hen. de Casewik, d.
975 *Egelric I., m., d.	1358 Tho. de Barnack, d.
984 *Egelric II., d.	1378 Joh. de Ashby, d.
992 *Osketyl, m., d.	1392 *Tho. de Overton. m., d.[12]
1005 *Godric II., d.	1417 Ric. Upton, m., d.
1017 *Brictmer, d.	1427 Joh. Litlington, d.[13]
1048 *Wulgatus, d.[4]	1469 Joh. Wisbech, d.[14]
1052 Wulketyl, deprived.[5]	1476 Ric. Croyland, S.T.B., m., d.
1076 *Ingulf, d.[6]	1483 Lam. Fossdyke, L.L.B., m., d.
1109 Joffrid, d.[7]	1487 Edm. Thorp, S.T.B., m.
1124 Waldeve, m., deprived.	1497 Phil. Everard.
1138 Godfrey, d.[8]	1504 Will. Geddyng.
1142 Edward, d.[9]	1507 Ric. Berdeney.
1170 Robert, d.[10]	1512 Joh. Welles, resigned.[15]
1190 Henry de Longchamp, d.[1]	

* Buried at Crowland. Those marked m. are known to have been monks of the house.
1. Monk of Evesham.
2. Murdered by the Danes on the steps of the altar, 870.
3. Chanc. to king Edred, and preb. of York. A wealthy noble who became a monk out of pity for the forlorn state of the foundation, and made over to it a tenth of his possessions.
4. Previously ejected from Penkirk. See p. 64.
5. Sacrist of Peterborough. He rebuilt the abbey.
6. The chronicler. A statue of him remains in the W. front.
7. Prior of S. Ebrulph in Normandy. He began the new church.
8. Prior of S. Alban's.
9. Prior of Ramsey.
10. Prior of Leominster.
11. Built N. aisle and infirmary; also drained the fens.
12. Became blind before his death.
13. Entertained Henry VI. here, and admitted him a member of the house. Visited also by Edward IV.
14. Prior of Freston, a cell to Croyland.
15. Surrendered abbey, 1539, retaining an allowance of 130l. 6s. 8d. He is called in the list 'Wellys alias Bryggys.' A punning motto of this abbot's, 'Benedicite, Fontes, Domino,' was carved on his chair, afterwards in the possession of bp. Dove.

RECTORS.

1539 Tho. Crowland alias Parker.[1]	1730 Jas. Benson.
1661 Will. Styles.[2]	1761 Will. Sandiver.
1670 Hen. Peru, A.M., r.[3]	1762 Jas. Thompson.
Radcliffe Searle.	1767 *Moor Scribo, d.
cir. 1707 ——— Postlethwayte.[4]	1808 Jas. Blundell, d.[5]
1721 Bernaby Goche, r.	1834 Joh. Bates, A.M.
1722 Culpepper Butcher.	

The first church was built by abbot Kenulphus in the 8th cent., and is said to have been of stone. This was completely destroyed by the Danes in 870. A new church was raised by Turketyl, about the year 945. As this church was in decay in less than 120 years it could not have been very substantial. Wulketyl, in 1061, commenced a new building which was entirely destroyed by fire in 1091. According to the chronicle abbot Joffrid commenced rebuilding the abbey in the year 1113, the foundation stones of the several parts of the building being laid by various dignitaries amid great rejoicings. A minute account is given by Peter of Blois. Of the church then commenced we have some remains. At the E. end of the ruined nave the W. arch of the great central tower is still standing. It is patched up with brickwork. Many of the details of this arch are very beautiful. One of the shafts on the N.E. side of it, now external, has an elaborate capital with minute carving, embracing distinctly, among other ornaments, the dogtooth. This is an earlier example of this ornament than has yet been recorded. The two nave arcades were originally alike, but before the church was completed the S. arcade was altered. The difference is observable to anyone noticing the two sides at the junction with the centre arch. But an explanation of the change could never have been given without recourse to the chronicle. Mr. Moore * has explained the reason of this very early alteration, by

---

1. Named in the list of pensions as appointed to serve the cure with pension of 10*l*. He was also to have a chamber and right of fishing.
2. Also warden of Brown's hospital, Stamford. Took up arms with the royalists, and escaped from Woodcroft when dr. Hudson was murdered.
3. Preb. Sexaginta solidorum, Linc. Instituted suit for tithes against sir Tho. Orby, and lost it. Rect. of Leverington, Camb., where he is buried.
4. Named by dr. Stukeley as minister at his visit.
5. Also inc. of Whaplode Drove.

* Paper on the Abbey by the Rev. E. Moore, amongst those of Linc. Arch. Soc., 1861. These notes are indebted to Mr. Moore's paper for several conjectures and facts.

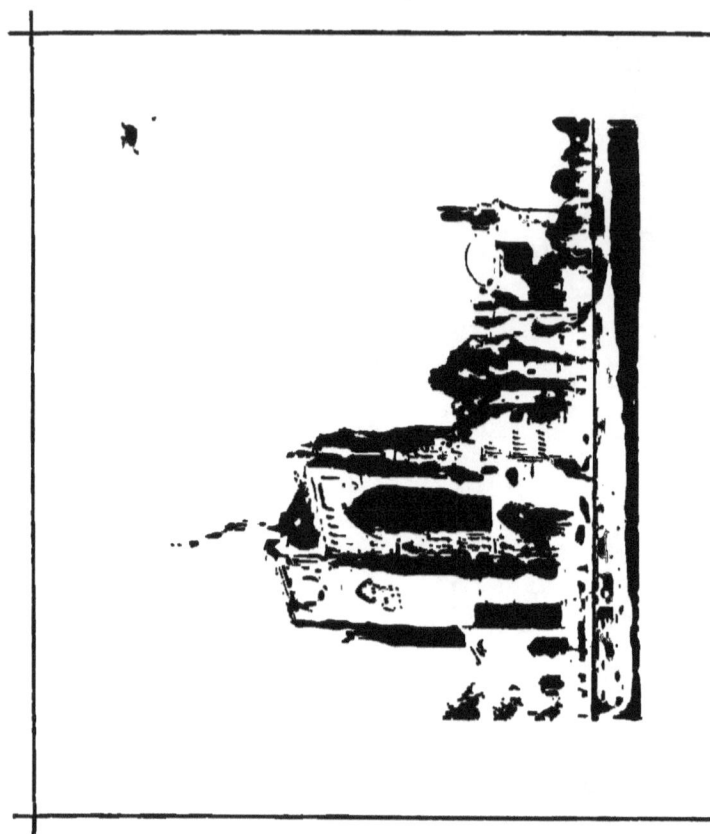

CROWLAND ABBEY, S.W.

quoting a passage under date 1118, describing an earthquake in England, which also overthrew the tower of Milan cathedral, 'and the new work of the church of Croyland, which as yet was weak in consequence of having no roof to hold it together, split asunder, most shocking to relate! in the southern wall of the body thereof.' The new arches of the S. side were built so lofty as to leave no room for a triforium. Besides this arch, the W. front of the S. aisle is part of Joffrid's church. This was later than the arch just spoken of. It consists of four tiers of arcades; all had originally shafts, but only those of the two middle tiers now remain. The arches in each row are different. There are zigzag round arches, plain pointed arches, intersecting arches, and plain round arches. Of this latter, the uppermost tier, only one arch remains. These, with two buttresses, are the only remains in situ of the Norman church. Many fragments are scattered about; and on the S. side several have been built into a low wall, where their beauty of execution is well seen. Of pure early English work is the W. front of the nave. This is the great charm of the ruins. It is richly ornamented in every part. There are five rows of niches, nearly all having the figures remaining in them. The great W. door is divided into two doors by a shaft, each with pointed arch; and above this is a large and deep quatrefoil adorned with sculpture of five scenes from the life of S. Guthlac. The two upper tiers of niches are not however of this date. They, and the great window now void of tracery, are of perpendicular work, late in 14th cent. The scenes in the quatrefoil, and the saints in the niches, have given rise to many attempts at explanation: at best all such attempts are mere conjecture, the carving being in many places so worn as to defy identification: the following is a condensation of the theory of Mr. Moore, who has given much time to their study.

Originally seven tiers: the two uppermost, in the gable, being now destroyed. They probably contained statues of our Saviour, and of SS. Mary & John. The mutilated statue on the bridge is possibly the central figure of all, our Lord in the act of blessing. The other figures, proceeding from N. to S., are thought to be S. Philip, S. James the greater, S. Thomas, S. Andrew, S. Peter, S. Paul,

(2 vacant,) S. James the less, S. Jude. Below these are K. Ethelbald, S. Bartholomew, S. Guthlac, K. Richard II., abbot Kenulph, K. William I., Q. Matilda, abp. Lanfranc, abbot Ingulf, (these last two do not agree with Mr. Moore's conjectures,) K. Edred, Siward, a bishop, S. John.

The last figure is one of four originally guarding the door. It fell down, but has recently been replaced.

Of the decorated work, during the 14th cent., there are no remains. But in 1405, during Overton's abbacy, considerable works were done, under the superintendence of William of Crowland, the master of the works. He rebuilt the transepts, with vaulted roofs; the Lady chapel, situated 'on the northern confines thereof,' probably occupying the same position as those at Ely and Peterborough; the refectory; the nave and aisles with their chapels. Three arches entire of the S. arcade of this nave remain. There were nine bays to the nave. In 1427 the tower, as it now stands, W. of the N. aisle, was built. But the completion of the whole design seems to have been reserved for abbot Litlington about 1464. The N. aisle (now the parish church) was vaulted by him. The W. porch and room above are later still.

In the interior there is not much to observe. The large bosses in the roof are very fine. To the N. of the present church, itself the N. aisle of the abbey church, is a chapel with groined roof, and considerable remains of inscriptions in black letter, but too much worn to be read. The eastern part is screened off by a perpendicular roodscreen of course removed hither. It had a roodloft. It still retains considerable remains of gilding and colouring. In the spandrels are good specimens of carving, especially noticeable are three fishes with interlacing tails, and a man punting.

We read much about the BELLS in the histories. Their sizes and names are recorded, as well as the date of their erection. One, called Guthlac, had been made by Turketyl, and when a fresh peal of six was added it was said there was not 'such a peal of bells in those days in all England.' At present there are five, thus inscribed:*

---

* It will be observed that in the 5th bell the rector's name is spelt inaccurately; also round a shield bearing England and France quarterly, the first bell has the motto, Jhu merci Ladi Help.

1. ✠ In multis annis Resonet campana Johannis.
2. THOS. NORRIS MADE ME 1674.
3. 4. Wᴹ HICKLING Wᴹ COOKE CHURCHWARDENS EDWᴰ ARNOLD LEICESTER FECIT 1788.
5. ✠ REVᴰ MOOR SCIEBO RECTOR ✠ WILLIAM COOKE AND CHARLES ASHBY CHURCHWARDENS ✠ E: ARNOLD LEICESTER.

But two MONUMENTS are of any interest. One, dated 1728—9, is remarkable as retaining the old formula of prayer for the dead (though the sculptor has indeed rendered it badly):

Beneath lieth Mary the Wife of ROBERT DARBY who dep. this life Jan : yᵉ 19th 1728—9 AGED 30 YEARS Cujus Animæ propitietur Deus.

The verb is mis-spelt 'propitieiur.' Six verses follow. The other is really singular. It is painted black on a white board with a black edge.

Beneath this place in six foot in length against yᵉ Clarkˢ pew Lyeth the Body of Mʳ: Abrᵐ: Baly he dyed yᵉ 3ᵈ of Jan 1704. Also yᵉ Body of Mary his wid: she Dyed yᵉ 21ᵗʰ of May, 1705 Also yᵉ Body of Abrᵐ. son of yᵉ sᵈ Abrᵐ & Mary, he dyed yᵉ 13ᵗʰ Jan 1704, also 2: wᶜʰ Dyed in there Enfancy, Mans life is like unto a winters day: some brake their fast and so departs away, others stay dinner then departs full fed: the Longest age but supps & goes to bed. O Reader then behold & see: as we are now so must you be. 1700.

The churchyard contains no ancient inscription. It is greatly overcrowded, and has lately been much extended. It was at the time of this extension that the fragments of Norman masonry already spoken of were collected and placed together. A dwarf wall, in great part composed of these fragments, marks the old boundary. A flat coffin-lid, in good preservation, is now placed on the top of this wall, immediately above the spot where it was discovered. To the W. of the church two stone coffins, now placed on the turf, indicate the line of the old churchyard. Other remains of floriated lids, and stone coffins themselves, are to be found in the farm premises of the parish. No inscribed stone in the churchyard is earlier than 1685.

The triangular bridge of Crowland is unique, and is in itself worth a long journey to behold. The chronicles, so early as 943, and again in 966, mention a triangular bridge, 'pons triangulus;' and if this reference be not retrospective, speaking of a point well known at the time the chronicle was written, as if the bridge had been then in existence, which is very likely, at any rate it does not refer to the present bridge, the date of which is about the middle of the 14th cent.

Four crosses at one time marked the extent of the abbey estates. Two remain to this day. One, on the Thorney road, like an obelisk, has been replaced; it used to lie on the ground; at its base are four shields, one having the abbey tokens. The other is towards Spalding and has this inscription, 'Aio hanc petram Guthlakus habet sibi metam.'

Since the dissolution, in 1539, the records (with one exception) are calamitous. In 1643 the town and abbey were garrisoned, and much destruction took place. At this time the great W. window was perfect. In 1688 the nave roof fell. The clerestory windows, large ones of four lights, were existing on both sides of the nave in 1735. Those on the N. side were taken down: those on the S. side fell this century. In 1748 the upper tier of statues was perfect. The whole of the W. front was, ten years ago, in a most precarious condition, and great fears were entertained that it would fall. This catastrophe has happily been averted. Mr. Scott undertook the task of preserving the front; and by a most careful process (detailed by Mr. Moore) the whole mass of the W. front was forced back into its original position. All defective stones were removed, and good ones substituted. Part of the W. front of the S. aisle was taken down and rebuilt. This was in 1860.

In Essex's collection (Brit. Mus. Add. MSS. 6769) are notes, etchings, and a plan of the abbey. The present nave is 144 ft. long, and the church 90 ft. long.

WOODSTON.

Woodston.

This name in Domesday is spelt WODESTUN; and at various times since it has appeared as WODESTON, WUDESTAN, and in other forms. The last syllable is doubtless the *town*, not the *stone*, so common about here. It is the pure Anglo Saxon suffix signifying an enclosure. Mr. Paley's conjecture that the former part of the word refers to the Saxon God WODEN, is extremely probable. The Rev. I. Taylor instances Wansford as evidence of the widespread worship of Woden, and he might have added perhaps Woodston.*

The church is dedicated to S. Augustine. This is most likely the English, not the African, archbishop. There are 28 other churches in England with this dedication. In 1291 the church was worth 8*l.*, and the abbot of Thorney had a portion of 6*s.* 8*d.* In the king's books the full value is 8*l.* 11*s.* 2*d.*, but besides the portion the procurations, &c., were 13*s.* 2*d.* The tenths were 15*s.* 1½*d.* The manor and church were amongst the first possessions of Thorney abbey.

The REGISTERS are singularly perfect and in very good order. From 1558 to 1812 are bound in one volume. Besides the entries proper there is much of value in this book. The archdeacon's injunctions in 1748; a list of 22 candidates for confirmation at Yaxley, 1745, 'from 12 years of age to above 20,' with a disquisition on the proper age for receiving the rite; a list of collections on briefs; some notes on the furniture of the church; a careful copy of all the inscriptions in the church; all these are to be found here, thanks to the care of a former rector. The interest of the volume may be judged from these extracts.

1636. 23 Jan. John Kisby Clarke of this Parish to 4 Parsons.
1692. 9 May. Thomas Kirby drowned at ye gravell ford.
1697. 12 Aug. Jane the wife of Mr. Judkin Feloniam in se comisit.

---

* In general when the name Woden is contracted into one syllable it is the *d*, not the *n*, that disappears. Thus Wednesday is pronounced We'nsday. In Hants a town of Woden is now called Wonston.

1699. 13 June. William Goodwin drowned at the Gravel ford of Woodston.
1734. 15 Aug. Robt. Alnwinkle a stranger found dead in the field.
1749. 24 May. Joh. Young a Black.
1752. 11 Oct. (baptized) Franc^s. s: of Rob. & Amy Dickens, Wood People.
1763. 10 Sep. Willm. Davis, a vagrant Soldier.

With one exception the above are from the burials. The briefs in 1707 were these:

8 June.	Collected for Darlington Church brief	1s. 11d.
20 July.	Shireland breife	8d.
25 May.	Perth Marston breife	4½d.
1 June.	Towcester Breif	7½d.
24 Aug.	Spilsby's Breif	22¾d.
24 Aug.	Littleport's briefe	22¾d.
7 Sep.	Broseby Church	4d.

The only part where the register is deficient is from 1590 to 1597.

In 1653 there are marriages before justices 'according to the late act of Parliament.'* As regards the visitation of archdn. Neve in 1748, after reciting what the rector and parishioners were to do respectively, the register proceeds:

Y^e expense in doing these things; on ye part of ye Parish, by a long course of neglect in others before you, being grown to a considerable article, & ye Parish having lately had its share of loss from ye Distemper amongst ye Cattle, Mr. Arch: Deac^n, at ye motion of ye Rect^r, thought fit to remit part of ye Execution to another year.

There are also these notes about the church furniture.

1732. Gilt salver & small wrought piece for offerings, given for Com^n. Service by Mrs. Walsham.
17—. She had also some years before new pewed the Church for the use of the poorer people; and gave the Branch.
1736. New pulpit cloth & cushion for desk all of Red given by same Lady.
1785. A new Altar erected by Inhabitants.
1789. A new Pulpit and Reading Desk d^o.

The inventories of church furniture for this county similar to those which have already appeared in the accounts of Northamptonshire churches have not yet been brought to light. There are a few slight memoranda in the record office of plate sold a few years before, in 2 Edw. VI.

Wodston. Solde by John Stappett and Willm Shepe Churchward^s ther wth thassent of all the parhiners vij old Broken lamps and other broken latten for iij^s viij^d iij . viii

---

* This was the act by which each parish was bound to choose a registrar. The names, parishes, &c., of the parties to be married were to be published thrice 'in the public meeting-place, commonly called the church or chapel, or (if the parties desired it) in the market-place next to the said church or chapel, on three market-days.' There was also this clause: 'Nevertheless, the Justice, in case of dumb persons, might dispense with pronouncing the words aforesaid; and with joining hands, in case of persons having no hands.' See also pp. 2, 64, 76.

The great benefactor of the place was Mrs. Walsham already named. In 1786 the donations to the parish are but two, both in the name of Walsham. Mary and John Walsham gave by deed, 1728, land for a school producing 16*l*. 5*s*. a year, and in 1744 Mary Walsham left for the poor 432*l*., producing 17*l*. 5*s*. 7*d*. This bequest was 'her stock of grain of that year on her Farm at Sexton Barns, Horses and Utensils of Husbandry.' The proceeds were to be distributed on S. Thomas's day. She had also, in her lifetime, given 100*l*. to the living, and laid the foundation of the school. In 1731 Joh. Wright left 30*l*., and in 1733, Tho. Wright, his brother, gave 5*l*. The meadow of Middleholm, 'granted to the men of Woodston,' was let for 20*s*.

In attempting to compile lists of incumbents for this county we meet with great difficulties. No history of the county exists that would assist us. It is only recently that Huntingdonshire has been made part of the diocese of Ely, and the ancient registers of the gigantic diocese of Lincoln are so voluminous as to preclude their being searched for a few isolated parishes. The lists, therefore, for this county are necessarily incomplete: but the following is believed to be correct for upwards of three centuries.

RECTORS.

1238 Walt. de Glovernia.[1]	1619 *Joh. Clement, A.M., d.[3]
1466 Ric. Andrew, d.	1653 *Sam. Foster, d.
1479 Tho Hutton, D.C.L.	1661 *Joh. Vokes, A.M., d.
Tho. Petye, d.	1702 David Standish, A.M.[4]
1503 Hen. Wilcoke, L.L.D.	1721 Fr. Whitstones, S.T.B., d.[5]
bef. 1534 Will. Haycock.	1730 *Rob. Smyth, A.M., d.[6]
1544 Joh. Wollaston.	1761 *Middlemore Ward, d.
1558 Ralph Bent, d.[2]	1780 *Joh. Bringhurst, A.M., d.[7]
1590 Walt. Baker.	1820 Mat. Carrier Tompson, A.B.,
1597 *Rob. Barnwell, d.	now A.M.[8]

* Buried at Woodston.
1. Presented by the king, the abbey of Thorney being vacant.
2. Minor canon of Peterborough. Buried in the cathedral.
3. Also rect. of Chesterton. Described in the parliamentary returns during the commonwealth as 'a constant preaching minister.'
4. Head master of the king's school and minor canon of Peterborough. Buried in the cathedral. The inscription on his tomb was this: 'David Standish A.M. Hujus Eccæ Min: Can: Publicæ Scholæ Moderator, Eccæ Parochialis de Woodston Rector. Excessit e Vita 22o die Octob: Anno ætatis 55 Domini 1720.'
5. Fell. of S. John's, Camb. Buried at Whittlesey S. Mary, where is a long Latin inscription to his memory.
6. An excellent antiquary. The good condition of the registers is due to him. He had made large collections for a history of the sheriffs of England from Hen. II., but 'it is much to be feared the MS. was destroyed by his drunken illiterate brother.'
7. Fell. of Corpus Christi, Camb.
8. Also vic. of Alderminster, Worc.

Of these rectors Ward has an altar tomb in the S. churchyard: Smyth has a tablet on W. wall of S. porch, on which he is described as 'a sincere honest man, and good christian, His utmost endeavours were To Benefit mankind, and Relieve the poor, He was a laborious & correct Antiquarian'; Foster, 'nuper hic fidus pastor migravit ad Agnum Dei,' Vokes, and Bringhurst, have memorials in the chancel.

The CHURCH is cruciform, with tower at the west end. The nave has aisles and two porches; the priest's door is N. It was entirely rebuilt in 1844: and for that date the work is highly creditable. A contemporary criticism speaks of it in high terms.*

<small>The church of *S. Augustine, Woodstone, Hunts.*, well known to ecclesiologists for its ante-Norman tower, has recently been rebuilt and refitted throughout, in a style and manner which deserves to be spoken of with high praise. The effect of the interior is most church-like, from the sombre light of the single lancets, the open roof, and the uniform open sittings, with poppy-head standards. The curious early font is completely restored. The tower has been rebuilt exactly on the original plan, with the exception of its now standing on four strong piers, by which a portion of the original masonry of the lower part is preserved.</small>

Some of the earlier work is preserved. At the W. of the tower is a large piece of the Saxon wall with one very small light.† The chancel arch is originally early English work, rather late. So is much of the chancel, though restored. An unequal triplet in the S. transept is also old. There are some old gable crosses. A few of these, having been blown down, are now used as headstones. In the rector's garden are fragments of 13th cent. piers from the old church. The present building is in the transition Norman style. All the windows of the nave are lancets. It is of four bays, having round arches, N., and pointed arches, S. The seats are all low and open, with poppy-heads. In the chancel the sedilia and piscina, if existing, are concealed by a large monument. The font is ancient but has been rechiseled. The tower now stands on massive piers; it is entirely within the church, and not pierced N. and S. The upper part seems original though not of Saxon date. The belfry windows of two lights, and the band of

---

<small>* Ecclesiologist, N. S., i, 138.
† It is said that this tower was destroyed on the ground that it was so insecure; but yet it was found impossible to pull it down without the aid of gunpowder.</small>

quatrefoils under the parapet, are preserved from the old tower. The side chancel windows are all of two lights. They have square heads and an external dripstone with notch-headed terminations. The E. window is perpendicular of three lights.

There are three BELLS all with inscriptions.

1. ✠ OMNIA : FIANT : AD : GLORIAM : DEI : 1608.
2. ✠ IOHANNES CLEMENT RECTOR PETRVS CHVNE CHWA 1636
3. GRATA SIT ARGUTA RESONANS CAMPANULA VOCE I. EAYRE S^r. NEOTS 1749.

Many of the MONUMENTAL inscriptions are curious, though none very ancient. In the churchyard are two old coffin lids with floriated crosses, neither in their original position. One, much mutilated, is used as a coping stone to the wall by the stile : the other lies under the arch that encloses the Saxon wall, at the W. of the tower. The following inscription is nowhere now to be seen : but it is worth preserving. It is entered in the register by rector Smyth as existing in his time; it was on a very large freestone, and written in Lombardick characters.

ORATE : P : ANIMA : FRATRIS : HENRICI : DE : IRTLINGBURGH.

The burial place of the Wrights is within the railings E. of the S. transept. There are some coped coffin-lids, moulded at the ridge, which expands into a shield for the name. Mr. Paley has given one singular inscription to a member of this family, of date 1659. In the chancel is a cumbrous monument to Mrs. Walsham. She was daughter to rector Vokes. Besides the benefactions to this parish she further left 6000*l*. 'to feed the Hungry and to Cloath the Naked.' Here also is buried her son, John Dickenson.* There is a tablet to Major Bringhurst, 'who fell at the ever memorable battle of Waterloo in Flanders.' An inscription to Mrs. Cooper, of Walthamstow, having recorded that she 'lived in Faith And

---

* Mrs. Walsham and her son have been previously cited, pp. 28, 29, as benefactors to the parish of S. John the Baptist, Peterborough. The son gave to the vicars as a residence his house in Westgate.

Devotion, In Charity and Meekness, As a Saint of the First times of Christianity,' a note in the register adds that she was 'of yᵉ Non-juring Persuasion' and justly entitled to the above character. She died 1711. On an altar tomb in the churchyard, 1778, is this sentiment:

O vain Man, a mark for Malice, thy Glory a blaze, thy time a Span, thyself a Bubble, is born crying, Lives laughing, and dies Groaning.
Who then to vain Mortality shall Trust,
But Limns the Water, or but writes in Dust.

The accumulation of soil on the S. side of the churchyard renders the S. porch useless. The arrangement of the plants and gravestones on the N. side exhibits greater care and taste than are commonly bestowed upon GOD'S ACRE.

Orton Longville.

The situations of the two Ortons on the high ground above the valley of the Nene, and above the main road to Northampton, may sufficiently account for the name, which is a contraction of OVERTON. The form of the additional names, given for distinction's sake, shews that they were added in Norman times. The two belonged originally, it is thought, to one man, and they may indeed have formed but one parish. When first possessed by two owners and made separate parishes, they would be naturally distinguished by the names of the owners. This parish, it is known, was in the hands of one Long: it is reasonable to think the contemporary owner of the other was named Walter, and that LONGVILLE and WATERVILLE expressed their separate properties.* It

---

* The name Walter was originally pronounced *Water*, and the *l* might easily be dropped in spelling Walterville. See the reference to this pronunciation in K. Henry VI., Part ii, Act iv, Sc. i. When the duke of Suffolk is taken, Walter Whitmore to whose share he is represented as falling, having mentioned his name, proceeds:
How now? Why start'st thou? What, doth death affright?
Suf. Thy name affrights me, in whose sound is death.
A cunning man did calculate my birth,
And told me—that by *Water* I should die.

ORTON LONGVILLE.

is singular that in the double name of each parish the final syllables mean the same. TON and VILLE both signify the TOWN; but one is Saxon and one Norman. On the assumption that this etymology is correct, two letters often inserted in the name are omitted. The spelling LONGUEVILLE is easily traceable to a false derivation meaning the *long village*, and the latinised form Iohannes de LONGA VILLA would encourage this.

The church at Orton Longville is dedicated to the HOLY TRINITY. In 1291 its value was 6*l*. 13*s*. 4*d*. after a portion had been deducted. In the king's books the full value was 12*l*. 19*s*. 8*d*., the synodals, &c., 13*s*. 2*d*., and the tenths 24*s*. 7¾*d*. The ADVOWSON is with the manor. Twice have the manor and advowson been confiscated by the king for felony.

The parish of Bottlebridge is now united with Orton Longville. The deed of bp. Gibson of Lincoln for their union is dated 1721. Amongst other statements are these:

Cum (ut informamur) ambæ Rectoriæ prædictæ jam vacent Cumq Ecclesia Parochialis de Bottlebridge prædict antehac ruinosa existens cum consensu tunc Episcopi Diœces : diruta et prostrata fuerit, ac materiales inde provenientes in reparanda et emendenda Ecclesia de Overton Longville antedicta in usum et Beneficium Parochianorum de Bottlebridge prædict fuerint adhibitæ.... paucæ admodum sint domus manconales.*

The site of the destroyed church is marked by a single upright gravestone with a much worn inscription in black letter. This stone has only lately been thus placed, having previously been utilised on the farm. Bottle is clearly a corruption of Botolph, the parish being always called in early times Botolph-bridge. Cotton † has a few notes about Bottlebridge. In his time, 1669, the church was in a ruinous state. There was an ancient mansion adjoining.

The place where yᵉ ancient house was is now converted into a Woad ground, Anno 1669. And yᵉ Chappell near adjoyning is gone to decay. This place, as

---

* 'Since, as we are informed, both the aforesaid rectories are now vacant, and since the parish church of Bottlebridge aforesaid being some time ago ruinous was by the consent of the then bishop of the diocese pulled down, and the materials thence procured were applied to the use and benefit of the parishioners of Bottlebridge aforesaid by repairing and enlarging the church of Overton Longville aforesaid.........and since there are (in Bottlebridge) very few houses fit to live in.' The present S. aisle of Orton Longville church was built of the materials brought from Bottlebridge.

† Brit. Mus. MS. Lansd. 921. Sir Robert Cotton, a very famous and learned antiquary, received his early education under Mr. English, head master of the king's school, Peterborough.

many other, may shew unto men the variations and mutabilities of all earthly structures. In a windowe in y⁰ Chancell are still to be seen two Coats, viz. B 3 Arrowes O.   A a Cross Lozengy, G.

In 1291 this church was valued at 5*l*. 6*s*. 8*d*. In the king's books, deducting a pension due to the prior of S. John of Jerusalem and the synodals, there remained 8*l*. 6*s*. 10*d*. liable to pay 16*s*. 8¼*d*. for tenths. At the parliamentary inquisitions in 1654 these livings were valued at 50*l*. each.

The earliest REGISTER is one for Bottlebridge, extending from 1556 to 1680. But it is imperfect; there are many large gaps. The earliest Long-Orton book is from 1559 to 1695. In the year 1636 there were several collections on briefs, but they are torn out. There are not many insertions of general interest.

1661. (Buried.) The daughter of Colonell Desborow.
1681. 19 Jan. Joseph Wright drowned was buryed.
1694. 30 Sep. Mʳ. Simon King Clerk buryed.
1714. 10 Sep. A Travellors child.

About 1740 the description 'beadswoman' often occurs.

The churchwardens' books abound with payments for destructive birds, &c. Sometimes a single bill 'for vermin' amounts to 23*s*. The fees were at this rate: old magpies, 2*d*.; young ones, 1*d*.; crows, 1*d*.; hedgehogs, 2*d*.; sparrows, per dozen, 2*d*.; eggs, per dozen, 1*d*.; hawks, 1*d*. In 1820 the molecatcher's bill was 4*l*. 4*s*. At the visitation in 1832 the churchwardens reported:

All well except an old clock that was not wanted, the repair of which the Archdeacon did not desire to be done and did not require any more presentment of the same.

In 1548 we find these notices of church goods sold.

Bottelbridge. Solde by Robᵗ Lamberd and John Bomber Churchwardens ther ij handbells for xxᵈ All wᶜʰ money they wᵗʰ other declare upon ther othes was bestowed on ij belle ropes.

Overton Longfielde. Solde by Willm Yearwell and Henrye Hoddye churchwardens ther ij great Candellstickes wᵗʰ other latten for vˢˡ ......put into the poore mennes boxe.

The chief benefactions to the parish are these. In 1654 lady Mary Armine gave 22*l*. a year to provide 8 poor widowers and widows 40*s*. each, and 15*s*. for a cloth coat or gown. Mrs. Walsham left 100*l*. to the poor. Rect. Stubbs and Will. Yarwell also left money to the poor producing a small yearly sum. The latter is for the parishes of Long Orton, Bottlebridge, and Cowbit, Linc.

In 1842 Chr. Jeffery bequeathed 100*l.* for annual distribution among the necessitous poor. There are also three acres of land, now called the Church Leys, left for the reparation of the fabric.

A chapter act dated 1 June, 1642, made a donation to the church the condition of renewing a lease :

<blockquote>
Mr. Smith of Overton Longville (if he will renew his Lease and amend his rent wch is now 2^s per ann. lesse than it should be and was of Old) shall pay only 40^s towards the reparation of the Church and have the Lease gratis for the terme in being.
</blockquote>

RECTORS.

ORTON LONGVILLE.	BOTTLEBRIDGE.
bef. 1534 Jas. Tunstall.	1312 Rog. de Northburg.[1]
1542 Tho. Skelton.	bef. 1534 Joh. Emeley.
1554 Geo. Pennington.	1542 Tho. Skelton.
1559 *Dionysius Ward, d.	1547 Rob. Webster.
1592 Everard Digbye.	1554 Edm. Fyrth.
1606 Edw. Wager.	1561 Mich. Chiltenden.
1637 Eusebius Hunt.	Joh. King, S.T.P.
1652 *Geo. Hamerton, d.[2]	1596 *Hen. Thorne, d.
1661 Edm. Spinkes, deprived.[3]	1624 Tho. Smith.
1663 Ric. Sawyer.	bef. 1654 Joh. Richardson.[2]
	*Simon King, deprived.[4]

*Ric. Caryer, A.M., d.[5]
1705 *Rob. Caryer, A.M., d.
1715 *Joshua Mann, S.T.P., d.
1718 *Joh. Taylor, A.M., d.
1721 Bernard Lewis.
1746 Joh. Naylor.
1761 *Jonathan Stubbs.
1780 Tho. Evans.
1799 Hon. Ch. Stewart.
bef. 1826 *Ch. Child, S.T.B., d.
1835 *Sam. Rogers, A.M., d.
1852 Joh. Bowen, A.M., r.[6]
1857 Ch. Geo. R. Cooke, A.M., r.[7]
1863 Joh. Watson, A.M.[8]

Inscriptions remain in the chancel to these rectors : Rich. Caryer, Rob. Caryer, 'Qui cum in eodem Officio

---

* Buried at the parish church.

1. This name is from the patent rolls, the presentation being made by the king. He had afterwards the living of Hemelden, and prebends in Sarum, Beverley, and S. Paul's. Made keeper of great seal, 1318, bp. of Coventry and Lichfield, 1821, and died 1360.
2. Described in parliamentary inquisition, 1654, as 'a constant preaching minister.'
3. Also rect. of Castor. Ejected under the act of uniformity. 'He was an able preacher,' says Calamy, 'and a person of great note.' See also p. 12.
4. In possession of the church of Bottlebridge at the restoration, but it is uncertain whether actually rector or not. Ejected under the act of uniformity. Calamy says he was 'an able scholar: a man of solid Judgment, and an honest Heart and Life; addicted to no Extreams.' He had lived with Baxter at Bridgenorth, and was subsequently minister at Trinity church, Coventry. After his ejection he lived at Orton, where his house was burnt to the ground in 1689, he being then over 80, and 'he was in a manner deprived of all his substance.'
5. Preb. of Lincoln and Peterborough.
6. Afterwards S.T.P., and bp. of Sierra Leone.
7. Now rect. of Chesterton.
8. Formerly inc. of Newborough.

post Patris Decessum hic obeundo Decenum (plus minus) absolvisset, cum Vita deposuit,' Taylor, Stubbs, Child, and Rogers. The tablet to the last-named, who was rural dean, is in brass.

The CHURCH has chancel with spacious N. chantry and S. priest's door, nave with aisles and clerestory, S. porch and N. door, and W. tower. With the exception of the extensive alterations made when the church of Bottlebridge was destroyed, it is almost all of one date, early in the 14th cent. The E. window, of five lights, is spacious. It has very large meshes in the tracery. The S.E. window, of three lights, is a very unusual but highly satisfactory design. It has very curious tracery. On each side of it externally is a niche with trefoiled head and moulding, conjectured by Mr. Paley to be the sedilia removed from within. The low side window is of three lights now blocked. Above is a window of two doubly-trefoiled lights with quatrefoil in head. Within, adjoining the low window is a stone seat, a similar one being on the N. side of the chancel arch. The door has an ogee arch. The chancel is embattled. There is a piscina within, and another in the chantry, with two niches. This was rebuilt in 1861, but the ancient work was not tampered with. It is divided from the chancel by a broad arch. The marks remain in the piers of the chancel arch from which the rood screen has been wrenched. W. of this arch are two curious little arches opening to the aisles, that to the S. trefoiled at each side. They are no larger than doors. The piers of the nave have quasi corbels with ballflowers. The clerestory windows are very small. The arch between the N. aisle and chantry is now blocked. The windows in this aisle are of two lights, and contain a few fragments of ancient glass. Cotton mentions three shields of armour, one belonging to the family of Wortley, as in a window in his time: and before the memorial window to the 10th marquis was erected one of these (described by Mr. Paley) remained in the E. window of the chantry. Close to the N. door is an excellent fresco of S. Christopher. The countenance is most expressive. The great size of the S. aisle is sufficiently accounted for by the extract from bp. Gibson's deed given above. We have no means of knowing whether the good windows at the E. end, which are of the same period as the rest of the church, and those W. of the porch, are removed from Bottlebridge, which is quite possible, or merely parts of the old S. aisle replaced. The two windows E. of the porch have had the heads altered in very poor style. The tower is of small size though of fair height. The large buttresses projecting N. and S. only give it an ungainly appearance. The internal measurement of the upper story is only 7 ft. 7 in. square. There is a small door to this story only 14½ in. broad. The buttresses to the chancel are placed at the angles. In the E. wall of the porch is a small circular window with a quatrefoil. The lower part of a good gable cross remains over the nave.

There are two BELLS. One is a sanctus bell, uninscribed, measuring 14½ in. in diameter at the mouth. The other is thus inscribed in old church text.

✠ Nomen Magdalene Campana Gerit Melodie.
It has also a foundry mark on a shield.

The MONUMENTS are numerous and costly. One is of the same date as the fabric and may be supposed to commemorate its founder. It is a cross-legged figure of a knight, under the arch dividing the chancel and chantry. Its date is determined by the armour. Above it hangs a helmet.* In the nave is a stone to Will. Yarwell, named already as churchwarden and benefactor, 1597. In the mortuary chapel the monuments are of large size. There are several hatchments here. A very elaborate tablet covered with shields, with marble table beneath, commemorates Eliz. wife of Hen. Talbot, younger son of George earl of Shrewsbury, 1629; Mary, her daughter, wife of sir Will. Armyne, 1674; and Talbott Armyne 'hæres ipsius Mariæ,' 1630. The slab and monument to sir Ch. Cope, of Bruern, Oxf., 1781, record that he

---

* Some portions of the armour, being much worn, have been misinterpreted and given rise to a most foolish legend. The anachronism of this story, which pretends that the knight here represented was killed by the Danes, is alone sufficient to condemn it. Cotton mentions a taberd hanging above it thus emblazoned: Argent, a chevron between 10 crosslets. 4, 2, 1, 2, 1. If this coat is known it might determine the person beyond dispute.

was 'distinguished By true greatness; If the great Man is the HONEST one!' A marble monument to lady Mary Seymour, 1825, has a seated figure. Under the E. window is a fine altar-tomb of granite to Charles, 10th marquis of Huntly, 1863. In the church are also inscriptions to Mary Wakelin, 1693; Mary, wife of Rev. W. G. Moore, 1826; Tho. Speechly, 1832; and others. The last-mentioned died at Bordeaux.* In the churchyard are several tombs to this family. The church was repaired and beautified in 1840. The S. porch was altered five years before. An organ was given in 1806 by the countess of Galloway.

Orton Waterbille.

An explanation of the second name of this parish has been attempted in the notice of Orton Longville. The more popular designation, CHERRY ORTON, is derived from a holt, or orchard, of cherries situated at the extreme end of the parish towards the other Orton.†

The ADVOWSON since 1480 has been in the hands of Pembroke college, Cambridge, to which it was bequeathed by Lawrence Booth, or Bothe, who was master of the college 1450—80, in which latter year he died. He was also bp. of Durham, 1456, lord chancellor, 1457 (for two years only), and abp. of York, 1462. The terms of his will describe his bequest thus:

Manerium illud egregium de Overton Watervile (quod inter hæreditamenta nostra longe est primarium) cum perpetuo patronatu Rectoriæ Ecclesiæ.‡

---

* The custom of recording a death in some church where the deceased was not buried (one of very doubtful propriety) is of comparatively recent origin. But at Marholm is a cenotaph of the 16th cent. The effigy in that church without name is known to commemorate William Fitzwilliam, earl of Southampton, K.G., lord admiral. He was chancellor of duchy of Lancaster, lord privy seal, &c. He died fighting against the Scots, and is buried in Middlesex. The monument is engraved in Hyett.

† The extent of the neighbouring trade in cherries is attested by the fair at Peterborough known as the 'Cherry Fair.' Near Cambridge is a village with the same distinction, Cherry Hinton.

‡ 'That splendid manor of Overton Waterville (which is of my possessions by far the most valuable) together with the perpetual patronage of the rectory of the church.' These particulars are from a MS. of the 17th cent. introductory to a terrier, in possession of the rector.

ORTON WATERVILLE.

In the same year the 'feoffees' of the abp. settled the manor on the college on condition of their founding two more fellowships.

The church is dedicated to S. MARY. The value in 1291 was 10*l*., from which was to be deducted a portion for the prior of Huntingdon of 1*l*. In the king's books the full value is 13*l*. 4*s*. 8*d*., and the tithe on the nett value was (xxv j ob' q') 1*l*. 5*s*. 1¾*d*. There was also a chantry of hardly less value than the rectory. In 1535 it was worth 10*l*. 6*s*. 8*d*. There were then two priests, Will. Emelton and Will. Nouman. In 1545 Will. Skakylton was appointed to the chantry, in which year all chantries were suppressed.

The REGISTERS commence in 1538. The first book contains upwards of two centuries, down to 1747. The next book, unfinished, goes down to 1812. From 1748 —54 they are imperfect. The title is as follows:

Regestum omnium tum Connubiorum tum Baptismatum et Sepulturarum que extiterunt in Overton Waterfield ab Anno Domini 1538.

A number of unusual christian names are to be found. In the 16th cent. these occur: Avys, Milsent, Custaunce, Lettys, Ursula, Sysselye, Maltum. This last is inexplicable. Later occur these names: Mirabella, Absalom, Thurstance, Maudline, Hierom. In 1590 a father and daughter were married on the same day. Among the burials we find:

1608. 7 Sep. Johes Taylor de Rabye in Com. Lynkolne morte obijt repentina in itinere versus Gunvile llerrye et sepultus est.
1620. 19 Jun. Michael Heiton molitor supra nonagenarium sepultus.
1621. 7 Mar. William Blaby of Stamforde travailinge towards Allerton suddainly upon y*e* breach of an impostume fell down in y*e* high way and died.
1622. 8 Apr. Nicolas Peter servante, about y*e* age of thirty. He gave five shillings to the Church, and as much to the poore.
       11 Mar.. Joane Neale wife of John shee died by casualty of fire in her owne house.
1633. 28 Dec. Henry Denis perished by water.
1654. 23 Aug. Widdow Carnall, very Aged.
1748. 17 Jul. Hall William He was unfortunately killd as he was stacking a rick of Hay by one of y*e* Waggon Horses getting between y*e* Ladder and y*e* stack and throwing him off y*e* Ladder.
1749. 11 Jun. Palmer John was killd by his Waggon laden with stone running over him w*ch* broke one Leg all to Peices, his other thigh, & bruised him in several Parts of his body.

At the bp. of Lincoln's confirmation in 1749, at Alwalton, 45 were sent from this parish, and two 'paid for want of certificates.' At the commencement of the second book is this note:

> The Customary Duties of this Parish are as follows viz
> Sermon Once a Sunday except on ye Feast day wch is ye Sunday next ye Assumption and then they claim two.
> Prayers every Holyday and upon Wednesdays and Fridays in Lent.
> Sacraments are generally double, viz two at Xtmas Easter & Whitsuntide and one ye Sunday after ye Feast of St Michael.
> Prayers twice a Sunday.

The following note of church goods sold was made 2 Ed. VI., but the day of the month is not given. The parish is called Overton Waterfield.

> Sold by Richard Slowe and Willm Bate churchwardens ther......a challise of Sillv^r waieng xxij oz a cope of Blewe velvet and a vestment of Blewe vellvett for vj^ll of the wch money they wth other declare upon their othes was spent upon the nedeful repairing their churche and on the poor lvi^sl viij^d.

In the abstract of charitable donations, 1786, the only benefaction named is that of Mr. Giddings, before 1611, to the poor, charged with repair of the church, producing at that time 12*l*. 10*s*. But in 1626 Will. Edwardes, of Watlingford, Herts., 'Shephearde,' left 5*l*.

> to be put foorth to use and to remaine for ever so longe as ye worlde endureth: and to bee dealte by ye minister, or three or foure sufficientest men of ye parish; and ye use to be dealte uppon Goode Fryday every yeare.

And in 1657 John Forster left 5*l*. to the poor to be distributed on S. Thomas's day; and 'Smith, Esq.,' gave 40*s*. to the church and poor. Bacon mentions a sum of 10*l*. annually for repairing the church, referring possibly to Giddings' bequest. More recently, as recorded in the church, Fr. Wright, 1857, and E. J. Wyman, 1859, left each 200*l*. to be invested for the poor and distributed at the discretion of the rector. Both these amounts were invested in consols.

RECTORS.

Joh. Hare, d.	1652 Nath. Gibson, A.M., deprived.[4]
1400 Joh. Fereby, S.T.P.	1662 *Tho. Ryder, A.M., d.
1545 Will. Barnaby.	1686 Tho. Browne, A.M., d.[5]
*Will. Millicent, d.	1706 *Tho. Thomas, A.M., d.[6]
1551 *Ric. Vasey, d.	1716 Roger Long, S.T.P., r.[7]
1569 Baldwicus Esdall.[1]	1751 Jas. Smyth, A.M.
1599 *Walter Whalley, S.T.B., d.[2]	1799 *Fr. Tennant, A.M., d.
1617 *Theo. Bathurst, S.T.B., d.[3]	1837 Joh. Mills, A.M.

* Buried at Orton Waterville.
1. Also vic. of Bottisham, Camb., 1573—76, and rect. Haddon 1589—99.
2. Afterwards S.T.P. His wife is mentioned as sponsor at the first using of the new font in Peterborough cathedral, set up in 1615. Ther. had previously been none. The present font, of 12th cent. work, was desecrated, and has only been recovered recently. This 1615

All of these rectors are believed to have been fellows of Pembroke college, Cambridge. To one only, Fr. Tennant, is there any memorial remaining in the church. A tablet, S. of the chancel, records that he was rector here 38 years, and died aged 84.

The CHURCH consists of chancel, nave with aisles, N. door, S. porch, and W. tower. It is mostly of the 14th cent. Some alterations, especially in the chancel, have taken place since; and there are detached pieces of earlier work. But the shell of the building is of the decorated period. The nave has on each side 4 bays. The piers are all octagonal, and swell out into the capitals at the top. The central pier on the S. side has an excellent capital carved. All are early decorated. At the E. and W. ends are smaller responds. On each side are three small clerestory windows; one has three lights, the rest two lights. At the E. end of each aisle is a very good net-tracery window, of three lights; and in the N. and S. walls are two similar windows of two lights each. Overlooking the chantry altars, in these walls, are two smaller windows, in unusual places. That on the S. side is very small; the other is larger, cinquefoiled in the head. Two elegant piscinas remain, and five brackets. In the chancel there are no remains whatever of the altar appointments. The whole E. end seems to have been rebuilt, perhaps shortened. The E. window is square-headed with three mullions, and on each side are two similar windows with one mullion, quite destitute of tracery. The roof is very low. There is one step to the chancel and one to the sanctuary. The priest's door is on the south. The original low side window remains at

font, now in the S. transept, was solemnly dedicated by the bp. in the presence of a large congregation. After singing a psalm, and offering prayer, 'mox ad Baptismum allatus est venerabilis viri magistri Joannis Bridgeman sacræ Theologiæ Doctoris ac Serenissimo Jacobo Regi a sacris, in ista Ecclesia primam tunc Præbendam occupantis, filiolus, qui imposito HENRICI nomine, Sponsoribus prædicto Domino Episcopo, & Humfrido Orme milite, & Elizabetha uxore D. D. Walteri Waley, in Christi ascriptus est. Cui et omnibus in posterum baptizandis benedicat Deus. Amen.'

3. Described in the investigation as a 'constant preaching minister.' A note in the register says he was 'an excellent Latin poet, and translated Spencer's Eclogues.'

4. 'A good scholar and an eminent preacher,' says Calamy. Ejected under the act of uniformity.

5. Afterwards S.T.P. He died in London.

6. The register says 'He was found dead one Sunday morning in yᵉ well, his shaving tackle being prepared he was supposed to have been drawing water for that purpose.'

7. Master of Pembroke, Camb. Afterwards rect. of Bradwell juxta mare, Essex.

the S.W. corner. The tracery is a double trefoil. Within is that very unusual feature, a stone stall, which occurs in three churches in this neighbourhood. Stanground and Orton Longville (see p. 138) have each similar confessional stalls. The chancel arch is of good decorated work. It has a round moulding, and the piers are halves of quatrefoils. The N. arcade seems a little earlier than the other : it has no termination to the hoodmoulds. The W. windows of the aisle are debased insertions. They are of two lights, with large trefoils, and ungainly quatrefoils in the head. On the nave roof are the dates of two repairings, 1758 and 1832. The font is octagonal on five shafts. There is a very fine pulpit. This pulpit, Mr. Paley says,

is a very fine piece of oak carving, apparently of the *renaissance* of the sixteenth century. Its details are similar to those of the celebrated screen in King's college chapel, at Cambridge. This pulpit is said to have been brought by a former incumbent from St. Mary's church, in that University. If so, it says little for the taste of those who rejected so magnificent a specimen of carving. Its form is octagonal, the panels and borders being very richly wrought, with bands of foliage in high relief. Over it is suspended an equally beautiful octagonal canopy, crested with the royal arms.

The S. porch is early English. The inner door has very deep hollows, and is continuous in its mouldings; in other words the jambs are not shafts with capitals, but mere continuations of the moulding round the arch. The outer door has good capitals, and three attached shafts. Both aisles have excellent decorated buttresses. They are gabled, and placed square at the angles. The tower is somewhat peculiar. It has no buttresses at all. The lower part might be of any date. It has very small windows. The upper part is perpendicular: it has a parapet with quatrefoil panels, and pinnacles with crockets. The belfry windows, which are transomed, are also of this period. Both nave and aisles retain their 14th cent. parapets.

There are four BELLS. The first has a fleur-de-lys at the end of each word. All are inscribed.

1. ✠ PROTEGE PRECE PIA QVOS CONVOCO SANCTA MARIA 1606 T N
2. THOMAS NORRIS MADE ME 1650.

ALWALTON.

3. SIC FIAT INTER CHRISTIANOS CONCORDIA RICH" CHAMBERS C: W: I: EAYRE FECIT 1754.

4. JOS: EAYRE S^T. NEOT FECIT. SAMUEL SHARMAN CHURCHWARDEN 1755

There are no MONUMENTS, and but one inscription worth preserving. It is on a brass in the N. aisle; a coat of arms also in brass has been removed; and the stone itself used a second time for an inscription in 1772. The words run thus:

Hic jacet Johes de Herlyngton qui obijt xij° die Januarij 3° Dni Millino cccc° biij°

In this aisle is a slab dated 1692; also a tablet 1772—1774, to Ric. Chambers and his wife.

The churchyard is spacious, but contains no tomb of special interest.

Alwalton.

This parish is somewhat under five miles from Peterborough, and is on the river Nene. The great north road goes through it. Its proximity to the great Roman station of Durobrivæ caused dr. Neve, rector here, to suggest as an etymology AD VALLUM, near the fortress. The name has undergone some variations. In Domesday it is spelt ALWOLTUNE. At that time there were two mills worth 40s., a fishery of 500 eels worth 5s., and 10 acres of meadow, but no church or priest. In Edward II's reign we read it as AYLWALTONE. In Richard I's reign it had been given to Peterborough abbey for augmentation of commons in the monks' kitchen. An occasional spelling, ADELWOLTUNE, most likely affords the key to the derivation. The TON is so common about here as a suffix that it is more probably of Saxon than Roman origin. Adelwold was bp. of Winchester. The place is frequently still pronounced as at one time written, ALLERTON.

The church is dedicated to S. ANDREW. The living is in the gift of the chapter of Peterborough. Its value in 1291 was 9*l.* 6*s.* 8*d.* In the king's books the full value was 9*l.* 19*s.*, and the tenths, after deducting procurations, &c., were 18*s.* 7*d.* In 1786 the 'certified value' was 60*l.*

The REGISTERS commence in 1572, and the first book goes up to 1681. At the beginning they are much defaced. These names occur: Faith, Temperance, Lettice, Pierie, Winnifred, Priscilla, Goodman, the last frequent. Amongst the descriptions of occupations are woolcombers and molecatchers. In 1654 Rob. Lawrance was chosen Register for Alwalton, Chesterton, Water Newton, and Sibson. There are no entries from the most ancient book of any general interest. The following are of later date: they include a memorandum about a legacy of 10*l.* to the poor. The second book begins 1697; so 15 years are lost.

1714. And they are desired at the beginning of a new Register Booke that shall be then concerned in the keeping of it to make a new recitale of the said Legacy & in whose hands it is lodged that the Interest may be continued to be paid for ever As they must Answere for such neglect to the Great God of Heaven of being instrumentall of defrauding the poore which God forbidd it should ever happen. Amen.

1747. 1 Feb. (Buried) Anne Wife of Tho. Frisby, she dy'd at Farcet of an inward bruise from a fall down stairs there.

1750. 1 Sep. Zachary Lee (or Ledbeater) my Servt. & faithful.

1753. 6 Aug. Anne Bayly Spinster. She was Sister to Thos. Bayly buried 1737. Who gave his Sister Anne sixty pounds on condition that at her death she shd give it to the poor of this parish; out of which she sav'd fifteen pounds which she added to the above 60*l.* & left the whole by will to the poor of the parish of Alwalton.

20 Aug. Thomas Robinson servant to Edward Pell Shepard kill'd by the fall from a Horse in Harvest.

8 Sep. Rich^d. Peach (hang'd himself)

1769. Elizabeth Shaw Daug^r of Robt and Rebecca Shaw baptiz'd at Whittlesea Novr. 1st. 1768 Christned at Alwalton June 18. 1769.

A vestry order, 27 Nov., 1777, shows how pews gradually encroached on the open benches. It provided

that Robt Pigott Esqr. of Alwalton in the County of Huntingdon, be permitted to build a Pew in the Wing of the North Ile of the Parish Church of Alwalton in the place of the two back Seats now (standing there).

Also that Willm Bradley of the same Parish have leave to erect a Pew in the place of those two seats next adjoining the Clark's Seat near the said North Ile.

Also that Richd Hetley of the said Parish Miller be allow'd to Erect a Pew, where the top Seat on the right hand of the Middle Ile now stands.

E. Keteriche as agent to the Rev$_d$. Tho$_s$. Marsham. Recr.
Willm. Bradley Chrchwarden.

ALWALTON.

The churchwardens' books are unusually entertaining. They are preserved from 1744. The extracts that follow are arranged in order of date with extracts from the overseers' books. The parish clerk was shaved at the expense of the parish (apparently by contract) for 4s. a year. A 'fullmire' named as a charge on the parish is a polecat, called in Lincolnshire a 'fomart.' Miss Baker says, '*Foumart* and *Fulmar* are correlative terms with us.'

		£	s.	d.
1744.	10 Nov. pead ye pinderd	0	5	0
1745.	6 May. Sould ye Goods of Dorety Hardey [every item is particularised, and the sum is]	3	2	3¼
	22 Sep. for making beatey Sudbery a peatecot and Stimpson 2 Shifts and a patecot and threed	0	1	0
1750.	31 Oct. p^d for one pound of Gunpouder and a pound of Shot to scare ye Wild Gees	0	1	2¼
	25 Dec. for killing a fullmire	0	0	3
1754.	9 June. P^d Goodey Brice for pipes & Tobacco when ye town Grass was Sould	0	0	3
1755.	An acc^t of the persons Names that are Requir^d to do their Statute Work With their Teams towards Repairing and Amending of the Road in Allwalton town Street on the 28th 29th and 30th of this Instant May [9 names follow.]			
1759.	A prayer for ye Takeing Lusiburge	0	1	0
	A prayer for ye Takeing Quebeck	0	1	0
	19 Dec. A prayer for overcoming our Enimies by Sea	0	1	0
1762.	19 Apr. [Memorandum, dated at Elton, in writing of lord Carysfort.] It is a shame that the Parish of Alwalton sends a Person to swear to the Truth of Accounts that have not passed through his Hands. It is the Duty of the Overseer of the Parish of Alwalton to account himself upon Oath, and to appear in Person on this day or within fourteen Days, or he will be sent to the Common Gaol according to Law. Carysfort. V. Jackson.			
1763.	Sparrow money dew to me about	0	11	0
1774.	paide Mr Sharman for repairing a Gunn	0	4	0
	for moing of thisels for the parish	0	0	8
	7 June. for the huencry	0	0	6
1775.	Swaring to the ten pound man	0	1	0
1783.	[Certain sums given to] D. Edis very impertinent about the money			
	12 June. Surplos washin and the clothes	0	2	0
	29 June. paid to Robt. Drake for a heghog	0	0	2
	12 Jul. D^o for a hedghog my self	0	0	2
	27 Aug. pade for a proair for the queen	0	1	0
1784.	P^d Robt Drake for Skareing the Gees	0	4	0
1788.	8 Apr. p^d Reeve for the town well Cerb	0	10	0
	p^d for the town peckax helving	0	0	6
1789.	13 Apr. Two Prayers for the King	0	2	0
1790.	25 Feb. p^d for the Constables staff	0	0	6
1792.	2 Feb. A jorney to Stilton to Draw the milisher But did not draw	0	2	0
	29 Feb. a jorney to Stilton to Draw the militia but did not Draw	0	2	0
1794.	11 June. Jurney to Yaxley a Confermation & Victuals & Drink	0	4	0
1812.	Ordered by the Vestry [to the Clerk] for good Behaviour	0	10	6

ALWALTON.

The following fragment of a vestry order is without date, but it is most likely about 95 years old.

And wee further Agree that the pindard shall Demand and have pade unto him the Sum of Sixpence for every hors mare or Gelding that he or his Wife shall Detain or Detect In the field or fields of Alwalton without either Shackel or Lock Shall pay unto the Afforesaid Tho. Spires or his Wife or his agents the Sum of Sixpence for Each head for such Default And further we Agree that all part or parties that shall Miss In form themselves of the A Bove writen order shall Not pretend to plead Ignorence this shall be a fixt upon the post of the Stox or otherwise the Coppy of it and for the other Defaults 2^d per head.

The following notice is dated 1548. It is from the record office.

Allwarton—Solde by Willm Whittyngton and John Syeaimt (?) churchwardens ther wth thassent of all the prishiners vij challises of Sillv^r for xxxiij^{sl} iiij^d ij candlestickes of Brasse and ij handbells for vij^{sl} } x^{lsl} iiij^d

Of the wch money they wth other declare upon ther othes that ther was Bestowed in glassing and mending the churche, hells, and churche wall xxvi^{sl} iiij^d and given to the pore ij^{sl} } xxviij^s iiij^d

Stolne out of the said churche ij Allte Clothes, ij towels, iij paynted clothes, a corporesse wth a rufe of redde velvett a veyle for lente a vestem^t of damaske and vij............

The list of benefactions in 1786 is identical with that now painted over the S. door. Mrs. Bailey left 60l.; Mrs. Gregory, Tho. Southgate, and dr. Neve, rector, each 10l. The proceeds are 4l. 10s. annually.* All is given to the poor.

RECTORS.

1419 Alan Kyrketon.	1685 Ch. Bifield, A.M., d.[4]
1552 Will. Rede.	1689 Will. Waring, A.M., d.[5]
1568 Will. Latimer.	1726 White Kennett, A.M., r.[6]
1583 Joh. Bill.	1729 ‡Tim. Neve, S.T.P., d.[7]
1594 Rob. Milner.	1757 Will. Brown, r.
1602 Joh. Palmer.	1763 Tho. Marsham.
1615 Tho. Bridgeman.	1800 Ben. Barnard, A.M., r.[8]
1632 Hen. Williamson.[1]	1801 ‡Hen. Freeman, A.M., d.[9]
1656 ‡Rob. Newcome, d.[2]	1832 ‡Joh. Hopkinson, A.M., d.[10]
1670 David Llewelyn, A.M., d.[3]	1853 Ed. Gray, A.M.

* This is erroneously put down in the parliamentary papers as 4s. 10d.

[1]. In his time the parliamentary inquisition was taken. He was reported as a 'preaching minister,' and the living valued at 70l.
[2]. He signs 'minister' 1656, but 'rector' 1660: somewhat significant. Previously rect. of Calcott, Hunts.
[3]. Preb. of Lincoln and Peterborough, vic. of Hamelden, rect. Tansover and Gretton, buried 'obscurely' in London.
[4]. Minor canon of Peterborough; buried in the cathedral.
[5]. Vic. of Peterborough, precentor of the cathedral, and master of the king's school. Buried in the cathedral.
[6]. Afterwards rect. of Burton Cogles, Linc., and Peakirk; also preb. of Lincoln, Peterborough, and S. Paul's. Buried in Peterborough cathedral.
[7]. Had been head master of Spalding school. Also minor canon of Peterborough, chaplain to bp. Thomas of Lincoln, preb. of Lincoln, archdn. of Huntingdon. See p. 33. Published sermon at visitation, 1747. His son, of the same names, was Margaret prof. of divinity at Oxford.
[8]. Preb. of Peterborough; afterwards rect. of Peakirk, and there buried.
[9]. Formerly fell. of Clare. Also vic. of Everton.
[10]. Also rect. of Etton, Northants.

There are tablets to the last two rectors; that to Hopkinson is in brass, and occupies the low side window. Of rect. Freeman it is said, 'his life was spent in active and constant usefulness.'

The CHURCH has a somewhat unusual plan. It is cruciform, the nave having aisles and S. porch, with W. tower. A good deal of the work is of transition Norman date, in parts approaching the more distinct features of the early English period. The nave consists of four bays on the N. side, the piers being circular with square capitals, and round arches. On the S. side there are only three bays, and here the piers still circular are lighter and more elegant than those opposite: the capitals also are circular, and the arches pointed. The inner door of the porch is of very late Norman, having the pointed arch, but it is enriched with much characteristic Norman work, and is unquestionably of the same date as the N. arcade of the nave. Hence it is clear that the original Norman church had only a N. aisle. This present inner porch door was the outer door of the first church. The present porch is modern; built at the restoration in 1841. The outer door of the porch then destroyed was of the horse-shoe form. There are three clerestory windows on each side, of two lights each, added in the 15th cent. The aisles are very narrow. The W. end being unencumbered with seats has a spacious appearance. In the centre is the font, a heavy square one. At the W. is a two-light perpendicular window. W. of the S. door is a stone beam, or quasi flying buttress, up to the nave arcade. The arches to the transepts are quite nondescript. The piers are very thin and lofty, they are divided into three, and have embattled capitals. But they might be of almost any date. The N. and S. windows are good geometric work. They are of three lights each, with trefoiled circles in the head. The design of that in the S. transept is well seen in the view given. The windows at the E. side of the transepts have plain intersecting tracery. The aisle windows are perpendicular. The chancel has some elegant decorated windows. These are lofty and of two lights each with geometric tracery, not all alike. The E. window has the net tracery. On both sides is a low side window. That on the S. has the iron stanchions left in the upper part. The lower part is occupied by the brass tablet already named. The piscina is apparently earlier than the chancel itself, and is of very singular form, having an inner arch. The sedilia however, three in number, are decorated. They closely resemble, as Mr. Paley has pointed out, 'those now built as niches in the outer chancel wall at Orton Longville.' Opposite is a founder's sepulchral arch, but no remains of effigy or coffin-lid lie beneath it. The seating is not what would be admired in a restoration of to-day. It is however a great improvement upon what went before. In the circular relating to the repairs, issued in 1840, is this passage: *

<small>The repairs had long been neglected, and at various times it had been disfigured by every possible enormity; by pews, or rather cribs, of every shape, size, height, and colour; by, what was called, a singing-loft; by bricking up one most beautiful arch, and by letting others go to decay; by broken floors, broken seats, and broken windows; by crumbling walls, and a roof scarcely hanging together.</small>

By these alterations 72 additional sittings were obtained. Amongst other works done at this time were the new roofs and stone parapet. The ends of the transepts were taken down and rebuilt. The tower is a beautiful specimen of 13th cent. work. The belfry stage is arcaded: and this, coupled with the projecting parapet above, and the bold staircase turret with conical top, has a most pleasing effect.

The belfry is provided with very sturdy beams. On the first is carved WI MI IO CH CH WA 1674. These are the first two letters of the christian and surnames of the churchwardens. A five-pointed star is cut after the initials. There are five BELLS.

1. ✠ THOMAS NORRIS MADE ME HS HG 1652
2, 3, 4. THOMAS NORRIS MADE MEE 1661
5. WILL WARING RECTOR JOHN COX CHVRCHWARDEN 1702

The MONUMENTAL remains are but scanty. Slabs within the altar rails to the family of Gregory, the earliest

---

* Quoted from the 'Ecclesiologist,' i, 79.

CHESTERTON.

being 1634, are the oldest extant. There are slabs in the body of the church to the names Bradley and Hetley. In the S. transept is a tablet to sir Richard Hetley, 1807. He was high sheriff in 1800. His father, mother, and six of their children 'lie buried in the Cathedral Church yard of Peterborough which is now no longer a Place of Interment.'

The CHURCHYARD has no tomb of general interest. It is not very spacious. The trees of the adjoining premises give it a secluded appearance. In 1749 the bp. of Lincoln held a confirmation in this church. Rich. Southgate, formerly librarian of the British museum, was born here. In Kerrick's collection (Brit. Mus. Add. MSS. 6739), is a sketch of the S. door. A sundial on the transept, dated 1735, has the motto 'Watch & Pray.'

Chesterton.

In name and position this place is alike Roman. Ermine Street, the great road from London to Lincoln, is one of the boundaries of the parish. The city and camp of the Romans was on both sides of the river, and as this river was the boundary line between the settlers of two entirely different peoples, the name of 'camp' is preserved on each side of the river in quite different forms. Mr. Taylor says:

> But as we pass from the Saxon to the Anglican kingdoms, we find *chester* replaced by *caster*. The distinctive usage of these two forms is very noticeable, and is of great Ethnological value. In one place the line of demarcation is so sharply defined that it can be traced within two hundred yards. Northamptonshire, which is decisively Danish, is divided by the Nen from Huntingdonshire, which is purely Saxon. On the Saxon side of the river we find the village of CHESTERTON, confronted on the other side by the town of CASTON, the two names recording in two different dialects, the fact that the bridge was guarded by the Roman station of Durobrivæ.*

In domesday it is called CESTRETUNE. There was then a church and priest. The names CESTERTON and CESTRETON also occur. The ADVOWSON is in the manor,

---

* Taylor's 'Words and Places,' pp. 259, 260.

and has accordingly passed through the families of Driden, Hewitt, Pigott, Gordon, and others.

The church is dedicated to S. MICHAEL. In 1291 the prior of Royston had a pension of 40*s.*, the prior of Huntingdon a portion of 20*s.*, and the abbot of Thorney one of 30*s.* The value of the rectory after these deductions was 12*l.* In the king's books the full value is 20*l.* 8*s.* 4*d.* : but the prior of Huntingdon's claim is not mentioned, and the other two are only 52*s.* : the procurations being 13*s.* 2*d.*, the full value is reduced so as to yield 34*s.* 4*d.* tithes. In 1786 the certified value was 61*l.* 10*s.*

The oldest REGISTER of Chesterton at present in the hands of the rector begins in 1734. This and later ones have been kept most imperfectly, and are in very bad order. An earlier register is now unaccountably missing. It has been lost comparatively lately, for it was in existence in 1831. The original answers of incumbents to a parliamentary enquiry as to register books extant in that year are preserved.* The letter from the late rector may there be seen: he returned one register as of vellum and parchment, containing baptisms, marriages, and deaths from 1561 to 1733 or 1734. He also very remarkably returns that there are no baptisms or burials from 1734 to 1769. This might easily be omitted, though not missing, by accident; but it seems impossible that a non-existing one can have been recorded. An old book belonging to Haddon parish is kept here, but that cannot be alluded to because it does not commence in 1561. There are no entries in these recent books that need be here recorded.

The churchwardens' accounts go back to 1776. Amongst the items these occur:

```
1778.  4 Apr.  A mop: and beer for washing the Church ........ 0 2 0
1779.  pade Richard peech for purls & kees for the bells ......... 0 0 6
1779.  21 Apr.  A vestry held this Day to Chuse parish Officers, and
                no pirson appearing I chuse myself tax gatherer for the
                year insuing.
                                        Henry Briggs Churchwarden.
1782.  Mr: Callow Bill for white washing and painting the Church  1 5 4
       To Ale for Ditto ....................................... 0 5 0
```

---

* Brit. Mus. Add. MSS. 9356. A previous enquiry in 1813 is recited and referred to.

1789. 25 Mar. paid Elleck Peach for bolts & purls for the great bell 0 1 0
       paid Wm Reve for putting The Claper in the Great bell .. 0 1 0
1794. 10 Jun. Journey to Yaxley 0 2 6

The charitable donations in 1786 were ' none.'

RECTORS.

bef. 1534 Joh. Browne.	1696 ‡Nic. Addenbrooke, A.M.
1544 Seth Halywell.	1730 Joh. Old.
1562 Ant. Bartlemew.	1753 Ed. Morgan.
1580 ‡Baldw. Esdall, r.[1]	1755 *‡Rob. Tench.
1586 Will. Acrod.	1786 *‡Joh. Fowke, L.L.D., d.
1629 Joh. Clement, A.M.[2]	1813 ‡Sept. Courtney, r.
Geof. Hawkins, A.M., depr[d].[3]	1819 *‡Lord Geo. Gordon, A.M., d
1660 Eusebius Hunt.[4]	1863 ‡Ch. Joh. R. Cooke, A.M.[5]

Memorials remain in the chancel to dr. Fowke, and to lord George Gordon.

The CHURCH consists of chancel, nave with aisles and clerestory, S. porch, W. tower and spire. The nave arcade, aisle walls, and tower, are of good early English work. No ancient windows remain in aisles or chancel. They have been replaced by round-headed windows without mullions. There are four bays of very fine detail. On the N. side are three octagonal pillars and two semicircular responds: on the S. side are five piers alternately round and octagonal. On this side three have very bold foliage carved in the capitals. The western pier has a fine base, the others are mostly concealed. In many features the work here seems better than on the opposite side. At the W. of the nave are visible some singular terminations to the tower buttresses. The tower arch is blocked up. Only one piscina remains, in the S. aisle. It is plain early English, and has a slightly projecting square bason. Both chancel and nave have now low flat ceilings; but in the nave the wooden supports to the wallpieces of the perpendicular roof remain. The chancel arch is early English: its mouldings are visible on each

---

* Buried at Chesterton.
‡ Also rectors of Haddon.
1. Fell. of Pembroke, Camb., vic. of Bottisham, Camb., 1573—76, and rect. of Orton Waterville, 1569—99. Buried at Haddon.
2. Also rect. of Woodston, and there buried. See p. 181.
3. There appear to have been three of this name, father, son, and grandson. One was ejected from this rectory in 1641, but another (or perhaps the same) appears in the list at the record office as rector in 1651. The former of these is probably the one buried at Castor, 1672, whose epitaph is given p. 21. In 1689 a Geoffrey Hawkins was rect. of Water Newton; he died in 1700, and was succeeded by his son, of the same names.
4. Also rect. of Orton Longville, 1637—52.
5. Formerly rect. of Orton Longville.

side, but the arch itself is wholly blocked in the upper part. The lower part is occupied by a screen in the Grecian style. The chancel has been entirely altered and retains no ancient features. In the clerestory wall over the S. aisle is a very small window, now blocked up, most probably originally to light the roodloft.* On the N. side is the pulpit of oak, standing on a platform, and richly inlaid with coloured woods. There are very few seats in the church, which therefore looks very spacious. They are mostly high pews, but a few open seats have been erected towards the W. end. The font is very small and ugly. There is a very fine S. door of best 13th cent. work. The mouldings are deep: the door itself narrow. On each side are two good detached shafts: at the angles one shaft attached. The capitals are formed into one continuous band. The bases of the outer shafts are concealed in part by the stone seats of the debased porch. Above the heads of the shafts there is excellent foliage; in one case a carved head. The clerestory windows are square-headed of three lights. The lowest stage of the tower has a tall thin lancet in each face: the belfry stage has a two-light window of narrow lancets, under an arch comparatively distant, which has shafts at the corners. A debased door, of the same character as the aisle windows, had been inserted in the S. wall of the tower, but it is now blocked. The tower arch, which is visible from the tower itself, is of the same date and very fine. There are some good buttresses, set square at the angles and projecting a long way. They are square above, but half octagons below. At the S.W. corner the two buttresses are developed into a bold staircase with narrow slits for windows. The spire is early decorated. It has small broaches, and below it is a corbel table of notch-heads. There are two rows of lights in the cardinal faces; all are of two lights, cusped, with quatrefoil above. They have acute gables. The masonry is everywhere excellent, and the whole forms a composition of great beauty.

---

* Perhaps the windows at Orton Waterville, p. 143, and the destroyed one at Whittlesey S. Mary, p. 103, were also for this purpose.

There are three BELLS, one only being dated. The first letter on the first bell is crowned. The third has fleurs-de-lys and ornaments between the words. The inscriptions are these, the first being unusual:—

1. ✠ O Trinitas Sancte Istam Campanam Conserba.
2. ✠ Sancta Margarita Ora Pro Nobis.
3. ✠ OMNIA FIANT AD GLORIAM DEI, 1621.

Amongst the MONUMENTS are three of great interest. The earliest is in the N. aisle, under a low sepulchral arch. It is indisputably in its original position, for the stone appears half covered by the arch, and yet the marginal inscription is quite perfect, whereas it would be in part under the arch, unless the arch and stone belonged to one monument. The legend reads thus :*—

orate . p . aia . willmi . beibyle . gnosi . qui . obiit . anno . reg . richardi . tertii . jo . cuius . anime . ppiciet . deus .

This would be 1483 or 1484. The family were long resident in the parish. They were connected by marriage with the families of Coles, Hewett, Driden, and others. A pedigree for six generations is given by Cotton in MS. Lansd. 921; and a fuller and more complete one is preserved in the visitation of Huntingdonshire, 1613, MS. Harl. 1179. They used the N. aisle as a burial place: and this seems to have been the Lady-chapel from the following extract from the will of Will. Bevill, the son (in all probability) of the one whose monument is preserved :†—

In the name of Almighty God. Amen. I, William Bevyll, of Chesterton, in the county of Huntingdon, Gentillman, of an holy minde and good remembrance, being the xxx day of the moneth of July, in the yeare of our Lord God MCCCCLXXXVII, make my testament and my last will in this wise. First, I give and bequeath my soule unto Allmighty God, his blessed Modyr and Mayd our Lady Saint Mary, and all the blessed company of Heven; and my body to be buried in the Chirche of St. Michael of Chestirton aforesaid, afore the autre of ye blessed Lady St. Mary the Virgin, with my best hors, in the name of my mortuary.

---

* 'Pray for the soul of William Bevill, gentleman, who died in the first year of king Richard the third, on whose soul God have mercy.'
† Nicolas's 'Testamenta Vetusta,' p. 780: quoted from MS. Cott. Julius, F. viii.

Also we learn from Cotton, as before quoted, that 'In yᵉ same Isle on yᵉ roofe Beyvyle is engraven on yᵉ Wood.' And the elaborate monument occupying the E. end of this aisle is a double one to this family. It is without inscription or date: but Cotton has preserved the date, 1611, and the coat of arms still to be seen, compared with the pedigree above mentioned, make it clear that this is a monument to Rob. Bevill, great-grandson of the Bevill whose will has been partly given, and his son sir Rob. Bevill, with their wives. On the monument are two couples kneeling towards a double faldstool, the men in each case nearer to it. Below are children: to the left two sons and seven daughters; to the right three sons and five daughters. Of the former two seem to have been twins and are curiously united on the monument. At the top is the coat of arms of the Bevills, the crest broken off, ' a chevron between three roundels.' Below this are two other shields, each having Bevill (with a crescent for difference) and another coat quarterly on the dexter side, impaling, the one, Laurence, and the other, Cole. This fixes the persons commemorated; for Rob. Bevill aforesaid married Joane Laurence of S. Ives; and sir Rob. Bevill, his son, married Mary Coles of Preston. Moreover the crescent for difference is accounted for, because Robert was not the eldest son. In 1494 Will. Beyvyll of Hunts. was admitted to the fraternity of S. Rhadegund de Thelilford. In this same aisle are several inscriptions to the family of Bailey. At the E. end of the S. aisle is a long Latin epitaph on a costly monument to John Driden, second son of sir John of Canons Ashby. His sister Honor was the fair cousin with whom the poet Dryden was in love: his mother Honor was daughter of sir Rob. Bevyll, and is one of the identical little girls represented on the monument in the N. aisle. This gentleman retained the old spelling of the name. The inscription is this:—

MS JOHANNIS DRIDEN Armʳⁱ. et natu secundi Johannis Driden ex Canons Ashby in agro Northamptonⁱ Bartˡˡ ex Honora F. et Cohœrede, e tribus unâ, Roberti Bevile Barᵗˡ. undè sortem maternam in hac vicinia de Chesterton & Haddon adeptus, prædia dein late per comitatum Huntington adjecit; nec sui profusus nec alieni appetens: A Litibus ipse abhorrens et qui aliorum Lites Æquissimo sæpe arbitrio diremit; Vivus adeò Amicitiam minimè fucatam coluit, et publicam Patriæ salutem asseruit strenue, ut illa vicissim Eum sumis quibus potuit Honoribus cumularit, lubens sæpiusq SENATOREM voluerit, vel Moriens, bonorum atq beneficiorum non imemor, maximè vero Religiosæ charitatis intuitu, largam sui census partem, ad valorem XVI Millium plus minùs Librarum, vel in Locis ubi res et comercium, vel inter Familiares quibus necessitudo, cum eo vivo intercesserat, erogavit: Marmor hoc Nepos et Hæres Viri multum desiderati, ROBERTUS PIGOTT Arm^r. P. Obiit Cœlebs III Non Jan Anno Dom MDCCVII Æt: LXXII.

The poet and his cousin were on terms of close intimacy the whole of their lives. Amongst the poet's works is an epistle 'To my honoured kinsman, John Driden, of Chesterton, in the county of Huntingdon, Esq.,' in which the latter is highly praised. This poem was acknowledged by a handsome gift. The writer and his subject are spoken of together in these lines:—

> Two of a house few ages can afford,
> One to perform, another to record.

And the following illustrate several of the expressions made use of in the above epitaph:—

> No porter guards the passage of your door,
> To admit the wealthy, and exclude the poor;
> For God, who gave the riches, gave the heart
> To sanctify the whole, by giving part;
> Heaven, who foresaw the will, the means has wrought,
> And to the second son a blessing brought;
> The first-begotten had his father's share;
> But you, like Jacob, are Rebecca's heir.

On the S. wall is a tablet to Ric. Edwards, who died 6 July, 1730, aged 63. This is also in Latin. He left considerable property to charitable uses: 'scivit quo valuit nummus, et QUI dedit.' Among the bequests enumerated here are 5*l.* for the poor of this parish; 110*l.* to poor widows of Brosley, Salop; and 400*l.* to found a school at Niend Savage, in the same county, for 20 boys, sons of parents of moderate means.

The churchyard is not very extensive. There are no burials on the N. side. There is a very small stump of a cross. The last rector is buried within rails at the E. of the chancel. The architectural defects of this part are happily concealed by ivy. Near the tower is a massive stone coffin, with lid in two pieces.

Elton.

For the beauty of its situation this village is without a rival amongst those described in this book. There are many trees, and the houses mostly are built on the slope from the high road, which is at a considerable elevation, down to the river. Above all stands the fine tower of the church surrounded with foliage. The name has become settled in its present form by gradual contractions. The earliest form seems to be ALLINGTON or AYLINGTON. Afterwards we find ELLINGTON, AYLTON, AILTON. The etymology may probably be referred to the same origin as the Allingtons in Kent, Devon, and elsewhere, the TOWN OF THE ÆLINGS. In Burgundy are places, as Alligny, thought to owe their names to this same clan.*

The church is dedicated to ALL SAINTS. In 1291 the value was 23*l*. 0*s*. 8*d*., and the abbot of Ramsey had a pension of 3*l*. 6*s*. 8*d*. In the king's books the full value was 27*l*. 9*s*., but the archdeacon's fees and the abbot's pension reduced its value so that the tithes were only 40*s*. There was a chantry connected with the college of Fotheringay, valued in the king's books at 6*l*. 13*s*. 4*d*., Robert Andrewe being its priest.

The REGISTER begins in 1560. The first page is very much worn, but the heading and dates are legible. It is entirely in English. Although the date of commencement is as above, yet it was 'made in the yeare of our Lord 1598;' at which time the copy on parchment of the old paper register was made. This caused the official return of the registers to parliament to say the register began in 1598. The first book ends in 1653. The form of entry is singular. 'One called John —— ;' 'An old woman named Mary —— ;' and the like. A few specimens are given.

1589. 28 Feb. Were buried a poor man called Edward.
1591. 18 Apr. Was baptised the daughter of Willm Dickenson Minister named ELIZABETH Parson there now xxvij yeares.

---

* See Taylor's 'Words and Places,' pp. 184—142, for a most interesting investigation of names of towns derived from families of settlers.

ELTON.

ELTON.

1596. The 11 daie of June was buried Elizabethe the Wieffe of Kelly (?) Lyon, who was cruelie murdered her throate Cutt the friday at nighte before beinge the 9 of June & soe found dead in the morninge beinge done by the hands of her owne husband. [In the margin is written] coniux a co(n)iuge interfecta.
1603. 4 Nov. A young wenche called Elizabeth Goodyn.
1625. 4 Apr. was buried one Henery Henson singleman.
1648. (Signature at foot of page runs thus:) Per me Skeffingtonum Bendish Ludimagistrum Ailtoniæ alias Allingtoniæ alias Eltoniæ in Comit. Hunt.
1651. 3 Jan. A vagrant girl perished and buried.
1660. 1 Apr. John Hollis mortally wounded at ffotheringhay same day Buried.
1664. 13 Mar. The right Revnd Mr Cooper the late most charitable and pious Pastour of this parish was Buryed.
1676. 19 Jan. John Edis being 80 years of age Decemb^r 19 last past and Clark of this Parish above 40 years.
1737. 24 Oct. (buried) John Dickins & Ellinger his wife both in a grave.
1745. 3 Apr. John Beaver from Duddington Drounded in Haddon Brook.

Skeffington Bendish was one of the 'registers' appointed under the act : both he and the other holders of the same office were far more conscientious in the discharge of their duties in this parish than in most. The books during the time the registers were laymen are in as good and complete form as when the entries were made by the parson. This is most rare. It is only in 1604 that the custom of signing the page commences. But the great value of the registers consists in a very extensive list of collections under briefs, most important. There is only room here for a few of the more remarkable and interesting.

		£	s	d
	Collected for Letters of Request Anno 1661.			
	Ffor Rippon Church Yorkshire	00	10	00
	Ffor Oxfordshire	00	09	08
	Ffor Hedon in Yorkshire	00	09	08
	Ffor Elmly Castle in Worcestershire	00	10	06
	Ffor the City of Chester	00	10	01
	Ffor Bridgenorth in the County of Salop	00	13	06
	Ffor the p(ro)testant church in Lithuania	00	11	03
1661.	2 Feb. Ffor the Improvements of fishing (amount torn away)			
	2 Aug. For Harwich in Essex	00	05	00
	22 Oct. Ffor the fire at St Martins in the fields London	00	07	00
1664.	14 Aug. Ffor Thrapston Bridge	00	03	07
	28 Aug. Ffor Basing Church in the County of Southampton	00	04	11
1665.	2 Aug. Collected for those that are visited wthin the Diocesse of Lincoln & London	01	11	04
	6 Sep. For the sd visited psons	01	18	00
	4 Oct. For the sd visited psons	02	05	07
	14 Jan. ffor Thomas Sloper Gent.	00	04	01
	8 Nov. For the visited	01	07	03
	6 Dec. For the s^d visited psons	01	15	02
1666.	4 Jul. Geven upon the fast day towards the relief of the poor visited people of Oundle 12 Strikes of wheat, 40 Strikes of Barley, 19 Strikes of Mault, 48 Cheeses and ½.			
	Collected for the Sad Fire at London	10	0	0

			£	s.	d.
1670.	30 Oct. A Catologue of the Inhabitants of Aylton alias Allington alias Elton in the County of Huntingdon who Contributed towards the Redemption of the English distressed Captives fro the Slavery and Bondage of the Turkish Infidels according to his Maties Letters Patents in that behalf read. [A long list of names concludes thus:] Sum totall		6	18	0
1671.	12 Nov. For the English captives und^r the Hungarians		00	05	01
1675.	12 Mar. For Northampton besides 10^{li} sent in by Sr Tho. Pooley Nov. 17th last Collected more		10	6	11
1679.	14 Sep. For St Pauls London		2	13	9
1680.	6 Sep. For redemption of English Slaves at Algiers		3	5	6
1681.	13 Nov. Towards training up Min^{rs}. for the Protestant Churches in Lower Poland		0	8	6
	11 Dec. For relief of the French persecuted Protestants		7	13	6
1682.	29 Oct. For a fire under Dyers hall, London		0	5	11¼
1685.	3 May. For Staverton in Northtonshire		0	7	1¼
	21 Mar. For Kirksanton in Cumberland damaged by water and sand		0	6	5
1686.	June & July. For the French Protestants		20	6	9¼
1694.	For a Fire at Wooller in Northumberland		0	6	0
1697.	26 Dec. For a Fire at Litchfield		0	5	8
1698.	12 Mar. For Soham in Cambridgeshire		0	4	0
1699.	23 Apr. For a Fire in Drury Lane London		0	5	4
1700.	Jun. For ye Redemption of y Slaves att Machanes		0	15	6
1701.	Sep. For Broughton in Northamptonsh^r		0	7	6
1702.	Oct. For a Fire at ye Citty of Ely		0	5	2
	24 Mar. For Lutterworth Church in Leicestershire		0	2	0
1704.	For the French Protestants of Orange		1	0	6
	For ye Widdows & orphans of y^{ose} y^t p(er)ishd in ye grt Storme		3	0	0
1706.	May. For a Fire at Inniskilling in Ireland		0	9	0

Collections for the great storm in 1703 were general. A similar entry occurs at Castor, pp. 12, 13.

A short note of church goods stolen from Ayltone is preserved in the record office, dated 2 Ed. VI.

Stolne out of the kepyng of Mr Robt Sappcottes a patten wth a challice waienge ij oz allso on other patten was stolne out of the keping of the p(ar)ish priste and the Baylif waieng iij oz.

The sacramental PLATE is massive. There are two patens, two chalices, and a flagon. All were presented by rect. Ball, as appears from this inscription : 'Ex dono Thomæ Ball Rectoris de Aylton 1670.'

There are three bequests to the parish of considerable value. Rect. Cooper (by deed in his lifetime) founded a hospital for four persons. This produced in 1786 25*l*. a year. In 1702 Tho. Seby left a rent-charge for the poor. In 1711 Fr. Proby gave land producing 7*l*. 10*s*. for the poor and a school; and Jane Proby the next year left 600*l*. original south sea annuities for a workhouse and other charitable purposes. Eighty years ago therefore the parish was in receipt of not less than 62*l.* a year from these bequests. Small legacies to the church, bells, high altar, and the like, as in previous cases, are not unfrequent.

RECTORS.

bef. 1534 —Brereton, S.T.P., or L.L.D.	1731 *Sam. Ball, L.L.B., d.
1552 Tho. Willan.	1737 Joh. Ball.
1561 Ric. Stephenson.	1738 *Joh. Forster, S.T.P., d.[6]
1563 Will. Dickenson.[1]	1787 Phil. Fisher.
1616 Will. Bendishe.	1842 Piers C. Claughton, A.M., r.
1629 Joh. Cooper, deprived.[2]	1843 Fred. Will. Faber, A.M., r.
1661 *Tho. Ball, A.B.[3]	1845 Piers C. Claughton, A.M., r.[7]
1708 *Tho. Ball, S.T.B., d.[4]	1860 Ric. Kempthorne, A.M.[8]
1723 Ric. Cumberland.[5]	

The CHURCH has a chancel with N. aisle used for vestry, nave with aisles, S. porch, W. tower. The tower is entirely within the church, the aisles extending to the extreme west. The vestry is modern, but built on the site of an old one, as is testified by the marks of the weathermoulds. A N. door is now blocked, and the chimney goes through it. The priest's door, S. of the chancel, is also blocked up. The chancel, though much altered, and the nave arcade are the earliest parts of the church. They are of early decorated work, dating perhaps from 1300 to 1320. The internal features of the chancel are in part hidden. In the S. wall are three two-light windows all different. That nearest the E. end has a double trefoil, the lights being very thin. The next has long thin lancets, divided by a thick mullion, and a quatrefoiled circle above. The last has much broader lights, and the tracery is of much later character approaching the flamboyant style, but the mouldings of all are identical. This window cannot be so early as the

---

* Buried at Elton.
1. Buried at Oundle.
2. Patron and rector. He was deprived under the act of uniformity, and succeeded by his son-in-law. Calamy says that he 'was a man of great Note in his country, for the Piety of his Life, the Prudence of his Conduct, and for his ministerial abilities. He was a grave venerable Person, of the Puritan Stamp.' (Calamy's 'Ministers Ejected,' 2nd Edition, 1713.) He was described as a 'preaching minister.'
3. Afterwards A.M. Probably also rect. of Gretworth. About 1678 he (with sir Edw. Turner) found a horse under the militia act.
4. Afterwards S.T.P. Son-in-law to bp. Cumberland. Also rect. of Gretford, Linc., and preb. of Peterborough.
5. Doubtless a connection of the bp. Was he son of the rect. of Peakirk, and afterwards bp. of Clonfert and Kilmore?
6. A sermon of his is extant preached at Huntingdon assizes, 1764.
7. Fell. and tutor of University coll. Bp. of S. Helena, 1859; now bp. of Colombo.
8. Formerly archdn. of S. Helena.

others. The low side window below is blocked up: it has the original iron stanchions remaining outside. To the W. of it there is visible a second opening, the use of which has not been satisfactorily established. There are three sedilia graduated, and a piscina. These have been restored. They are cushioned, and have a desk. The heads are cinquefoiled, and they are divided by thin shafts. The E. window is an unfortunate insertion of much later date. The hoodmoulds of the windows are terminated by heads both internally and externally. In the N. wall is an aumbry, or credence-table, restored. Round the E. end are some hangings. The altar levels are original: the steps are shallow and very broad. The seats in the chancel are ranged stallwise. The staircase to the rood-loft is N. of the chancel arch. W. of the arch the door still remains. There are two small apertures visible from the chancel, which seem to be for lighting this staircase. A third opening is possibly for a squint; or the upper one may have lighted a priest's chamber over the vestry. The chancel arch has continuous mouldings; the thin inner shafts supporting it are new. They have the nail-head under the capitals. The chancel is twisted to the north. The nave is of four bays. The piers have a quatrefoil section, and are not more than 8 feet high. They stand on square bases. The font is central, and stands on a new base of clunch, apparently in imitation of an early English one. Some old open seats remain with square ends. They have been well repaired. Alternate ones, towards the nave, have the linen pattern: one only has it in the aisles. They are in their original position as testified by the shorter ones near the pillars. There is a modern lettern, and oak pulpit. In the aisles is the stringcourse marking the old pitch of the lean-to roof. The present aisles are wholly late perpendicular work. Within the vestry is preserved the old altar-table; a marble slab on iron frame work, very similar to that still used at Chesterton. About the end of the 17th cent. these were very commonly erected, as is seen in many of the London churches. The porch is large, and has three fair niches. The tower is lofty; standing too on high ground, and the churchyard sloping away rapidly to the west, it forms a very striking object. It has three bands of quatrefoils all round. It has battlements, the centre one being pierced. It is of much smaller size above than below. The buttresses are curiously arranged. There are none to the lower stage: but as the section of the tower gets less at the first stage, quasi-buttresses rise here from the corners of the lower storey. It is entirely of 15th cent. date.

The belfry is large and contains five BELLS, but of these two have been recast. The first has long ornamented spaces between the words of its inscription: the second has two texts in Lombardick letters, and its founder's name in small capitals below.

1. THOMAS NORRIS CAST ME 1631.
2. ✠ IESVS SPEEDE ME OMNIA FIANT AD GLORIAM DEI
  THOMAS NORRIS CAST ME 1631
3. THO: ROBINSON & W-M: DEXTER CHURCH-WARDENS 1746 T: EAYRE OMNIA FIANT AD GLORIAM DEI
4. THOMAS NORRIS CAST ME 1631 RECAST BY G. MEARS, & CO., OF LONDON, 1864.
5. W PIX TH BARKER CH WN 1631 RECAST BY G. MEARS, & CO., OF LONDON, 1864.

In the chancel are MONUMENTS to the Ball family. Three were rectors: and the stones mention their degrees, connections, and preferments. A stone also commemorates Tho. Ball, D.D., rect. of Eriswell, Suff., and Great Malsingham, Norf., who died 1789. There is a tablet to the 'Rev^d. and learned' Joh. Forster, 49 years rector. Members of his family are also buried here. In the S. aisle, over the E. window, is a stone carved thus in thick letters, 'Sir Richard Sapcote knyght,' and beneath is a coat of arms impaled. It is without date; but sir Richard was sheriff of Cambridge and Huntingdon shires in 1470, and his widow, dame Isabel, died 1493.

The hall was once the seat of this ancient family. We learn * that in this hall there was, formerly:—

A private Chappell of singular workmanship and most artificial glasse windowes, erected by Lady Elizabeth Dinham, the widow of Baron Fitzwarin, married into ye said family. The Chappell is now in a ruinous condition.

Another monument is recorded as having been erected to a member of the family, but it does not seem to be now in existence. It was on the S. side near the E. window, 'about a white raised marble,' and was inscribed 'Here lieth ye bodie of Robert Sappcotts of Elton, Esq. who died ye 4th of January 1600.' The will of dame Isabel, who lived at Burley, Rutl., provided:—

My body to be there buried. To three priests to say masses for the souls of Sir John Fraunces and Sir Richard Sapcote, my husbands....

In 1507, sir John Sapcote, kt., left to his wife all his plate at 'Allington, in the county of Huntingdon,' for her life. And sir Richard Sapcote, in 1543, desired by will to be buried at Fotheringay. Lord Denham and lord Vaux had each daughters who married Sapcotes: and John earl of Bedford married a daughter of sir Guido Sapcote.

In the S. aisle are also numerous hatchments. There are many tablets to members of the family at the house, some with long epitaphs. Amongst the persons thus commemorated are these: Tho. Proby, 1684; sir Tho. Proby, bart., 1689; John Proby, and his daughter, 1710—11; various children between 1670 and 1680. On the tablet to John Joshua earl of Carysfort, K.P., 1828, are considerable notices of the family. In the chancel are memorials to John Joshua, lord Proby, 1858, eldest son of the 3rd earl of Carysfort, and to Hugh Proby, drowned in Australia, 1852. Over the Proby pew in the S. aisle there have been two banners, but they are now gone. In the S. porch is the matrix of a brass.

In the CHURCHYARD, near the porch, is a stone coffin with a coped lid, much worn. It bears a floriated cross, with the flowing ornament at the middle which is the

---

* Cotton's Notes. Brit. Mus., MS. Lansd., 921. In his time, 1668, it was the seat of sir Tho. Proby, bart., 'where he hath lately built a neat house.' In MS. Lansd., 1179, is a careful pedigree of the Sapcotes, dated 1611. There are also drawings of 11 coats of arms in the chapel of Elton house, and of others in 'the Parlour windowes.' Three were brought from the church.

WATER NEWTON.

subject of so much controversy. It is 5 ft. 11 in. in length. Recently two Norman headstones have been dug up. One is but a small fragment: the other has the circular cross in the head quite perfect, and a considerable part of the interlaced stem. It is in two pieces, the part containing the cross being 22 in. long, and the diameter of the circular head 17 in. The lower part is 2 ft. 5 in. long at its extreme length, and from being interlaced to its foot, and, having no signs of ever having stood in the ground, it seems likely that it fitted into another stone, and was indeed the churchyard cross itself. Though these two stones are clearly part of one composition, yet there are several inches missing between them: they do not join on to one another. It is very similar to one discovered at Helpston, mentioned on p. 97, and figured in the plate of memorial stones there. These are now placed in the S. aisle. Other stones of the like character, or coffin lids, were unhappily destroyed by the workmen. Drawings of nine fragments of coffin lids are in Gough's collection in the Bodleian library. Six were nearly perfect. There is also a copy of the stone coat of arms in the S. aisle, and of the monument to Rob. Sappcotts mentioned on the previous page as being apparently no longer in existence. It may possibly be concealed under some of the pews. In 1861 the church was visited by the members of the Archæological Institute.

Water Newton.

This is a very compact little village on the great north road. The population is small. Originally known as Newton only, the prefix was adopted to distinguish it from another Newton, now called Wood Newton, not many miles distant. The prefix marks its peculiarity, the houses being almost huddled down by the water's edge, on the right bank of the Nene. The ADVOWSON has been in the hands of the lord of the manor, and has consequently been never long in one family. Within 150 years the families of Turner, Edwards, Austin, and Knipe, have presented.

The church is dedicated to S. REMIGIUS. His feast was on 1st October, on which day his name still appears in the calendar of our Prayer-book. The parish feast is held still about that time. There are but seven churches in England with this dedication; 4 in Norfolk, and 2 in Leicestershire. S. Remigius was abp. of Rheims, A.D. 500, and died it is said in 533. He was only 22 years of age when consecrated. He baptized king Clovis: and the cruet he used is still preserved at Rheims, and has ever been used for anointing the kings of France at their coronation. But there was also a bp. of Lincoln of this name in the 11th cent., and to him some of these dedications may refer. He died in 1091. The value of the rectory in the king's book was 8*l*. 12*s*. 4*d*.; the abbot of Thorney having a pension of 30*s*., and this with fees reduced the amount so that the tithes were but 12*s*. 11*d*. In 1654, when the parliamentary inquisition was taken, the value was 60*l*., and in 1786 was 59*l*. 8*s*.

The earliest REGISTER is lost. The present commences in 1687 and extends to 1812. There is also a marriage book from 1755. The title of the former one runs thus:—

The names of such as have been Christened maried and buried in Water-Newton orderly succeeding one another.

In so small a parish one would not look for many entries of importance. One or two may be given.

1738. 6 Sep. (buried) an unknown travelling man.
1783. 2 Oct. the Stamp act took place.
1783. continued. rien de tout.
1787. a poor Stranger, drown'd in the River on Sept[r]. 21st, buried Septem[r]. 23[d].

The constable's book dates back to 1797; the churchwardens' book does the same. The following extracts, with the exception of the first two, are from the latter.

Tho[s] a Becket Sessions July 15th Weekly money	3 3	2
1804. 5 Feb. Gabriel, for the Pound Gate	1 3	10
1803. 30 Mar. Gabril French for wood and workmanship, Clarks seat	2 6	6
1813. 18 Apr. Ringing on Acc[t]. of Buonapates Dethronement		
1817. Paid the last Churchwarden Shaws Rate w[h] he refuses to pay	0 15	0

1819.	14 May.	Paid Batley for ringing Bell untill Midnight on the Funeral of His Majesty Geo. 3rd, ...	0	5	0
1824.	24 Dec.	Mr. Thos. Cooke for Hanging the Bells of New and repaing the Frams as by Bill agreement	11	5	6
1834.	21 Mar.	Mr. Robertson for King Arms	8	15	0
1840.	25 June.	Postage. Forms of Prayer on Her Majesty's escape from assassination	0	0	4

The following note, dated 2 Ed. VI, is from the record office. The name is there spelt Waternewston.

Solde....a vestment for vij^{sl} ij paynted clothes for ij^{sl} vi all^{ter} clothes for iiij^{sl} x towells for iij^{sl} iiij^d surplesses for iiij^{sl} all wh money they wth other declare upon ther othes was bestowed upon the repa(rat)ion of ther churche } xx^{sl} iiij^d

The charitable donations were returned in 1786 as 'None.'

RECTORS.

bef. 1534 George Tatym.	1732 *Rob. Fuller, A.M., d.²
1606 Joh. Hanger.	1735 Sam. Ball.
bef. 1654 Chr. Wells.	1738 Joh. Old.
bef. 1689 *Geof. Hawkins, A.M., d.	1753 *Ed. Ketteriche, A.M., d.
1700 Geof. Hawkins.¹	1807 *Randolph Ric. Knipe, A.M., r.
1720 *Ric. Southgate, d.	1846 Randolph Knipe, A.B.

The plan of the CHURCH is very simple. Chancel, nave with aisles and clerestory, S. porch, W. tower and spire. The tower itself is the earliest part, being of transitional Norman date. It seems to be very early in the 13th cent., and so to be properly classed amongst early English work, but it retains many features of the earlier style, like certain parts of the western transept at Peterborough. The tower is without buttresses, but about 3 feet from the ground there is a very considerable slope in the masonry which has in part the same effect as a buttress. The width of the tower from north to south, on the ground, is 17 ft. 6 in., but above this slope the width is only 15 ft. 9 in. The tower is of less width than the nave. The belfry windows are round-headed, but are divided into two lights which are pointed. On two of the sides they have the zigzag ornament. The N. and S. walls have on the ground floor a small lancet. The tower is surmounted by a broach spire; but this is of decorated work. It is of no great height. There are four two-light spire-windows, the heads having square

---

* Buried at Water Newton.
1. See note p. 153.
2. Fell. of Emmanuel coll.

sides, like those at Castor. Below the spire is a corbel-table of notch-heads. The nave is of four bays, of distinct early English work. The arches are semicircular and the piers octagonal, except one of clustered shafts in the S. aisle. At the E. end of the N. aisle the arcade is terminated by a respond: in the three other cases the arch dies into the wall. The chancel is in an unsound state, the walls being very insecure. There is a great deal of ivy about it, of which some would say that it assisted the decay of the walls, and others that it held them up. The E. window is of three lights under a depressed arch. The lights are cinquefoiled, and the quatrefoils in the tracery are much elongated. Externally are two small buttresses at the E. end. A third, at the E. of the N. aisle, makes up the whole number of which the church is possessed. The roof is tiled, but that to the nave is of lead. Some features of interest are to be seen within. The floor is much raised above the original level. The piscina is trefoiled: the three sedilia, aumbry, and two brackets, are tolerably perfect. The brackets are of considerable beauty, that on the S. side being very large and fine. The windows in the aisles are square-headed of two lights. They are original, the hoodmoulds and notch-head terminations being clearly of early date. There is no W. window to the S. aisle. At the W. end of the N. aisle is a remarkable little room, now used as a vestry. Within memory it was a pigeon-house. It is entered from the church by a narrow door, and lit by a small lancet in the W. wall about 4 inches wide. The eastern wall of this room, though ancient, is later than the nave arcade, for the capital of the last nave arch is within it. The exterior wall of the N. aisle is extended westward 4 ft. 1 in. further than the S. aisle wall. The S. porch is of good decorated work: the doors are excellent. The inner one has continuous mouldings, round and massive; there are stone seats, and the base of a holy-water stoup in the porch: the outer door has large semicircular piers, with good capitals and chamfered moulding to the arch above. The mouldings of both doors are terminated by a mask. The roof is of simple laths. The central stone of the outer gable of this porch has remains of paneling, suggesting that it may have been the upper part of a niche, perhaps in the same position, the lower part and figure having been removed. The clerestory windows are early decorated of two lights, with intersecting tracery: their hoodmoulds are terminated by carved heads. There is massive coping at the ends of the S. aisle. Six of the bosses on the nave roof have well-carved figures. Along the interior walls of the aisles there were stone seats: one of these has been removed for the sake of the materials.

There are three BELLS, one having a date only. The first is the most ancient, and the inscription is in very early Lombardick letters: the legend on the second is in old English, having enriched capitals.

1. ✠ AUE : GRA : PLENA : DNS : TECUM
2. ✠ Sancta Maria Ora Pro Nobis.
3. 1665.

The earliest dated MONUMENT is a plain slab in the chancel with this inscription round the edge:—

IOHN . HARBOTTILL . OF . BASTON . IN . THE . COVNTY . OF . LINCOLNE . GENT . WAS . BURIED . THE . SIXTE . DAY . OF . FEBRUARIE . ANO . DOMI . M . DC . XLVI . & . OF . HIS . AGE . XLIII .

On a window-ledge in the S. aisle is a female effigy of much older date, but unaccompanied by name or date. It seems however to have been erected about the middle of the 14th cent. It is of small size, but it is not necessary to infer from that circumstance that it commemorates a young girl. In the chancel are memorials to Ed. Keteriche, rector for 54 years, 1807, and to Rob. Fuller, 'nuper hujus Ecclesiæ Rectoris, Et Coll. Emman. apud Cantabrigienses olim Socij,' 1735. There are also numerous tablets to members of the Knipe family, including one to the late rector, 1847. In the nave and aisles occur flat stones to the families of Edwards and Fuller. Two curious Christian names, Easter and Original, are to be seen. In a niche on the W. side of the tower there is a figure remaining. It is however so mutilated that it cannot be said if it is sepulchral or not. The figure and niche are both later than the tower wall. In a square frame below them is an inscription evidently sepulchral, but its connection (if any) with the figure above is unknown. The letters are in five lines, and of the early Lombardick type in use at the close of the 13th cent. The words read thus:—

    VOVS : KE : PAR :
    ISSI : PASSEZ :
    PVR : LE : ALME :
    ……… OMAS : PVR :
    DEV : PRIEZ :

This may be compared with the Helpston inscription given on p. 96. To the S. of the tower is an old stone coffin, containing bones. It is massive; and the lid is raised on two large pieces of wood.

Cotton mentions sir John Whitbrooke, knight, of this parish, in 1613: in the Harleian MS. 1179, is a sketch of his arms and a pedigree.

Ramsey.

From the ancient records of this town, as far as we can learn, there does not seem to have been at any time an intimate alliance between the abbey and the parish. The church to which the ensuing notes refer is not uncommonly considered to be the remains of the abbey itself: curtailed in dimensions, but still retaining the shell of the monastic church, in the same way as the present parish churches of Thorney and Crowland have been, so to speak, manufactured out of their respective minsters. But this is not the case. The present church at Ramsey formed no part of the abbey buildings. It is said indeed that stone from the abbey at its dissolution was used in repairing it; but with this the connection ceases. The abbey church was far larger and more

RAMSEY ABBEY.

magnificent; it stood moreover some distance to the south, but the exact site has not been described. But a very few notes about the foundation of the abbey will not be out of place, although not strictly speaking within the limits of the subject.

The abbey then was founded in the year 969 by earl Aylwyn, cousin to king Edgar. He enjoyed the remarkable title of 'alderman of all England.' In the charter of confirmation of Henry VIII., in his first year, previous charters are recited, and the story of the foundation told. The paper commences: 'Because it is manifest by the increasing disturbances of this world that the end of time is now near at hand and the great day of Judgment is perceived to approach, as the Gospel-Trumpet then soundeth to forewarn the Faithful.' The story in a few words is this. Aylwyn was afflicted with the gout. A fisherman plying his trade for the earl in Ramsey mere had a vision of S. Benedict, by whose direction the earl went to see the way the beasts lay down at night, such position marking the site of the abbey. By obeying these directions Aylwyn was cured, and at once proceeded to clear the ground for his foundation. In five years it was dedicated. It had the privilege of sanctuary. Valuable grants were made to the abbey from time to time. It gloried in the possession of the bodies of kings and martyrs. In 1114 the church was restored, perhaps rebuilt. Soon after it was despoiled by Magnaville, earl of Essex. It grew too rich: 'Ramsey the rich' was its description in a local rhyme. The abbots were among the earliest to obtain a seat in parliament. The royal entertainments were numerous. 'Considering the frequent coming of ourself and our most dear consort Philippa, Queen of England, to the Abbey of Ramsey,' is a reason assigned in one charter for the grant of fresh privileges. In the year 31 Hen. VIII. all the possessions of the abbey were granted to Richard Williams, alias Cromwell, in consideration of his services, 'and also in consideration of the sum of 4963*l*. 4*s*. 2*d*.' Beyond the walls of some large room, probably the refectory, of 13th cent. work, now divided into separate rooms and used for cellars and offices, there are no remains of this wealthy abbey. There is an arcade round the walls of very elegant early English arches, of course much mutilated. The large sepulchral monument now standing at the end of a passage in the house, and said to represent Aylwyn, is also very manifestly of the same date, about 1240. It most likely was erected at that time by the monks, in honour of their founder.*

The parish church is dedicated to S. THOMAS-A-BECKET. Instances occur where churches, after the archbishop was canonized, had their dedications changed in his honour. Clapham, near Bedford, is one of these. But in the present instance the style of architecture corresponds with the exact date. S. Thomas of Canterbury was murdered in 1170, and canonized by pope Alexander III. in 1173. The parish church of Ramsey was finished within a few years of that date, and dedicated to the new saint. There are said to be upwards of 60 churches in England with the same dedication. In 1291 the parish church was valued at 6*l.* The patronage, since the dissolution has been with the owner of the abbey estate, having been included in the original grant:—

Our Rectory appropriate of the churches of Ramsey and Bury in the said county of Huntingdon, with the advowsons and right of patronage of the said churches.

The REGISTERS are voluminous, and in very excellent preservation. Not only are the entries for the latter part of the 16th cent. copied from an older book, as is always the case, but these books afford the clearest evidence that in many cases until recently all the entries for the whole year were made at one time, from a rough copy. The books commence in 1559. The extracts that are here given have some interest.

1557. M^m that there were noc burialls sett downe in the old Regester for all this yeare.
1608. 17 Dec. (Buried.) Wyllyam Love a very old poore man who lived uppon ye almes of ye towne.
28 Dec. John Randall son of Rob^{te} Randall who had ye falcing sickness.
1610. Tho. Wodham cominge out of ye Turfen wth his boats laden wth hassocks ye xxjst of August, in a terryble winde & tempest was drowned in Ugmeare whose bodye was not found before ye vth of Septemb^r. &

---

* Several excellent drawings of this tomb are in the Gough collection in the Bodleian.

RAMSEY.

was buryed ye vi^th of ye same moneth Willm Carryer de Yaksley Coroner at ye same tyme who viewed his bodye.

1615. 24 Nov. Walter Sampson alis Creede Steward to Sr Oliver Cromwell knight died at Hinchinbrooke ye xxiij^th of November & was buried in ye p(ar)ishe church of All Saints in Huntingdon.

1619. 13 Sep. John Gillon housholder perished by water.

1623. Matthew Boothe, John Warwick, Thomas Lambert, William Garner, and Margret Smythe the xxx^th of August who were all five in a boat & by mishapp were drowned in the streame called Roman streame being in the p(ar)ish of Ramsey.

1636. William Rawson servingman was buried the 30th August who was burned the day before in a great soar fyer wherein ther were xv comoning tenements burned in the littell wyte¹ besydes other that were in pt burned.

1654. 16 Nov. Thomas Clifton labourer being digging of sand, was by ye fall of earth y^t gave suddenly slayne.
18 Nov. Thomas Smyth labourer digging sand at ye same time, had his life (?) mortifyd his body broken.

1656. 27 June. Henry Stimpson a distracted p(er)son.

1658. 2 Sep. the Lady Ferrers was Buried at ye foot of ye crosse in ye Church-yard.²

1660. (among the births) the year of his Majesty K. Charles 2. his happy restauration, & returne after his long exile, wch was on 29th of May. Vivat.
(among the burials) & Regis Caroli 2^di Reg. 12° & in Anglia redit^s suj auspicatissimj & mensis Maij die 29°.

1661. 6 Jan. Michael the sonne of Luke Sherman being detained from baptisme till ye age of 9 or 10 years did then receive that holy Sacrament.

1664. 25 Sep. George Blench by the overthrow of a Cart perished, & was buried. A morte subitanea Libera nos Domine.

1665—6. Col. William Cromwell Gentleman departed this life Febr. 23.—9 in ye morning & was buried Febr. 24—9 of clock at night 166⅚. ye yonger son of Sr O. C. [Sir Oliver Cromwell.]

1666. Ramsey visited wth ye plague this year.³
16 Jul. Elizabeth the wife of Thomas Middleton was buried in her own Gard(en).

1667. 19 Sep. Thomas Wisditch a mason, falling on high from an house Sep. 17. died that night.

1668. 13 Aug. Robert ye Sonne of Edward Hendry was privately baptized by a Romish priest.

1669. 16 Apr. William the sonne of William Hanns, a child (being killed by an horse running away with his rider).⁴

1670. 22 Jul. John Hardy, killed by M^r. H. Wilcox, was buried July. 22. 1670.

1673. Peter ye Son of Peter behague Jane the wife of John Arx & Sarah the wife of Richard Bradford drowned in Ramsey-mare Apr. 9. were found Apr. 10. & were buried April. 11. 1673. 2 more were drowned at ye same time one of y^m found, & was carried to be buried at Peterburgh—ye other not yet found. Ap. 10.—Ann ye wife of Walter Sprung drowned wth ye fore-mentioned, found Apr. 21. buried Apr. 22—1673.

1674. Note y^t: ye Register of the Marriages was losst (among many other loose Papers) in M^r. Robins his Sickness &c.⁵

1706. 7 Apr. Henry Evans. (nulli pietate secundus)

---

1. The Great White and Little White are the names of two streets in Ramsey; the former running from the Station to High Street, the latter branching out from it. The word is sometimes spelt Whyte.
2. The grave-stone placed over lady Ferrers' grave was removed to the church. The inscription is gone; but copies have been preserved. This stone will be noticed below.
3. The persons who died of the plague are frequently entered as 'buried the same day.' It is but seldom, as in the next entry, that the interment is elsewhere than in the church.
4. A long original prayer, praying that the 'innocent blood' may not be required at the hands of the people of Ramsey, follows this entry.
5. John Robins was incumbent, and died at Ramsey in 1675.

1716. 22 Aug. Aribella a Vagrant.
1719. 15 Nov. Charles Denson Blacksmith a Benefactor.
1720. 24 Sep. A vagrant Stranger.
1721. 12 May. John Walton killd in a Mill.
1724. 15 Sep. Thomas Story Carpenter killd in a clay pitt by a fall of ye earth upon him ye 10 of 7^{br} at 9 in ye morn but lived till ye 13.
When at ye same time & ye same falling of Earth one Robt Offly Carpent^r serv^t to Jacob Berrye was killd outright & found dead under ye ruins & was buried at Wistow in ye county of Huntingdon his father & mother living y^r.
Ramsey May ye 29th 1731. Memorand. On the 21st day of May 1731 a Sudden & terrible fire Begun about 2 of ye clock in ye Afternoon in ye house of W^m. Pain of Ramsey aforesd Taylor by ye Carelessness or neglect of 2 of ye Daughters of ye s^d Wm Pain wch in ye space of 5 or 6 Hours burn't down & wholly consumed above Fourscore Houses besides Granaries full of wheat Mace & Oats, Barns Stables & Outhouses household goods Beds Bedding Brass pewter & all manner of wearing apparel &ct to ye utter ruin of an innumerable number of poor miserable people.
Note not one house standing in ye high street from ye schoole house to ye high Bridge on ye North side of ye s^d street nor from Richard Badsons house on ye south side to ye wid^w Priests at ye George Except a part of John Beards house & Samuel Phillips & wch were much Shattered all ye west side of ye g^t white from ye turning of ye corner in ye high street down to an house of Mr Overalls wch tho not consumed was in part pulled down. God be praised no one person Burnt killed hurt or Bruis'd.
For behold ye Lord will come wth fire & wth his chariots like a whirlewind to render his anger with fury & his rebuke wth flames of fire. Is: 66: 15: Lord have mercy upon us.
1735. 21 Feb. Mary wife of Rich^d. Neal drowned going in a small boat f^m. Ramsey Market Barnaby Brity who was wth her w^n. y^e. boat sank narrowly escaping.
1759. 13 June. A young Man unknown, murder'd in M^r. Blot's Farm at Higney, was found in the Wood June the 7th. and buried at Ramsey.
1783. 9 Sep. A Stranger Man said to come from Soham.
1784. 7 Feb. William Son of John Childs } Both Drowned the same day in different places by the Ice breaking.
Thos son of Thos. Belshaw

The entries from 1642 to 1653 are missing. In 1653 John Adamson was appointed register, and in 1657 Tho. Huxley. Several curious names occur, especially for women, such as these: Euphrania, Theodosia (frequent), Theophila, Tryphena, Lora, Pleasant, Damaris, Canina, Carina, Hensibob. The last might well puzzle any one. It is a monstrous combination of two names into one. At the end of the second book is a list of parishioners confirmed 3 Aug., 1671, at All-hallows, Huntingdon. The third book opens with an inventory of church goods in 1673. Some very full accounts of parochial perambulations are also given. Paupers supported by the parish are frequently described as 'a towncharge.' In 1630 one whole page of the register is entirely re-written, the parchment being in bad condition so that the first transcript is hardly legible. At the top is this note: 'This year 1630 is playner wryten next following.' The number of persons drowned is very great. In reference to the great fire in 1731 the following passage may be quoted. It is from Steele's Collection in the Bodleian Library. The entire loss, after deducting upwards of 2000*l.* repaid by insurances, was given at 11,675*l.* 12*s.* 11*d.*

This poor town was greatly impoverish'd before by the contrary Element, their crops of corn, and the cattle having been destroyed by the overflowing of their low lands, which have lain under water for 3 years: so that they are now in general a very miserable people, and will be more so as the winter comes on.
Immediately after the said sad fire, Nicholas Bonfoy, Esq; sent the poor sufferers 20 guineas, Will. Marshal, Esq; the same sum, Rob. Pigott, Esq; 50*l.* The town of Godmanchester, 27*l.* the town of Huntingdon, besides great quantities of provisions, 30*l.* The town of Whittlesea, 70*l.* the town of Chatteris, 23*l.* the town of Wistow, besides provisions, 10*l.* Sir Will. Lemon hath also given them leave to dig what sand they have occasion for in his Lordship of Warboyce, towards rebuilding their several habitations.

The following items are extracted from a book containing the churchwardens' and overseers' accounts for the year 1682—3:—

To Goode Skiner for four Children		5	2
Allso one that was too Little		2	2
ffor Beare bread and Grave for buring of a child from Mary Skiner	00	01	06
for ye bell going about	00	00	02
for those that Laid out thorntons boy	00	00	06
for berring [burying] in beare 9^d bread 3^d Candle 1^d tobacco 1^d	00	01	02
To Those that Carried him to Church beare 8^d thred 6^d	00	01	02
To those that sat by at Good hardis Child Day	00	01	00
ffor sending the bell about ye towne for The townsmen to meet to mak Book	00	00	02
Paid to ould frior for scouring ye Dike before the Dore	00	00	06
for Berring the stranger	00	01	00
Given to John Mast for haveing Rob. Sharpe's prentice back to Whittlesey	00	00	06
ffor sending the bell about The towne for The Towns men to meet	00	00	02

A charge for tobacco of this date must be somewhat unusual.

There are two notices of the ornaments of this church in the record office made in the reign of Ed. VI. The earlier is dated 1548, and refers only to two articles sold.

Ramseye. Solde by Thomas Ainsworth & John Writte churchwardens there wth the assent of all the poshn^{rs} (parishioners) on coverlett for vij^{sl} on old paynted clothe for iiij^{sl}. } xj^{sl}

All wch money they wth other declare upon ther othes was bestowed mountyng of scriptures about the churche there. } xj^{sl}

The later one is of the date 1552, as appears from comparing it with other inventories of that date of exactly similar form, as that of Brinckton, 13 July, or of S. Ives, 17 July, 1552. The part containing the date is torn away; and the inventory is much mutilated in other respects. A few conjectures are supplied in brackets.

In pmis (a chalice) Sillv^r double gillt w....
Itm iij b(ells)....d on sanctus bell and vi....
Itm on sute of whitte silke, a cope, a vestm^t, ij......stoles.
Itm on blew vestm^t of vellvett wth albe and...... ij copes of w......
Itm on redd vestm^t wth floures of golde ; ......silke wth albes......
Itm on vestm^t of grene tiffenie wth albe and ......phanell: on redd vestmt of satten a bridges wth albe amesse stole and phanell,
Itm ij olde russet coopes: a vestm^t r......silke wth albe and amesse: on vestm^t of blew satten a br(idg)es wth albe:
Itm x towells; on vaile: and a p...... clothe: iij pyllowes of silke: on of vellvett:
Itm ij canapies for the pyx thon of silke (tho)ther of clothe: another of lynnen clothe wth iiij......bedes: another of satten bridges:
Itm ij crosse clothes on of blew silke on (of y)allow silke: ij latten basyns: iiij candellstickes of latten:
Itm iiij allter clothes of lynnen, and ── wrought wth redde silke at the endes: iiij (corpo)resses wth cases:
Itm a streamer of yeallowe silke: (clo)thes to hange before the alter, on of green and whitte, on of whitte and redde on other green and blewe: on p(yx) of copp and gillt: a littell peare of sillv^r to putt in the pyx:
Itm a paier of shettes: a paire of organes: xj sleaved surplesses: vi rachettes:
Itm on handebell: and ij sacring bells:
We the said Comissioners according to the kings ma^{ttes} instructions anexed to the comission have assigned and appointed for the Divin service in this church of Ramsey on Challice waieng xxv oz, iij surplesses, and iij allter clothes for the table of comunion.

The sacramental PLATE is valuable. So far back as 1713, as appears by a note in the register, there existed a large flagon, and three chalices with covers all of silver. The oldest has RAMSAYE on the cover. A second has 'The guift of Elizabeth Margetts' on the chalice, the cover plain. A third has both chalice and cover engraved 'Donum Joannis Tidmarsh de Ramsey in Com. Huntingdon.' On the flagon, besides a coat of arms, is this inscription :—

  Ex dono Rob^{ti}. Pigott Armigeri
  Hæredis et Virtutem et Census
  Johannis Dryden Armigeri Ecclesiæ
  Et Parochiæ de Ramsey in Agro Hunt.
  Benefactoris Munificentissimi.
    Anno Dom
     1713

A plate and paten have been given by Mrs. Fellowes in the present century.

The most considerable of the charitable gifts, as returned in 1786, were these. 3*l*. 10*s*. a year left by Mark Woolley, 1695; 15*s*. a year by Tho. Thirkell, 1715, in land, for the poor and a sermon: 7*l*. a year by Ch. Denson, 1718. Wm. Myles, 1600, gave 40*l*. for the poor, and Coulson Fellowes and others, 1750, gave 122*l*. for a workhouse. There is also a free school: at the above date it was in a poor state:—

Being subject to be overflowed with water, the school house is in a very ruinous condition, and the school unsupported.

N.B. The school, though ruinous, is let for two guineas a year; formerly let for 60*l*. a year; and the fen-lands, formerly 40*l*. a year.

This parish came in for a share of the large amount bequeathed by John Driden† for charitable purposes. In 1555 Rob. Pickard left 4*d*. to the high altar at Ramsey. And two extracts from wills of the same year may be given as examples. The first is that of Rob. Nelson, who says:—

I bequethe my sowle to almyghtye god in trynytye, and my bodye to be beryed in the parysbe churche of Ramsey, and I geve to the reparation af the sayd churche vj^s viij^d And to the poore people of Ramsey at the day of my buryall xl^{sl} and xx^{sl} at chrystmas next to be distributed by the dyscretion of my executors and sup(er)visors......Also I wyll that my mortuarye be p^d accordinge to the lawes of this realme, in consideration of my tythes and offerings negligently p^d or forgotten.

The other is the will of John Thresser the elder:—

My bodye to be buried in the churche yerde of Ramsey......Moreov^r I wyll, and ordeyne Mr Stockewth, and Sir Roberte Wynde curate my executors whom I wyll Shall sell the Residue of my goods unbequethed to pay my debts, and to see my bodye honestly brought to the erthe, and w^t the residue to discharge my funeralle, and do other works of m^{r}cye as they shall devyse best for my sowle, and all Chrysten sowles.

INCUMBENTS.

bef. 1555 Rob. Wynde.	1686 *Will. Hume, r.²
bef. 1597 Will. Mott.	1689 *Ric. Askew, d.
1599 Rob. Ennyle.	*Will. Searle, d.
1600 Hen. Sampson.	1733 *Pet. Cowling, d.
1610 Geo. Stuke.	1737 Tho. Whiston.
1618 Will. Harvey.	Joh. Peverel.
1632 Joh. Pindar.	1788 *Hen. Mawdesley, d.
1633 Will. Baker.	1840 Edw. Forbes, A.B., r.³
1661 *Joh. Robins, A.M., d.¹	1847 Ch. Hippuff Bingham, A.M.
1675 Edm. Gibbs, r.	

† See pp. 156, 157.
* Buried at Ramsey.
1. Also preb. of Lincoln.
2. Stated by Cole to be buried here; but he certainly did not die incumbent.
3. Now A.M., chaplain of the English church, Rue d'Aguesseau, Paris.

The CHURCH has chancel, nave with aisles and clerestory, N. and S. doors, W. tower. The chancel is very short; it is much raised above the level of the nave floor, and has a groined roof with plain intersecting ribs, not moulded. Both chancel and nave are of transition Norman date, and a very excellent example of the style. The nave is of seven bays, the piers being all alike, but the capitals are alternately round and rectangular: moreover to each opposite pair of pillars the capitals have similar, though not exactly identical ornaments. All the arches are pointed, and there are no mouldings to them. Another bay is concealed under the tower. The W. door is of the same date, though at first sight it seems of more distinct Norman work, for it is deeply recessed, and has the characteristic foliage of the earlier date: but the shafts have bands round them at the middle, which is an unmistakeable proof of later work. The chancel arch is of the same character as the nave, but is much loftier, and the capitals of the piers that support it are as high as the top of the nave arcade. These piers have more numerous shafts, and more richly ornamented capitals than the nave piers. A perpendicular clerestory with seven small windows has been added; it is rather low. The aisles are also of perpendicular date: they have three-light windows, one to each bay, all exactly alike. The chancel had at one time aisles, but these have been destroyed. On each side are to be seen clear traces of them: they had lean-to roofs. The E. end is unaltered, and is a very curious one. There are three round-headed lancets, at a considerable distance from each other; above them, but not exactly in the centre, is a pointed oval window known as a vesica piscis. All these, internally, are deeply splayed. Externally another round-headed window is in the gable, above the groined roof. Between the lancets, and at the outside, are very shallow buttresses. There is no division in the roof externally between the nave and chancel; and this gives the whole an ungainly appearance of undue length. The eastern bay of the nave was formerly included in the chancel, which was thus made to assume proper proportions.

There was a screen the whole width of the nave and aisles, at the first pillar from the chancel arch. The E. ends of the aisles were thus made into chantries; which were also themselves divided from the enlarged chancel by screens. Cole, who visited the church in 1744, has described the arrangement.* At that time the screen was adorned with the royal arms, the ten commandments on one side, and on the other a frame thus inscribed:—

The Beautifying of this Church was ye gift of ye Honourable John Driden Esqr. Henry Smith, Henry Johns Ch. Ward^s. 1700.

A curious double piscina in the chancel, under one arch, projects out from the wall: so do the three sedilia below, which are very plain, and appear to have had no canopies or divisions between the seats. They are graduated. In the chancel stands a very fine lettern, now disused. It has a rotating desk, and the stem is supported by buttresses of open tracery, topped with figures.† Two old volumes are placed on it, both imperfect. A fragment also of the chain by which they were attached, remains. They are the paraphrase of Erasmus, and Comber on the prayer-book. There are low open seats throughout the church, with poppy-head finials. The central passage is made far too narrow. The church was restored by Mr. Fellowes in 1844, as appears from a grateful memorial from the parishioners erected in the S. aisle. A W. gallery for the organ extends the whole width of nave and aisles. There is a fine hexagonal font of blue marble, having shafts at each angle. The central shaft and base are new. This has but recently been restored to its proper use.

In 1744 there were several objects recorded by Cole which have now disappeared. No vestiges of the screens remain. In the middle lancet of the E. window were two crucifixions. A large hatchment obscured the upper windows. In the N. aisle was a coat of arms in coloured glass, of which Cole gives a sketch. A fragment of an inscription was in the same window: 'Orate p(ro) a(n)i(m)a Mag(ist)ri......Rectoris.' In the E. window of this aisle

---

* Brit. Mus. Add. MSS. 5806.
† This lettern, and that in the neighbouring church of Bury, are figured in the Glossary of Architecture, pl. 104, where the date assigned to the Ramsey lettern is about 1450.

were the remains 'of a beautifull Crucifixion.' The tower is said by Willis to be 64 ft. high, and to have been built about the year 1673, by the inhabitants with stone brought from the abbey. From a number of nondescript features in it this seems very probable. Within the belfry in particular it can be seen that the windows are evidently made up from old materials. Before the erection of this tower the steeple was a low wooden building, which contained four bells. These were recast into five when the tower was built.

There are now seven BELLS. The inscriptions on six of them are given below. There is no great variety in the legends. The seventh bell is the sanctus bell, much smaller than the rest, and hung higher. It is uninscribed. The beam of the belfry towards the staircase has these names deeply cut:—

    1672   NEVILL JONES E   } CHVRCHWARDENS.
              THOMAS WALLIS

After the first name is a figure representing E, apparently meant for a contraction for 'Esq.' Above the door, used as a lintel, is a portion of a coped coffin lid, bearing a floriated cross.

1. 1810.
2, 3. R: TAYLOR. S^T. NEOTS. FOUNDER. 1810.
4. R: TAYLOR. FOUNDER. 1810.
5. THOMAS. POOLEY. &. HENRY. PARKER. CHURCHWARDENS. 1810.
6. THOMAS. POOLEY. &. HENRY. PARKER. CHURCHWARDENS. R: TAYLOR. FOUNDER. 1810.

The MONUMENTAL remains are of no special interest. At the E. end of the N. aisle is a large slab, removed to this spot, having an incised cross. The design is very fine: the brass has been taken from it, and all the inscription is gone. Cole mentions another similar slab near this one which had been brought from the churchyard. He describes it thus:—

On a black marble slab, removed out of yᵉ Church yard as yᵉ Clark inform'd me near where yᵉ Cross at yᵉ East end of yᵉ Church yard stands, is part of an Inscription to be seen, with a large Cross on it: partly cover'd by Pews and broken.

If still existing it is now wholly concealed. Cotton * has also given the inscription in a more perfect form: it bears a pretty punning motto. The inscription is this:—

Per Crucem ad Coronam. Hic infra jacet Elizabetha filia Edmundi Lucy Militis et Uxor Joh(ann)is Ferrers Militis, quæ vitam æternam Expectans animam suam Deo primo Septemb: 1658 ætatis suæ 70 placide reddidit. In luce tua videbimus Lucem. Mori lucrum.

The first four words refer to the original position of the monument near the churchyard cross. A note in the register referring to this lady has been given above. In the chancel are two mural tablets to W. H. Fellowes, M.P. for the borough and afterwards for the county of Huntingdon, 1837; and to Emma Fellowes, his relict, 1862. In the floor of the N. aisle occurs the name Descow, 1770; near it are tablets to Smyth, 1848, and Day, 1867. A few other inscriptions are preserved in Cole now concealed or lost. One was to Peter Cowling, Minister, 1737; on it was this line: 'John Hall erected this stone.' Hall was parish clerk, and 'made an apology,' the account proceeds, 'for yᵉ Impropriety of erecting a Stone wᶜʰ was to be laid on yᵉ Ground, and laid yᵉ Fault on yᵉ Stone Cutter.' Another was to Will. Crane, gent., an attorney, 1724: another to Will. Searle, minister, 1733.

The churchyard is large. The S. porch was destroyed at the restoration in 1843. There is one perfect coffin-lid, coped, bearing two crosses and the wavy line at the middle of the stem; but this has been utilised as a modern monument. Fragments of two others remain, one forming part of the stile near the W. door. Many of the tombs have an effective brick arrangement resembling the coping of an ancient gravestone. The lofty stem of the churchyard cross stands near the E. end. Cole records that near it was a handsome black marble altar monument. This has wholly disappeared. It had this inscription:—

Here lyeth the Body of Lucy Carr yᵉ: only Daughter of Sʳ. Edmund Carr Knight & Baronet of Steyford in Lincolnshire. She deceased Octo: 18 in yᵉ year of our Lord 1689 aged 66. being yᵉ Wife of Henry English Esquire.

---

* Brit. Mus. MS. Lansd. 921.

On the external S. wall of the chancel is the word 'Resurgam' in a frame. Beneath it are buried, but without memorials, three of the incumbents.

The remains of the abbey gateway are very near the church. They are of 15th cent. workmanship, and form a most pleasing object.

Ramsey S. Mary.

This parish and church owe their existence to the munificence of the late Mrs. Fellowes. There were houses, ten years ago, which were at least four miles from any church. More recently another district has been formed at Pond's Bridge, half way to Whittlesey: divine service is already conducted, and a church will ultimately be erected there. This will be three miles off Ramsey S. Mary, and will relieve moreover the extensive parishes of Whittlesey and Farcet.

The patronage belongs to Mr. Fellowes. There has been only one appointment.

INCUMBENT.
1859 Will. Collins, A.M.

The CHURCH consists of chancel with N. vestry, nave with aisles and S. porch, tower and spire W. of the N. aisle. The main entrance is from under the tower, which forms a sort of N. porch. The vestry also has a door. It is built in the decorated style. The nave is of five bays, one on the N. side being taken up by the tower, and having no arch to the nave. A somewhat ungainly buttress, supporting the tower, stands where the last pier should be. All the piers are octagonal. The aisle windows are all of two lights, trefoiled, with geometrical tracery in the head. Above the vestry roof, which is at right angles to the chancel roof, is a small triangular window to the N. aisle. The E. window is a handsome one of three lights. The other chancel windows are more enriched than those in the aisles. All the chancel windows have stained glass. A single lancet on the N. is a memorial, 1862, and has a wise virgin with burning lamp. One of two lights opposite, also a memorial, 1863, has the Sower, and the Good Shepherd. A third has Christ receiving children, and raising Jairus' daughter. The E. window has some very good glass. The chief subjects are the Resurrection, Crucifixion, and Ascension. Below the central scene is a smaller one of the anointing our Saviour's head. This window is to the memory of the foundress. There is an inscription beneath to this effect; and this appropriate text is added: 'This also that she hath done shall be spoken of for a memorial of her.' At the E. end of the S. aisle is another memorial window to this lady, bearing this inscription :—

✠ IN GRATEFUL MEMORY OF EMMA FELLOWES WHO FOUNDED THIS CHURCH TO THE GLORY OF GOD A: D: 1859 ✠ FROM THE INHABITANTS OF THE DISTRICT AND OTHERS INTERESTED IN HER PIOUS WORK ✠

The scenes in this window have relation to the subject of the memorial: both are from the Temple at Jerusalem: one representing its building, the other its dedication. The roof is plain, but has a good effect. All the wall-pieces are supported on stone corbels, well carved. They have heads, male and female alternately. The corbels to the aisle roofs have ornaments. The chancel arch is deeply moulded. The hoodmould ends in carved heads. The arch is supported on large corbels, representing angels playing musical instruments, their wings extending backwards and embracing the wall. There is one step to the chancel, two more to the sanctuary. Except two Glastonbury chairs the chancel is without seats. The colouring at the E. end is well arranged. Besides the commandments, &c., there is much pattern work in colours, and some texts. The vestry is divided from the chancel by a screen. The seats throughout are of stained deal, low and open. At the W. of the nave is an octagonal font. The panels are carved alternately with foliage and scenes. These latter are the Nativity, Baptism, Crucifixion, and Ascension.

The tower is surmounted by a broach spire, slated. The buttresses are set square at the angles, as in the geometrical period. The belfry windows have two lights, and are doubly trefoiled. Above them is a plain corbel table. The second stage has a shaft at the angles. There are two BELLS inscribed alike.

1, 2. G MEARS FOUNDER LONDON 1858.

The church is built of brick with windows and facings of stone. The roofs are all of acute pitch. All the hoodmoulds are terminated in carved heads. All the gables have crosses. The burial ground is on the south. It is almost a model of a quiet country churchyard. The graves have little edgings of raised tiles, and plain crosses at the head, inscribed with name or initials. There are but few of the large gravestones, and these not offensively obtrusive. Nearly all have flowers nicely tended.

The W. elevation is the only part of the design at all unpleasing. This is due to the inadequate size of the two windows, which leaves a large surface of plain wall unrelieved. They are also too high from the ground. Though this church would make an excellent subject for a picture, it has been thought more desirable to give a view of the perpendicular gateway of Ramsey abbey, the beautiful oriel window in which would not be easily surpassed.

Yaxley.

Norman Cross, where the road to Peterborough branches off from Ermine Street, the great north road from London to York, is in this parish. The houses are grouped about the first rising land above the level of the fens. It had at one time a market on Thursdays; but this has long been discontinued. A dispute with the men of Peterborough about the market has been noticed above, p. 26. The annual fair is on Ascension-day. The variations in spelling the name have been considerable. In domesday it is IACHESLEI. Afterwards it appears as GEAKESLEA, JAKLE, JAKELE, JAKESLEIA. In this case

YAXLEY.

the EY, or *island* is more manifestly appropriate than in many villages in the neighbourhood. It can be readily seen that the elevation is sufficient to insulate the town. But these changes in the spelling render the etymology uncertain. The first syllable may be AC, an oak, as in *acorn;* or AX, water, as in the isle of AXHOLME; or GEAK, a cuckoo. The last syllable also, but for its occurrence in so many places near as EY, or EA, might appear to be LEY, a meadow.*

The ADVOWSON is now in the crown. The rectory was appropriated to Thorney abbey in 1315. So that the value given in the taxation of 1291, 35*l*. 6*s*. 8*d*., is that of the rectory. The abbot of Thorney then had a pension of 1*l*. 6*s*. 8*d*. In the king's book the value of the vicarage was 11*l*. In the parliamentary investigation, about 1645, the church is said to be worth 8*l*., the vicarage a donative of 10*l*., increased by 30*l*. by the commissioners ' at Goldsmith Hall, out of Rectories of Fenstanton and Hilton.' In 1786 the clear yearly value was returned at 30*l*., but the living was then augmented by another 70*l*. The church is dedicated to S. PETER.

The present REGISTERS begin in 1653. In one or two places they are deficient. The earlier ones are known to have been burned. A few only are worth transcribing.

1695. 6 Jul. Ann Tompson bur: neith: in Lin^n. or Wool^n.
1754. 1 June. Henry Jordan, Cord-wainer. He cut his Throat wth. a Razor, & was brought in by ye Jury a Lunatick; & Orders were given by ye Coroner for him to have Christian Burial.
       3 Jul. Thomas Bailey, Aged 20: Killed by a Cart.
1781. 24 Aug. Anne—Dau^r of—one—Allen—a—Stranger.
1784. 1 June. John Voy Shepheard he Hanged him Self with a board and was brought in by the Jury Lunatick & Orders were given by the Coroner for him to have Christian Burial.

In 1802 was baptized a daughter of lord viscount Melsintown. A remarkable feature in this register is the number of trades called by unusual names. Some, it will be seen, are essentially trades of the fen. These are examples: boat-wright; sedge-merchant; fellmonger (tanner); thatch-threadmaker; tinkerwoman; ragman; turfman. The churchwardens' books, which commence

---

* See a discussion of the etymology of Yaxley, Suffolk, in the East Anglian, vol. ii.

1776, contain the customary payments for hedgehogs and sparrows. There are also notices of parish meetings as far back as 1733. At a vestry meeting of 18 Apr., 1811, it was resolved :—

That the Church Yard in its present ruinous State is highly indecent, and detrimental to the Respect which ought to be shewn to a Burial Ground. That temporary Repairs will not be sufficient to remove the evil, and that a new Wall in particular is absolutely necessary. That the Inhabitants of the Parish being chiefly Tenants at Rack Rent are not able to defray the Expenses of the same And that the Land Owners in the Parish not usually resident be solicited to aid them by whatever Contributions they may be pleased to assist.

The result of this appeal was the collection of a sum of 110*l*. 13*s*. 6*d*.

The present PLATE is wholly modern. Some was sold in 2 Ed. VI. as appears by the following note :—

Solde by Thomas Cloppwell and Robt Bethedge ch(urchwardens) there, ij challises waieng xxj oz for xl^{sl} all (which money was) bestowed upon necessarie repa(rat)ion of their churche. Allso they have declared upon their othes that Mr Comme of the said town dyd take ij bells out of the churche for my Ladie Elizabethes grace, of the wch her grace hath given on to the p(arish) of Thorny at annye (c)asuallties of fyer.

The principal donations to the parish were those of Francis and Jane Proby, 1711 and 1712, for the schools. In 1786 these produced 38*l*. a year; now considerably more. In 1714 Eliz. and Rob. Marriott gave 60*l*. to the poor. An unknown donor had given land producing at the time of the abstract in 1786 the sum of 6*s*. 8*d*. a year. It was 'supposed to issue out of the parsonage of Gasley.' Both donor and donation are now alike unknown. Sir Will. Gedney, in 1540, made a bequest to the parish :—

I bequeth my soule unto Allmighty God the whiche shall redeme me and all the worlde. Item I bequeth to the hye aulter wher I shall departe in the honor of the blessyd passyon of Chryste xv^d. Item I bequeth to the towne of Yaxley for to be dellt amonge poore peple 6^s. 8^d. Item I bequeth to the towne of Glynton for to be delte among poor peple v^s.

In 1554 John Bryngton left 10*s*. to the repairs of the church : and in 1555 Will. Ashwell left a larger amount :—

My bodey to be buryed in the churche of Saynt Peter in Yaxley wth. my dewty done there unto. Item I geve and bequethe to the poore of the said Towne of Yaxley xl^{sl}.

Besides the vicars in the following list, Robert, clericus, de Iakeslea, occurs in a deed dated 1170 ; and in 17 Ed. III. one John is styled chaplain of Yaxley.

Of all these vicars one only, Jonathan Styles, is known to be buried here; and he is commemorated only by a slab with initials.

VICARS.

bef. 1534	Ralph King.	1687	Edm. Annis, A.B.
1553	Ric. Dunne.	1705	Jas. Dayson.
1572	Joh. Payne.	1714	*Jonath. Styles, d.
1574	Hen. Gallant.	1722	Rob. Newcome.
1583	Joh. Savage.		——Saunders, d.
1585	Tho. Bradehurst.	1745	Joh. Wakelin, A.M., d.[2]
1623	Tho. Jeffrey.	1760	Peter Peckard, S.T.P., r.[3]
1626	Rob. Edmonds.	1777	Fr. Lernoult.
1639	Geo. Nelson.[1]	1806	Ric. Buck.[4]
1662	Tho. Stringer.	1828	Geo. Freer.
1669	Joh. Andrew, d.	1835	Ch. Lee, A.M.
1687	Joh. Clayton, A.M., r.		

The CHURCH is cruciform. It has chancel and nave, both with aisles and clerestory, transepts, N. door and S. porch, W. tower and spire. The chancel is of three bays, the eastern one on the N. side being walled, but on the S. side is an arch, an unusual position. All are of same date, early English. The piers have a quatrefoil section. The chancel arch, of the same date, is very good. The inner order is supported on inverted cones, that on the S. side terminating in foliage. The arches from the chancel aisles to the transepts are also 13th cent. work. The E. window is later: it has five lights, and has flowing decorated tracery of great beauty. The two windows to the W. of the S. chancel aisle are early decorated in date. They are each of three lights, not cusped, but pierced in the heads. The E. and S.E. windows of this aisle are later, and almost of that foreign style known as flamboyant. The N. chancel aisle is of the earliest decorated work. The E. window has three lancets doubly trefoiled, having thin cusps and separate dripstones. Two windows to the N. are of the same character. The N. transept is early English, as evidenced by the lancet in the E. wall, and the remains of one in the W. wall: but the N. window is an insertion in imitation of those in the N. chancel

---

* Buried at Yaxley.
1. Deprived by parliament in 1641. In Walker's *Sufferings*, p. 319, it is said that ' he was Harrassed out of this Living; being *Plundered*, and forced to *Fly in Disguise*.' His place seems to have been supplied by one Edward Fludd, ' a preaching minister.'
2. Also rect. of Fletton, and there buried.
3. Dn. of Peterborough; see under Fletton.
4. Also rect. of Fletton.

aisle, but later: the space between the heads of the lancets in this being pierced, and the central lancet being more nearly of a height with the outer ones. One window in the N. chancel aisle is a four-light perpendicular window under a four-centered arch. It seems indisputable that the chancel aisles originally had separate gables. This would give the E. end of the church a very grand effect. At the E. end may be seen the stringcourse shewing the roofs were of much higher pitch, the ridge remaining the same. When the roofs got out of repair the clerestory was added to the chancel and a low pitched roof placed on it: and the aisle roofs were sloped up to it, their walls also being heightened. The walls within, N. of the chancel, exhibit the moulding from which the original aisle roof sprang. The aisle roofs are too high for the clerestory to have the proper effect from without. The result is a very awkward one. The nave is of four lofty perpendicular bays. It is divided from the chancel by a screen of 15th cent. date. The top beam is gone, and its appearance consequently ungainly. It has a poppy-head in the centre. Above the chancel arch are the royal arms. The door to the roodloft is visible on the N. side: also in the aisle the lower door, blocked, and one step remain. The wallpieces of the roof are supported by shafts rising from the ground. The inner mouldings of the arches are supported also by embattled shafts; and between these and the former a curved moulding runs from the ground round the entire arch. Between the transepts and aisles are two arches on each side: the one nearest the nave has straight sides, and is of the same date as the nave; the one nearer the aisle wall is small and very acute. This suggests the idea that the aisles have been widened. The two easternmost nave arches do not open, as is generally the case, opposite the centre of the transepts. Perhaps this was to gain more room for the roodloft. In the S. transept is a large decorated window of four lights, with net tracery, the meshes being large. It is very like the E. window at Orton Longville. The S. aisle has two plain windows of three lights each, under depressed arches, with cinquefoiled cusps. The earliest part of the church, and the most distinctly early English in character, is the W. end of the S. aisle. Here are two windows, one in the S. wall and one at the W. end, of triple lancets. They are unequal, and have a triple dripstone, with notch-heads. The buttresses here are set square at the angle, and are of good detail. The interior door also of the S. porch is early English. This was probably the external door of the original porch. It is now much mutilated. On each side were three banded shafts. Two only remain perfect. The door seems to have been trefoiled, like that at Whittlesey S. Mary in the same position, and like the N. door at Etton church. The moulding above the door remains. The existing porch is perpendicular. It has three niches, and on the roof three nondescript animals. The centre one is chained and has a fine crest. Under the N. transept window is a dwarf buttress. A similar one existed under the window of the S. transept but has been removed: remains of the masonry can be seen. The E. window of this transept is a lancet. The buttresses here, and to the S. chancel aisle, are set square. This usually betokens early work. Those at the E. wall are gabled and rather elaborate. At the N.E. and S.E. are sitting animals, as on the S. porch. The eastern walls of the aisles slope up to the chancel roof much more than the roofs of the aisles themselves do. There is a bent stringcourse below them. In the centre of this sloping parapet on the S. aide is a square stone cut in a quatrefoil forming a finial cross.

The eastern end is raised, but the levels are not the original ones. The S. chancel aisle has two piscinas and aumbries. This shews that the E. end of the aisle was added, and the altar which stood at the old end removed further east; or else that the last bay was an enclosed chapel. The former would be the more probable were it not for the open arch by the high altar. There are the remains of two excellent brackets. In the chancel are two brackets, and quasi canopies. The N. chantry has three early English sedilia, very perfect. They are graduated, and have trefoiled canopies, with gables, surmounted by fleurs-de-lys. The design includes a piscina

E. of the sedilia. Above the arches to the chancel are remains of some remarkable frescoes. The groundwork has five-leaved flowers. Three figures are pretty distinct: one is in a pilgrim's dress: the other two are the Saviour and Mary Magdalene, 'Touch me not.' The Saviour holds a staff surmounted by a cross. These are but a portion of a considerable number uncovered. Each transept had an altar under the deeply splayed lancet. The piscinas remain. In the N. transept there is also an aumbry. The N. door is considerably above the level of the church. Internally, to the E. of the door, is a niche. In the N. aisle are a few open seats with plain oak backs, original. They are open below. The windows here are of three lights. There is some good stall-work in the chancel.

The tower is included within the church, and has arches N. and S. as well as to the nave. It is of four stages. There is a small W. door, and a three-light perpendicular window above it, having narrow lights but large external splay. The second stage has simply a thin slit for light: the third is quite blank: the fourth has three-light trefoiled belfry windows with transoms. The parapet above is dated 1709. This is the date of some repairs. There are eight large gargoyles. The spire is crocketed. From the tower there spring flying buttresses pierced with quatrefoils. The spire has two-light windows at the foot, and single lights above. There are large pinnacles at the corners of the tower.

Of the five BELLS, two are cracked or broken. All were recast at the same time. All are inscribed.

1. HEN. CLINTON. COMES. LINCOLNIENSIS. BENEFACTOR. JOHN CHILD SIMON BROWN; CHURCH WARDENS: HENRYCUS. PENN. FUSORE. 1721.
2. HIC. EST. DOMUS. DEI. ET. AULA. CŒLI. JONATH. STYLES. VIC. 1721.
3. GLORIA. DEO. EXCELSIS. 1721.
4. DOMUS. MEA. EST. DOMUS. ORATIONIS. 1721.
5. MEMENTO. MORI. JOH. PROBY. ARMIGER. MANERII. DOMINUS. BENEFACTOR. 1721.

On the tower is a sundial with the motto ' Post est occasio calva.'* It was renewed in 1818, which date is painted upon it.

Several of the MONUMENTS are of considerable interest. Under the W. tower are two pieces of a coffin-lid with floriated cross of 13th cent. work. Near the S. porch, in the churchyard, are two of decorated date. One is too defaced for the pattern to be seen : the second is coped, and has two fine crosses and an ornamented stem. In the N. chantry is the upper part of a slightly coped coffin-lid also enriched with ornaments. Here also is the matrix of a floriated brass cross, with place in the head for a figure, perhaps a priest. There are memorials to the families of Weston and Burton in the N. chantry : Bowker in nave : Child and Squire in S. chantry. The E. window of this chantry is of stained glass, a memorial to a member of the last-named family, 1849. In the N. chantry is a tablet thus inscribed :—

Inscribed at the desire and at the sole expence of the French Prisoners of War at Norman Cross To the Memory of Captain John Draper, R.N. who for the last 18 months of his life was agent to the depot, In testimony of their esteem and gratitude for his humane attention to their comforts during that too short period. He died Feb. 23. 1813. Aged 53 years.

But the most remarkable of all the memorials is in the north transept wall. It is without inscription. On the stone are carved two arms in relief, holding a heart. A trefoiled canopy surmounts the whole.† It is of decorated date. Behind this stone was discovered a cylindrical box of wood, now in possession of the vicar. It is cracked, but quite sound. It is $4\frac{1}{2}$ in. high and 4 in. in diameter. We frequently find hearts buried by themselves in a different place to the body. At Woodford, Northants, a heart has recently been discovered. Bruce's heart was to be taken to the Holy Land, but the Douglas was slain while discharging the mission. The heart of

---

* This same motto occurs at Horton, Dorset. The full line of which it is a part is inscribed over the grammar school at Guilsborough, Northants, and runs thus :—
Fronte capillata, post est occasio calva.
Bacon quotes it in his 21st Essay in this form : 'For *Occasion* (as it is in the common verse) turneth a Bald Noddle, *after she hath presented her locks in Front, and no hold taken.*' It is just like our modern phrase 'Take Time by the forelock.' The author is Dionysius Cato. See Notes and Queries, 2nd S. vi, 290. Some dial mottoes are very apt. At Elsworth, Cambridgeshire, is this one : 'Mox Nox.'
† Engraved in Bloxam's Architecture, 10th Ed. p. 414.

Cœur de Lion was buried at Rouen. Abp. Rokeby's heart was buried at Halifax, and his body at Dublin. The heart of lord Edward Bruce, killed in Holland, was brought to Culross to be buried.*

The churchyard, from whence is a fine view over the fens, is crowded. It contains, except the coffin-lids already named, no memorials of great interest. There are a few coped brick graves like those at Ramsey. The following verse occurs on a tombstone. It is the only one in the neighbourhood, but it is not uncommon elsewhere.

> Here I lie without the door,
> The church is full, will hold no more,
> Here I lie, the less I pay,
> And yet I lie as warm as they.

Stanground.

This parish has always been held with the curacy of Farcet. The two have an extensive acreage in the fens. In domesday the name appears as STANGRUN. Other varieties are STANGRUND, STANDGROUND, and once, in the parliamentary return about 1645, the name occurs as two words, STANDY GROUND. The meaning may be *stony*, referring to the ground just by the village as opposed to the fen lands near; or it may be derived from the *stone* cross, which was erected as a boundary mark between the parishes on the road to Fletton, called the 'maiden's cross.' The earliest notice of the parish, except that in domesday book, is in an inquisition dated 4 Ed. I. In this 'Stangrund and Farsheved Hamlett' are described as one town, 'una villa.' Stanground was part of a settlement upon the princess Elizabeth for her maintenance, during the reigns of Ed. VI. and Mary.

The church is dedicated to S. JOHN BAPTIST. In the taxation of 1291 the church was worth 20*l*., besides the abbot of Thorney's pension of 4*l*. 13*s*. 4*d*. This was of course the rectory. In the king's book the vicarage,

---

* See also p. 55, note 19; Gentleman's Magazine for 1789; Chambers's Book of Days, ii, 414.

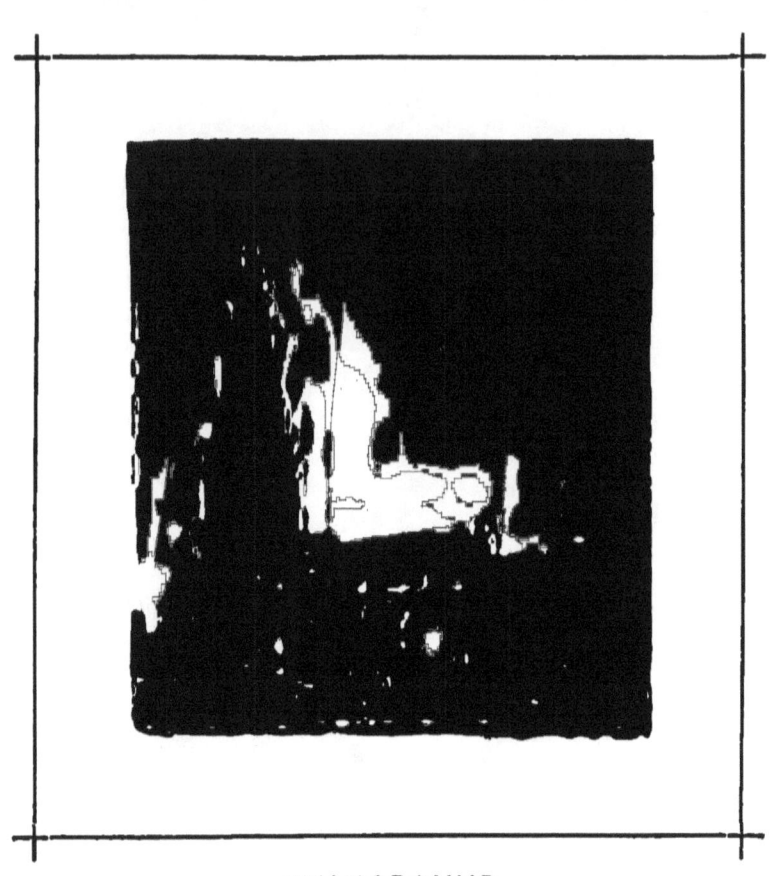

STANGROUND.

with Farcet, is given at 6*l*. 6*s*. 10*d*., the tenths at 12*s*. 8¼*d*. There were no procurations or synodals. The living was in the gift of Thorney abbey. In 1402 the rectory was appropriated to the abbey and the vicarage ordained. In this deed it is provided that the abbey shall build a manse with a hall, two rooms, two cellars, kitchen, stable, garden, and gates. The religious were also to distribute 5*l*. yearly among the poor. The abbot paid the king 100*l*. for the licence to appropriate the rectory. In 1538 the great tithes were let to the vicar, Andrew Pollard, to improve the vicarage, at 12*d*. a year for his life. In 1588 sir Walter Mildmay made a grant for increasing the vicarage, and bestowed it on Emmanuel college, Cambridge, of which he was the founder. Considerable litigation towards the end of the last century with regard to the tithes resulted at last wholly in favour of the vicar.*

The REGISTERS commence in 1538. The earlier part, for about 60 years, is copied from older books. This was done by Rob. Smith, who has made an entry to that effect, and has entered the names of all members of his family (particularly his grandchildren), in fine prominent characters. The first book extends to 1643, but the last two years are incomplete. The next two books commence in 1652. There are some entries of interest.

1612. 21 Feb. John Charleton for tythes forgotten 3s. 4d. ex testamento.
1618. 18 Feb. Guy Chesham annu(m) agens supra centesimu(m) sepultus fuit.
1630. 27 Dec. Lawrence Bate the husbande of Alice.
      30 Dec. Alice Bate late wife of the sayed Lawrence.
1668—9. 3 Feb. Tho. Jeanes Doct^r of Physick being accidentally drowned and taken up hard by the Town, was here buried. [In another column is this note:—] in his journey homeward from a certain Noble Patient in a dark Night without a Companion. Ant: Wood.
1689—90. 24 Mar. Hannah Sinke was then whipped according to law & sent away wth a pass to Sunderland in the Bishopricke of Durham where she said she was born, the pass was signed by
                                    Oliver Pocklington Curate.
                                    Joshua Laxton Constable.

---

* The abbey had two fens, 'Brodde Fenne, and Fleg Fenne,' about 800 acres in extent. These were part of the Bedford level. In the time of the abbey all was under water. Between 1630 and 1640 there was a prospect of their being drained. In 1634 a set of 'adventurers' was incorporated to drain them, 'from these lands being covered with water, little advantage redounds to mankind, except some few river fish and water fowl.' The drainage having been effected, vicar Salmon claimed tithe on the improved lands. The countess of Westmoreland disputed the claim. In 1640 the sum of 25*l*. was agreed upon as a composition. This payment was continued till 1773 when the vicar demanded tithes in kind. Lord Brownlow resisted this claim, and even disputed the above composition. The question was tried at Huntingdon, 1780, and finally decided before the lord chancellor in 1792. Copious notes on these questions are preserved in the vicarage; they were prepared by vicar Devie.

194   STANGROUND.

1701. 7 Dec.   Mrs. Katharine Womack, Relict of Lawrence L^d B^p of St Davids aged 79.
1704. 29 Aug. A Gentle woman. A stranger.
1712. 17 Nov. (buried) Edm. Crane supposed to be married.
      22 Dec. Joseph Jenning stole M^{rs}. Margarett Bellamy. At Night.
1720. 3 Feb.   John Roper, Jersey-Comber.
1731. 2 Aug.   The Rev^d. Edmund Jeffery vicar of Southwick in ye county of Northampton.

There is a considerable list of collections under briefs. They are mostly stated as being for certain places, without any object mentioned. A few are more explicit. Some extracts are given.

Year	Entry	Amount
1661.	29 Sep. Collected uppon the briefe for Bridgenorth in our County of Salop	0 9
1662.	1 June....for the Inhabitants of Markett Harborough and littel Bowton in the County of Leichester	7 6
1663.	28 Feb.....for John Ellis of Milton in the county of Cambridge	6 10
	17 Mar.....for Harwich Church in the County of Essex	5 0
1665.	6 Aug. Bramble hanger breife in the parish of luton in the County of bedford	3 10
	2 Aug....towards the reliefe of those that are visited with the Plague on Weddensday being the first fasting day	8 0
	[Similar collections for three more Wednesdays in the following months.]	
	3 Oct. fflootburg brefe in the County of Lancaster	3 0
1669.	17 Feb.....fore the towne burton upon stather in the partes of Lindsey in the couentey lincoln	00 03 01
1687.	8 Jul.....for White Chapel Breife	11 2
1690.	31 Aug. East Smithfeilde Breif in Middlesex	5 11
	4 Nov.....upon y^e. second Breife for releife of ye Irish Protestants ye summe of	1 0 9
	1 Dec......for ye Borough of Southwarke in Surry	9 1
	23 Dec....towards ye Relef of the suferers in Ellsworth in Cambrigshire	2 0
1694.	29 Sep.....up^n ye brief of ye French Protestants	8 8
	....for ye City of York	6 3
	....for Jos. Peters	4 3½
1708.	12 Dec.....for ye head of ye Canongate at Edinburgh in north Brittain called Scotland. A loss by fire	03 06
1709.	4 Sep.....for Harlow Church in ye county of Essex burnt by fire	00 01 11
1711.	27 Jan.....for Long-Melford Church	00 01 6
1712.	10 Aug.....for Charles Empson of Booth in ye Parish of Howden in ye County of York, loss by fire & water	00 02 9
1715.	3 Aug....for ye Cowkeepers brief	6 9 3
1716—7.	....for ye Reformed Episcopal Churches in Great-Poland & Poland-Prussia &c.	11 4 0
1720.	10 July....for ye sufferers by Thunder, Hail, &c. within ye several Parishes and Townships of Wheaton-Aston, Eapley & other Townships in ye County of Stafford	0 4 3
1722.	2 July....for an Inundation in ye County Palatine of Lancaster	0 3 7

The following notice of goods sold bears date 2 Ed. vi.

Solde by John Spayn and John Gainthropp churchwardens ther, on Sauntus Bell and on Crosse of Copp for xl^{al} } xl^{al}

All wch money....was Bestowed on ye rassing of a water Banke in the comon ffen....

Solde by the said churchwardens, candlestickes old paynted clothes and sensers wth other old Implements for iiijli } iiijli

All wch was putt into the poore mennes box, wh was robbed on S Peters even before the first Inventorye made.

The charitable donations apply to both parishes. Most are recorded on a board in the N. aisle. Ed. Bellamy, 1557, bequeathed money for apprenticing a boy from each place in turn: Tho. and Joh. Coveney, 1680, gave money to the poor, producing in 1786 30s. a year: the gifts of Will. Bellamy, 1704, and of Rob. Bellamy, 1779, produced each 40s.; and that of Mary Walsham, 1744, realised 7l. 10s. Rob. Tompson, 1710, gave 5l. but it has been lost. There is also '10s. a year more, left by a pauper, in land.'

RECTORS.

c. 1220 H. de Gravell.
      Will. Copmanford, d.
  1296 Will. Sparby, d.
  1318 Tho. de Clopton, r.

1320 Tho. de Nassington, r.
1320 Tho. de Clopton, r.
1365 Joh. de Drantfield.

VICARS.

1409 Joh. Machon de Melton.
bef. 1534 *And. Pollard, d.
  1545 Griffin Jones.
  1546 Edw. Wilkinson.
      *Tho. House, d.[1]
  1554 *Hew. Smyth, d.[1]
  1561 Tho. Howlatt.
  1573 *Will. Longe, d.[2]
  1602 Sam. Starling, f.
  1631 *Elias Petit, d.
  1634 *Hen. Salmon, S.T.B., f.[3] d.
  1654 Sam. Craddock.[4]
      Joh. Gibbon.

1650 Ric. Kidder, S.T.B., f., dep.[5]
1662 *Will. Forster, S.T.B., f.
1680 *Will. Makernesse, S.T.B., f, d.
1680 Jas. Wolfenden, S.T.P., f, d.[6]
1684 *Joshua Radcliffe, S.T.B., f, d.
1690 *Sam. Doughty, S.T.B., f, d.
1720 *Joh. Chapman, S.T.B., f, d.
1731 *Wil. Whitehead, S.T.B., f, d.
1755 *Joh. Brigham, S.T.B., f, d.
1766 *Jas. Devie, S.T.B., f, d.
1809 *Hen. Y. Smythies, S.T.B., f, d.
1842 Rob. Cory, S.T.B., f.

* Buried at Stanground. Those who were fellows of Emmanuel college are marked f.
1. These two were probably vicars, and are so recognised in Devic's list. The former is entered in the register as 'clark,' the latter as 'Sir Hume Smyth.'
2. In the register appears under date 8 Feb., 1602, this entry, 'Tho. Scot Clark,' buried. Vicar Longe was buried 17 Feb., 1602.
3. Described in the parliamentary returns as a 'preaching minister.'
4. Also rect of North Cadbury, Somerset. This and the following are named by Devic as vicars, but without date.
5. A very celebrated man. He was born of puritan parents, and sent up to Trinity college, but the master refused him. Ultimately he went to Emmanuel. Ordained deacon and priest in one day by bp. Brownrig, of Exeter. This was in 1658: he was born 1633. In 1662 he was ejected from Stanground under the act of uniformity. Rect. of Raine, Ess., 1664–74: min. of S. Helen's, London, before that, but never instituted: also preacher at the Rolls. In 1674 made rect. of S. Martin, Outwich: soon afterwards lecturer at Blackfriars: preb. of Norwich, 1681. He had been offered living of S. Paul, Covent Garden. Dn. of Peterborough, 1679: bp. of Bath and Wells, 1691. An autobiography of him appears in Cassan's Lives of the Bishops of Bath and Wells. Cole has preserved some ridiculous gossip about him said by Cassan to be wholly untrue. He was made bishop after an ejectment. Was offered the see of Peterborough. There is a portrait of him at Wells. He published at least 12 books, besides several tracts and sermons. He was killed in bed, 26 Nov., 1703, by the fall of a stack of chimneys of his own house. This was in the great storm mentioned before. See pp. 12, 13, 160.
6. Buried at Whittlesey, S. Mary.

Memorials to a considerable number of the vicars remain in the church. Nearly all the inscriptions are in Latin: many are somewhat lengthy. The earliest is a brass in the S. chancel wall to Elias Petit, in English. He was '4th sonn to Valentine Petit of Dandelyon in the Isle of Thanet in Kent Esquire.'* A tablet to Will. Forster records that he was 'Pastor Vigilans et fidelis. Vir plurima eruditione ornatus, Mira Suavitate morum præditus.' Will. Makernesse, 'Vir pientissimus,' has a stone on the chancel floor: he died on the twenty-third day after induction. On the same stone is the epitaph of Joh. Chapman. In the N. aisle is a tablet to Will. Whitehead. Of him it is said:—

Loco, quem tenuit, Dignus certe fuit, altiore etenim non Indignus merite censendus, Morum CANDOREM, Integritatem Vitæ, Sensit Vicinitas, Senserunt Parœci........Apud Bathon^m vanâ spe convalescendi Illusus, Fato tandem cessit........Bibliothecam quam Satis instructam, reliquit, In usum Successorum moriens Legavit, Rectoribus de WOODSTON et FLETTON, Ut Integra semper descendat, Curatoribus Institutis.+

The last vicar has a tablet in the chancel.

The CHURCH has chancel, with chantry and vestry, N., nave with aisles and clerestory, blocked N. door and S. porch, W. tower and spire. The chancel has no windows on the N. side; on the S. are three early decorated windows of two lights; their hoodmoulds have the notchhead. There is a S. priest's door; and a low side window of three lights, square-headed. This is now filled with plain quarries. Within it is faced by a stone stall looking east. There is a somewhat similar stall on the opposite side. The stall on the S. side has been restored, but the base is unaltered, and shews from its character that the chancel arch, window, and stall, are of one date. There are two masks on the N. side, one to the hoodmould, and one to the inner moulding: and the base of the chancel arch is adapted to it. The staircase to the roodloft remains on the N. side: it is now used for the modern

---

* A short account of this family, and of their ancient seat at Dandelyon, is to be found in Lewis's History of the Isle of Tenet.

+ 'He was certainly worthy of the position he held, and indeed deservedly thought not unworthy of a higher: the neighbourhood and the parishioners alike knew the candour of his manners, the integrity of his life......Attracted to] ath in the vain hope of getting well, he at length yielded to fate......He left a well-selected library, which he bequeathed at his death for the use of his successors, and appointed the rectors of Woodston and Fletton the guardians of it, so that it should continue to descend entire.' This library consists of a thousand volumes.

stone pulpit. This staircase projects into the chancels and has the appearance of being supported on shelves. It is lit by a small cross slit. There is a piscina of two drains of geometrical date, exactly like those in the cathedral; it has been restored. There are also three graduated sedilia, undivided, under one plain arch. The aumbry opposite has marks of a shelf. On the N. side of the chancel are some stone seats restored. The steps are new but retain the original levels. The E. window has five lights: it is plain (but seemingly not later than the others), with intersecting tracery, the lower lights being twice cusped. It is now filled with stained glass erected in memory of Susanna Apthorp, 1863, by her nephews and nieces. The design includes a crucifixion, our Lord in glory, and the twelve apostles. The reredos is modern and fairly effective. It has marble shafts. The vestry has an early geometrical window of two lights, with a circle in the head, but the mullion is gone. There is a door and squint from the N. chantry to the chancel. In the chantry are a piscina, the remains of a roodscreen, and a small bracket. The nave is spacious. It is filled with low open seats with poppy-heads. A few in the S. aisle are original: one is a singular design of four fishes, two upright and two curved. The door to the roodloft is visible just above the door to the pulpit. The break in the mouldings of the chancel arch shew were the loft was. The nave is of four bays. The bays on the S. side, and two on the N. side, have plain piers, the moulding of the capitals coinciding with that of the arch above: the half-pier against the tower on the S. side, and the three easternmost on the N. side, have floriated capitals. The piers on the S. side are loftier than those opposite. All seem early geometrical in date, about the year 1290. The corbel supporting the E. end of the S. arcade is decidedly early English in character. In the S. aisle are two rough massive brackets: also an elegant sepulchral arch. The aisle windows are of three lights; some have intersecting tracery. The solitary fragment of ancient stained glass is a red shield in the S. aisle bearing three lions. The tower arch has circular piers. At the W. is a two-light window of stained glass. The tower is twisted to the north. The clerestory windows are over the arches: they are square-headed, plain, of two lights, and seem early. The early English font, ornamented, stands W. of central pier of N. arcade. A stained glass window in the N. aisle is to the memory of the widow of R. T. Cory, D.D., master of Emmanuel, and her two granddaughters. The spire is of great height, and is conspicuous for its elegance. There is a row of ballflowers below the cornice. On three sides are small circular windows. There are four BELLS with inscriptions.

1. ✠ MEROREM MESTIS LETIS SIC LETA SONABO 1617.
2. ✠ MEROREM UT MESTIS LETIS SIC LETA SONABO 1612 E N E H TOBIAS NORRIS ME FECIT.
3. ✠ SARVE GOD AND OBE THE PRINCES 1788.
4. HENRY YEATS SMYTHIES. B. D. VICAR. JOS^H. WARWICK. CHURCHWARDEN. 1832.

Besides the MONUMENTS to vicars already specified there are a few to be noted. The oldest has its name obliterated. It is on the floor of the chancel, and bears a floriated cross. The legend is round the margin. The date, 1443, is tolerably clear. On a brass in the wall is this inscription:—

Hic jacet corpus Roberti Smith genosi qui obiit 4 die Dec. A° D^{ni} 1556. finibus exiguis clauduntur corporis artus viva vivet * virtus spiritus astra tenet.

Alice Smith, wife to Tho: Smith son to ye abovesaid Robt Smith who died ye 5th of Sep. 1595.

    Whose constant zeale to serve the Lord
    Whose loyal love to husband dere
    Whose tender care towards children al
    Remaine alive though corpse lye here.

There are other memorials to the same family, and to Coveney, 1665 and 1668. Cole has preserved the following inscription in the nave: the entry in the register referring to this accident has already been given:—

H S T. Jeanes D^r. Phys: Londini natus: Plurimis ultra citraque Academiis educatus, & noctu obequitans aquis inopinatim submersus vicinis.

In the vicarage garden is preserved a wayside or churchyard cross. It is of the Maltese pattern and

---

    * Mr. Paley has pointed out that this word is a mistake for 'viret.'

FARCET.

stands on a modern base: down the sides are ornaments resembling Norman work. This cross was only rescued from desecration in 1865 by the present vicar. It was discovered by him on the Farcet road, where it was used as a bridge over a ditch.

Farcet.

Owing to the large extensive fen district in Farcet fen, the acreage here is about double of that in Stanground. The position of the church and village is similar to Yaxley. They are on the extreme edge of the higher ground, the fen coming close up to the foot of the ridge which slopes down from the road itself. The name of the place has undergone some curious changes in spelling. It has gradually dwindled from four syllables to two. FEARRESHEVOD, FEARRESHEAFDE, FAIRSHEVOD, FARSHEVED, FARSEID, FARSETT, and other varieties occur. And the earliest form has suggested the very probable Saxon etymology meaning the head of the ferry, or ford.

The living has always been attached to the vicarage of Stanground. In the ordination of the vicarage it is provided that the vicar 'shall provide a fit chaplain in the chapel of Farcet belonging to the said church, at his own costs and charges, according to the custom of past time, to administer the divine offices.' * A meadow in Farcet king's delph was assigned to the almoner of Thorney. In 1659 Oliver St. John, chief justice, held some of the adventurers' lands in Farcet fen. In 1306 the towns of Stanground and Farsheved were presented for wasting 100 acres of alders and rushes in Farcet fen. Also the abbot of Thorney was presented for making a 'purpresture' † in the king's forest, and enclosing it with a double ditch on the side towards Farcet, 2 miles long and 2 furlongs broad, 'to the detriments of the king's deer.' The great increase in value secured for the living by

---
* 'Unumque Capellanum idoneum in Capella de Farshed ad dictam Ecclesiam pertinente suis sumptibus et expensis juxta morem præteriti temporis inveniet divina ministrantem.'
† An enclosure. Johnson gives *purprise* in the same meaning, from the French *pourpris*, and law Latin *purprisum*.

vicar Devie, was mainly due to the improved value of the lands drained in Farcet. Most of the documents relating to the lawsuit were printed in the pamphlet published by him in 1782. The countess of Westmoreland was granddaughter of sir Walter Mildmay,* who made the grant of the living to the college. When Salmon was vicar he had demanded of her, among other things, 14 nobles for serving Farcet church. She replied that it was a benevolence 'during one man's life,' though afterwards continued; and that when the vicar had declined to receive it as a benevolence payment had been refused. This very question had been raised before and decided against the vicar by the bp. of Lincoln. The special grant to which the countess alluded was to sir Chr. Barton: and it is certainly specially provided that it is for his life only. It runs in these words:—

In stipendium Xpoferi Barton clerici celebrantis infra Capellam Beatæ Mariæ de Farcett in comitatu Huntingdon coram parochionalibus ibidem ad iiij^l: xiij^s: iiij^d. per annum sic sibi concessum per quoddam scriptum sigillo conventuali nuper Monasterii predicti sigillatum cujus datum est primo die Septembris anno xxx^o regis Hen. viij. habendum et tenendum durante vita dicti Xpoferi.

The church is dedicated to S. MARY.

The REGISTERS commence in 1813. Previously they had been kept at Stanground. Among the list of collections on briefs in the Stanground books are a few belonging to Farcet. The following are from them.

1661.	24 Feb. Collected at Farsett uppon the breife for the Royal flishing traid	8	9
1670.	21 Mar. Kerkles Breife in ye Countie of Suffolke	5	8
	24 Oct. Isleham Breife	1	9
1675.	30 June....Walton in the County of Norfolke	4	8
1682.	10 Oct.....for Lishton breefe	4	0
1700.	9 June....for ye redemption of slaves	1 6	9

In the Farcet chest the documents, though of no very great interest, are a model in respect of the care taken of them. They are well preserved and properly tabulated. A letter from the secretary of the bp. of Lincoln, 1723, mentions the inefficient performance of the curate's duties, and adds that the bishop expects his 'Order should be Immediately and effectually comply^d wth.' Another paper records a proceeding in the court of arches before

---

* He was member for Peterborough in queen Mary's first parliament; and in 4 and 5 Philip and Mary was one of the knights of county of Northants. He was chancellor of exchequer for life, and was buried in S. Bartholomew the Great, London.

sir John Lambe against Ed. Bellamy for 'the agistment of Dry Cattle, tithe of Milk, Wool, Lamb, Calf, Eggs, and Goslins.' Sir Walter Mildmay gave to Christ's college, Cambridge, 20*l.* a year out of the manor of Farcet, for founding a Greek lectureship and six scholarships, and for a preacher's stipend.

Amongst the PLATE is a curious old chalice of silver, rather ungainly, of cylindrical form. It has a carved rim, and bears this inscription between double lines round the centre : * THE * TOWNE * OF * FAVSET.

The returns of charitable bequests in 1786 gave two belonging to Farcet. Ed. Bellamy, 1657, left rent-charge of 3*l.* a year for apprenticing a boy : and Tho : Andrew, 1700, left land for a school producing 11*l.* 14*s.* a year. By a copy of his will in the Stanground register it seems this land consisted of 10 acres in Whittlesey fen, and that he also left 4*l.* to the town stock, the 'rent' of which was to go to the poor.

The CHURCH consists of chancel with S. chantry and vestry, nave with aisles and clerestory, S. porch, and W. tower. The alterations that this small church have undergone are considerable. The changes would appear to be somewhat in this manner. Originally the plan seems to have been a simple nave and chancel, most likely Norman, with an apsidal termination. The tower was then added, about the year 1200, at the W. end of the nave. It was not quite so wide as the nave, and a small piece of the nave wall projecting from the tower is still visible in the aisle. During the next century a S. aisle was added, and the present S. nave arcade erected. Possibly at the same time the chancel itself was rebuilt and enlarged. The S. arches of the nave, three in number, have round arches and are rather broad : but they, and the chancel arch, are of early English date. The arch under the tower, towards the S. aisle, is pointed. Still later, in the 14th cent., the S. chantry and S. porch seem to have been built. In the perpendicular period a clerestory was added. The present N. aisle and arches were built in 1852 by the present vicar. A note in the register preserves a minute record of the works done at that time, and also at the restoration nine years before. In 1843 the seating was renewed and other improvements effected. The E. windows were repaired by the Rev. E. Cory, the curate, 'instead of the parish who are bound by law to repair them.' In 1852 the chancel and chantry were rebuilt, and the N. aisle added, by the vicar. The old nave roof, 'rotten and dangerous,' was removed. The whole N. wall was taken down. It had one window below and two above. These latter were used as lights to the new aisle, and circular windows were inserted in the clerestory. At the N. E. corner of the nave stood a thick projecting staircase for the roodloft. The nave was at the same time repaved. Some of the carving from the old roof is preserved in the new ones. Some of the roodstairs also are adapted for the pulpit. In the chancel are a piscina and a stone seat with arms projecting from the wall. This was placed in its position during the above restorations: the seat itself is perhaps a fragment of the stone seats which once may have gone all round the chancel. On the N. side is an aumbry. In the S. aisle also is a trefoiled aumbry. The E. window has stained glass by Wailes. The seats are all low and open. The font is octagonal, and very plain. The tower has the early shallow buttresses characteristic of transition Norman work. The lancet in the lower stage is deeply splayed within. In the second stage is a single thin lancet. The belfry floor has round-headed two-light windows, the lights being pointed. At the sides are shafts like the mullion. The tower is surmounted by a nondescript parapet, with poor pinnacles and metal crosses. Below it is the original corbel-table. From within this parapet rises a short pyramidal leaded spire. In the first floor there remains a blocked door leading to the old roof. There are three BELLS. The inscription on the tenor, which has been recast, is copied from the old one. On a beam are these letters and date: AF CW 1668.

1. ✠ PRAISE ✠ THE ✠ LORDE.
2. T A 1653
3. Omnia fiant ad Gloriam Dei. A S 1621 Recast A S 1854

FLETTON.

In the chancel is a slab to the Rev. John Montfort, curate, 1785. Memorials also remain to members of these families: Bird, Bellamy (with coats of arms), Bowker, Kisbee. In the churchyard are numerous stones to the Speechley family. The following inscription is rather quaint.

HERE LIETH THE BODY OF
M^{RS} DOROTHEA WRIGHT
WHO DIED AUG. 4. 1674.
SHEE DID GOOD BY
HEALEING.

Fletton.

The church and rectory of Fletton, nestling close together under the shadow of some noble trees, form one of the prettiest objects within a walk of Peterborough. They are less than two miles off; the bridge fair of Peterborough is held in the parish of Fletton. In domesday book the name appears as FLETUN: subsequently the varieties occur of FLECTON, FLETTUNE, and FLETTON. It is the town by the fleet, or brook running down to the main river, and its name still, as of old, describes its situation. A piece of land called 'the fleets' was allotted to the inhabitants of Stanground in lieu of their ancient right of common, in the act for enclosing the lordship of Fletton. The church is dedicated to S. MARGARET. In 1291 it was worth 6l. 13s. 4d. In the king's books the full value was 9l. 16s. 9d.; and the tithes 18s. 4$\frac{1}{2}d$.

There are no very early REGISTERS. The earliest book commences in 1616, but entries from 1606 are copied into it. Great parts of the pages are left blank, with dates, as if it was intended to copy in the entries from loose sheets or a rough copy. Some years this has been neglected, and in 1609 is the note, 'Desunt omnia.' There are no entries whatever from 1642 to 1648, and but an insignificant number in the following years. Three entries only are worth transcribing.

1665. 28 Apr. (buried) Elianora Ellis, Virgo sexagenaria.
1677. 15 Oct. (buried) A traveller out of Nottinghamsh.
1728. 30 Oct. (married) * * * * & Mary Thacker.

Did the bridegroom in the last instance escape before his name could be ascertained? The undesirable name of Sapphira occurs.

In the church are four boards with the parochial benefactions painted on them. In the official returns in 1786 the following annual receipts appeared:—8s. from John Henry's bequest: 4l. from that of Hen. Walsham: 10s. from Will. Charlton: the same sum from Charlton Wildbore: 5s. from two unknown benefactors. The bequest of Frances Proby was also named, but no return was made. From the inscription on the board in the N. aisle we learn that she left 200l. in 1711: by 1775 this money had accumulated to 1212l. 19s. 6d., which sum, by an order in chancery, was invested in government securities, and the proceeds divided thus: 12l. to the schoolmaster, and the rest for apprenticing children, and for the poor. Ultimately it was invested, so as to produce 40l. a year, in old south sea annuities. Besides the above, Mary Walsham in 1744 left 100l. to the poor: and Rob. Wright, 1815, left 10s. a year. In the same year 'Mrs. Sarah Preston, Spinster,' left 20l. a year to the poor; but 'By the Statute of Mortmain this bequest is rendered void.'

RECTORS.

bef. 1531 Ed. Eyre.
1558 Will. Baker.
1558 *Joh. Ellys, d.
1634 *Will. Loe, d.[1]
1651 *Tho. Rayment, d.
1693 *Joh. Wright, A.M., d.
1730 *Joh Wakelin, A.M., d.[2]
1760 Peter Peckard, S.T.P., r.[3]
1798 Ric. Buck.[4]
*Jas. Jackson Lowe, A.M., d.
1830 Ed. Rutter Theed, A.M., d.[5]
1851 Chr. Carr, d.[6]
1856 Will. Judd Upton, A.M.[7]

---

* Buried at Fletton.
1. Described in the parliamentary returns as 'a preaching minister.'
2. Also vic. of Yaxley.
3. Fell. of Brasenose; rect. of Abbot's Ripton, 1793—98; vic. of Yaxley, 1760—77; preb. of Southwell; dn. of Peterborough, 1792—98; master of Magdalene, Camb., 1792—98. Wrote life of Nicholas Ferrar, of Little Gidding. A sermon of his is reviewed in Gent. Mag., vol. 65. He lost his life from cutting a wen on his cheek in shaving. He lived three years after the accident. His fortune was left to his college at Cambridge. A capital portrait of him is at the rectory.
4. Also vic. of Yaxley.
5. Also vic. of Selling, Kent.
6. Inc. of Newborough, Northants., 1830—31.
7. Inc. of Greensborough, York, 1850—56.

Within the altar rails are memorials to two of these rectors, Wright and Lowe. In the vestry is a slab to rect. Wakelin, 'Worthy in every Relation of Life to be remember'd with Regret.' His daughter, aged 4 years, had died two days before him.

The CHURCH is of the simplest plan. Chancel with N. aisle, nave with aisles and clerestory, S. porch, W. tower and spire. The arches of the chancel aisle are now entirely blocked, and the chantry itself used as a vestry, entrance being obtained from the N. aisle. The blocked arches of the chancel are the earliest part of the church. They are early Norman. There are two round arches, with slightly ornamented capital to the central pier. To the E. of these bays is a blocked priest's door. The N. side of the nave is now of three bays, also Norman in date, but later. The two eastern arches are massive; the capitals are fluted. The W. arch is very broad; and in fact a pier has been removed, and a single pointed arch of early English date extended over the space for two arches. The following remarks by Mr. Paley on this question are a triumph of architectural research :—

<small>These aisles remain, but one pillar and two arches have been removed towards the west, and a wide obtuse arch of early decorated date spans the vacant space. The capital of this pillar was carried to Stanground, and there at this day it may be found, inverted, at the north-west corner of the nave, where it forms the plinth or base to a decorated arch coeval with this.</small>

The capitals to Norman work are mostly ornamented with inverted cones. The nave arches have no hoodmould above, as those in the chancel have. The chancel arch is early English. It has semicircular piers and a pointed arch. The S. and E. sides of chancel have net-tracery windows of the middle of the 14th cent. On the S. side also is a decorated stringcourse. There are no signs of piscina or sedilia. Two panels of the roodscreen remain, the upper part being sawn off. A fragment of the cresting is preserved under one of the blocked arches. The clerestory has three S. and two N. windows, all of two lights and square-headed. In the vestry are the door and steps to the roodloft. The steps are very steep and awkward. The pulpit and desk are accessible only from the N. aisle. Beneath the sounding-board at the back is a carving of the annunciation. Above the chancel arch are the ten commandments (their proper position) surmounted by the royal arms of the Hanoverian period. Between the two tables is a painting of S. John. On the S. side of the nave are two octagonal stilted piers; the three arches are of inelegant shape. At the ends of the aisles are triplet lancets; one is trefoiled. The arches are acute, and the eyes pierced. These windows belong to the early decorated period, and are comprised under a single dripstone. The seating is very bad. At the W. end are remains of some original benches, very low, with poppy-head finials squared at top, all different. In the N. aisle is an octagonal font of debased character. Its sides are fluted, and stem is thin. The tower arch is blocked; in front of it is a gallery for the organ.

The tower seems in a somewhat dangerous state. There is a good deal of patching visible from the interior. The spire itself is most elegant. Below the cornice is a row of ballflowers. The original Norman corbel table is preserved under the roof of the chancel: and some pieces of very early sculpture have been built into the walls.

The belfry has very strong beams, but is in a very dirty state. The floor of the lower story is dated 1741: The ladder from it to the bells has the date 1777. There are three BELLS all inscribed. The first is in ancient Lombardick characters; the letters are distant. It is difficult to assign any meaning to them. The next has enriched capitals, and has a foundry mark of three bells and a crown. The third has ornaments between the words.

1. ✠ S P A L L E
2. WILLIAM WATES MADE ME. 1590.
3. OMNIA FIANT AD GLORIAM DEI 1620.

The first of these inscriptions is difficult to explain. The letters are quite distinct. It is possible that the bell may have been dedicated to S. Paul, and that the letters are intended merely for the saint's name. Bells are not uncommonly found with simply the name of the saint upon them, without the addition of any prayer, as 'ora pro nobis.'

The MONUMENTS, besides those already mentioned of rectors, are but few. In the vestry are slabs to the wife of rect. Wakelin, and to his relict. The very numerous virtues of the former are recorded at length. There are numerous slabs to the Wright family. The names of Henery and Wildbore are also preserved. The stone in the nave to Charlton Wildbore, the benefactor already named, is almost too worn to read.

Near the S.W. gate of the CHURCHYARD is a fine ancient coped stone. It is not in its original position. It bears a floriated cross with crosslets. Under the W. window of the church is a Saxon churchyard cross, very interesting. It was erected by, or in memory of, Ralph, son of William, if we may trust the modern sculptor's rendering of the ancient inscription. This new inscription is cut on a pedestal which has been placed beneath it. The stem is enriched with characteristic carving. The top of the cross itself is gone. It was originally a massive cross in a circle. It is very similar to the celebrated cross called the 'Four-hole cross' standing in the middle of the Bodmin moors in Cornwall; and the upper part is broken in exactly the same way. The carving on the stem is similar to that on the recently recovered cross at Stanground, but the general character of this cross shews it to be of an earlier date. The few fragments of Saxon work built into the exterior chancel wall are of contemporary work. The stem of the cross gradually slopes from the pedestal to the head. There can be little doubt that this cross was in existence in the 10th cent.

Cotton says 'There have been Flettons lords hereof.' The village was given, as Alwalton, for the monks' kitchen. The church and rectory are in a most beautiful situation, partly hidden among trees.

It will perhaps be well, at the conclusion of the notes relating to the Huntingdonshire churches in this series, to repeat the remark made at the commencement as to the difficulty of consulting any copious collections for the county. It seems unaccountable that so small and compact a county, so near to London and Cambridge, should be without a history. Such however is the case. And after consulting the records of a few Northamptonshire parishes, so ably and thoroughly preserved, the want of such a history is doubly felt. Nor are extensive materials for such a history known to exist even in manuscript. It would be a most useful work for any antiquarian residing in the county to undertake, and one that would thoroughly recompense the leisure hours bestowed upon it.

Additions and Corrections.

Page 1. Since these notes first appeared the tower arch of Marholm church has been opened. One of the frescoes was found to be upon the part blocked up, and has consequently had to be removed. The upper part of the arch has been restored: the capitals of the piers are original and of good Norman work, justifying the opinion given on p. 5 of the early date of the tower.

Page 2. A few extracts from the overseers' books may be added :—

		£ s. d.
1772.	P^d Wm Griffin in ye Snow for want of Bisness ..	0 5 0
1777.	P^d. M^r. Wright for Inoculating the Poor	6 : 1 : 3
1783.	Paid for Ale when the Widows were flitted	0 2 2
1784.	To Rum for Ben: when Ill	0 1 0
	To P^d for Ale when some dodders were loaded ..	0 0 6
1790.	To Peter York for flitting the Poor	0 2 0

In 1771 one 'Molly' appears very frequently on the books as receiving money on all possible pretexts.

Page 3; *line* 9. For 1558 read 1552.
———— *line* 16. Sey is a kind of fine woollen stuff, formerly used by millers for bolting cloths. Johnson spells it *say*.

Page 4. Tho. Cheswick occurs as rect. of Marholm in 1565.
———— *line* 19. For Shapman read Shapland.
———— *note* 11. Chr. Hodgson was buried at Marholm, not at Castor.

Page 8; *line* 19. For xxxi read xxbi.

Page 13; *line* 17. For 1558 read 1552.
———— *note* 8. The word in the inventory certainly refers to towels, not bowls.

Page 14; *line* 37. Joh. Gayton was also probably rect. of Peakirk.

Page 15; *note* 13. Will. Jeffery was also preb. and chancellor of Sarum.

Page 16; *note*. For 9769 read 6769.

Page 27; *line* 25. For Delarne read Delarue.

Page 30. John de Ronds occurs as vic. of Peterborough in 1278.
———— *note* 5. Gunton was a native of Peterborough. His father left 20*l*. to the poor of Priestgate lane. He published, besides the History of the Cathedral, 'God's House with the Nature and Use thereof.'

Page 34; *line* 24. For Delarne read Delarue.

Page 55; *line* 29. For Will. read Ric.

Page 56; *note* 7. Bp. Lindsay seems also to have had rectory of Molesworth, Hunts.
———— *note* 8. Bp. Dee left several sums of money to the poor of Castor, and 100*l*. to the repairs of the Cathedral.

PAGE 57; *note* 7. Dean Nevill is buried in a chapel at the W. end of the nave at Canterbury, which he had restored. At his funeral a question arose as to whom the pall belonged: it was resolved that anything laid on a grave 'about and above' the choir belonged to the precentor, and anything in the body of the church to the sexton.

———— *note* 10. Bp. Lamb is buried in the Melbourne chantry at Hatfield.

PAGE 60; *line* 14. Joh. Gayton was also probably vic. of Peterborough.

———— *line* 28. Also rect. of Alwalton. See p. 148.

———— *note* 11. Perhaps also vic. of Brixworth, 1621.

———— *note* 17. Dr. Wollaston was never vic. of Wisbech.

———— *note* 14. Bp. Gordon died in 1779, not in 1709 as given in this note. In the copy of Baker in the cathedral library are a few portraits and views inserted: amongst them is an excellent engraved portrait of Nat. Spinkes. He holds a book in his hand inscribed on the edges 'Sick Man Visited.' Below the portrait is this engraved notice of him: 'This very Eminent Divine was Venerable of Aspect, Orthodox in Faith; his Adversaries being Judges: He had uncommon Learning and Superior Judgement. His Patience was great, his Self denial greater, his Charity still greater: His Temper sweet and unmoveable beyond comparison. His exemplary Life was concluded with an happy Death July 28, 1727. in his 74. Year.'

PAGE 79; *line* 17. William Jones, rect. of Paston, was a very celebrated author. He is generally quoted as Jones of Nayland, from one of his preferments. He was rect. of Pluckley, Kent, 1765—77, and vic. of Stoke-by-Nayland, Suffolk. In the obituary notice of him in Gentleman's Magazine, 1800, is a list of his works. They are very numerous. The most noted of them, and the one for which he is chiefly honoured, is the 'Catholic Doctrine of the Trinity.' He was also F.R.S.

———— *note* 10. For exigno read exiguo.

PAGE 90; *line* 2. Joh. Girdlestone was also inc. of Thorney. He resigned the living of Eye.

PAGE 93; *note* 6. For vic. read rec.

PAGE 95; *line* 10. The stone coffin was found at the E. end of the N. aisle, not of the S. aisle as here represented.

PAGE 99; *note*. This note was written on information supplied by those imperfectly acquainted with the facts of the case, and conveys a wholly inaccurate version of the occurrence. The author greatly regrets its insertion, since it has done injustice to the memory of one who long and manfully, to his own great loss, defended the rights of the church. The true statement of the facts is as follows. The lords of the manor of Whittlesey were entitled to the great tithes of S. Mary's, and used to pay the vicar 200*l*. a year. They also leased of the vicar of S. Andrew's the small tithes for 20*l*. a year. The vicar having always given a receipt for this amount 'in lieu of small tithes' it was evident that the small tithes were allowed to be his property. In 1805, Mr. Moore, then vicar of both parishes, was induced to make a claim for a more adequate payment, and the lords assented to the appointment of an arbitrator, who fixed the sum of 200*l*. a year, instead of 20*l*., as a fair equivalent. This sum was paid regularly during Mr. Moore's life. But it was known that even this increased amount was not equal to one half the real value of the small tithes; and therefore Mr. Cook, when the lords offered to continue that payment to him, most properly declined it. For three years he made every effort to obtain an amicable settlement of the case by arbitration or otherwise, but in vain. He was forced at last to file a bill in chancery, the lords continuing to receive the small tithes without paying anything to the vicar. In this litigation 25 years were spent: and when the suit terminated in the vicar's favour, he was only able at common law to recover the amount of the tithes for seven years, the impropriators having received 490*l*. a year the whole time; and so Mr. Cook served the parish for 18 years without any remuneration whatever, the lords wrongfully appropriating what was proved in the event to be the property of the vicar.

PAGE 100; *line* 1. Ed. Grouud was not in holy orders: he was churchwarden.

PAGE 101; *last line.* In the will of John Woodfowl, 1454, he describes himself as 'chaplain and hermit of the chapel of S. Mary of Heldernall.'

PAGE 102; *note* 4 is incorrect.

PAGE 105; *note.* It appears that both churches were destroyed by fire in 1244. In MS. Cott. Nero C. vii, an illuminated record of the annals of Thorney, are these entries:—
A.D. 1244. Hoc anno scilicet ydus Apriles per infortunium incendii combusta est fere tota villa de Witleseye cum duabus ecclesiis, et cum duabus grangiis abbatis blado plenis, et insuper xiiij homines combusti sunt.
A.D. 1277. In crastino apostolorum Petri et Pauli per infortunium incendii combustum est totum manerium de Witteles.

PAGE 107; *line* 4. Two entries respecting the family of Hake, as connected with the parish of Whittlesey, occur in the Peterborough registers:—
1599. 6 June. William Hake Esquire died at Kilthorpe was solemnly brought through Peterborough and buryed at Wyttlesey the vi of June.
1613. Nov. Mistress Lucy Hacke the wyfe of Mr William Hacke a Gentelwoman of good presence, yet not quoze, of a sharpe and quick apprehension yet no scoffer; personable and full of favour, yet most chaste, dyed in childbed the 24 of this present, and was buryed at Wyttlesey the 25th daye, whose death was much lamented in Peterbor. [In the margin are these lines:—]
   Juno, Minerva, Venus, terræ tria Numina quondam,
   Unica pro tribus elucet nostra Lucya.

PAGE 107. Cole, vol. 24, mentions a deed of bp. Fordham, 1404, altering the date of dedication feast of S. Mary's to 21 Sept. He quotes also a licence of the same bp., 1406, to Adam Herberd, Joh. Backhous, Will. Pelle, Joh. Grounde, Will. Fysher, and other inhabitants of S. Mary and S. Andrew of Whittlesey, living in the street or hamlet of Estreyc, to hear mass in the new chapel there for three years.

PAGE 117; *line* 25. For 1821 read 1853. Joh. Wing, A.M., appointed in 1821, has been omitted in error. He was also rect. of Thornhaugh, Northants.
——— *line* 11. Alan Kirketon, or Kyrketon, had been rect. of Alwalton.

PAGE 121. At one time a common epithet for this town was 'Curst Croyland.' It is suggested in Notes and Queries, 1st. S. x. 146, that this is a corruption of its ancient epithet 'courteous'; 'Croyland as courteous as courteous may be.' And it is singular (Ib. 275) that in Holm-Cultram are some lands, formerly belonging to the abbey, still called 'Curst Lands.'

PAGE 139. There seems to be no existing memorial to the countess of Carlisle, buried at Orton Longville in 1742, or to Robert viscount Morpeth, 1743.

PAGE 148; *line* 29. Alan Kirketon, or Kyrketon, was afterwards abb. of Thorney.
——— *line* 32. In Gough's Collection for Hunts. in the Bodleian it appears that in 1742 Joh. Forster, A.M., was rect. of Alwalton and also of Walsoken in Norfolk. In this case Dr. Neve must have resigned.
——— *line* 38. Dav. Llewelyn was also, for a very short time, rect. of Peakirk.

PAGE 151; *line* 13. For Kerrick read Kerrich.

PAGE 153; *line* 7. Joh. Old was also rect. of Water Newton.
——— *note* 3. In Walker's Sufferings, p. 265, the Geofrey Hawkins ejected from Chesterton in 1641 is said to have outlived the usurpation, and to have become rector of Water Newton. But it seems more probable that the latter was son of the former, especially as a clergyman of the same names is buried at Castor in 1672. Of the ejection here Walker says: 'Driven from this

living in 1641, by Steward of Mannor; who took no care to put any one into his place, but seiz'd the whole profits for his own use; and afterwards by an enclosure alienated almost the whole Glebe, which to this day is not restored to the Parsonage.'

PAGE 158; *line* 11. Sept. Courtney was A.M., and afterwards vic. of Plymouth, king Charles the Martyr, and of Compton Gifford, Devon.

PAGE 160; *line* 25. The word Machanes also occurs p. 12. No such name is to be found in gazetteers. But I have been informed in Notes and Queries, that the place meant is Mequinez, a large city in Marocco.

PAGE 161; *line* 5. Sam. Ball was also rect. of Water-Newton.

PAGE 167; *line* 18. Sam. Ball was also rect. of Elton.
——— *line* 19. Joh. Old was also rect. of Chesterton.

PAGE 200; *line* 26. For Tho read The.

Index 1.—Persons.

Abree, 57
Acharius, 55
Acrod, 153
Adamson, 174
Addenbrooke, 153
Addison, 100
Adelwold, 145
Adulphus, 55
Adyson, 3
Affen, 30
Affordeby, 14
Ainger, 116
Ainsworth, 175
Aldwald, 113
Aldwin, 113
Aldwinkle, 130
Alexander, 16, 105, 114
Allen, 185
Allington, 93
Alnewyk, 48
Alpyng, 48
Amitius, 66
Andreas, 30, 55
Andrew, 15, 131, 187, 201
Andrewe, 158
Angel, 65
Angeli, 55
Anketill, 30
Annis, 187
Apthorp, 197
Armyne, 139
Arnold, 127
Arwinus, 55
Arx, 173
Ashbey, 122
Ashby, 123, 127
Ashton, 55, 73
Ashwell, 186
Askew, 177
Aslakeby, 14
Aspden, 2
Augusta, 14
Austhorp, 14
Austin, 52, 166
Aveling, 107
Aylwyn, 171
Ayre, 72

Backhous, 211
Backhouse, 109

Bacon, 101
Bagley, 20, 54
Bailey, 148, 185
Baker, 131, 177
Balderston, 60
Balguy, 34
Ball, 23, 54, 60, 79, 160, 161, 163, 167, 212
Ballard, 93
Baly, 127
Bardenay, 123
Bardney, 48
Barker, 24, 61
Barnaby, 142
Barnabye, 24
Barnack, 123
Barnard, 66, 70, 148
Barneby, 65, 79
Barnes, 108
Barnwell, 78, 131
Barr, 98
Bartlemew, 153
Barton, 200
Basevi, 90
Basset, 93
Bate, 12, 20, 66, 142, 193
Bateman, 70
Bates, 12, 124
Bathurst, 142
Batley, 167
Baudrie, 78
Baxter, 137
Bayly, 146
Bayston, 30
Bayte, 115
Beale, 52, 77, 102, 104, 109, 110, 112
Beard, 174
Beaumont, 57
Beaver, 159
Beawater, 102
Beby, 18
Becket, 71, 118, 172
Bedford, 116, 118, 119, 164
Behague, 173
Beharrell, 34, 110
Beivyle, 155
Beleby, 18, 102
Bell, 90

Bellamy, 194, 195, 201, 203
Bellars, 92, 96
Belshaw, 174
Bendishe, 101
Benedict, 31, 46, 55, 71, 171
Bennet, 71
Benson, 124
Bent, 131
Beonna, 55
Berdenay, 123
Beresford, 15
Bernard, 39
Berrye, 174
Bethedge, 186
Bevill, 155, 156
Bevyll, 155
Beyvyle, 155
Beyvyll, 155
Bifield, 148
Bill, 148
Bingham, 177
Bird, 203
Birde, 48
Bishop, 100
Blaby, 141
Blacker, 4, 37
Blake, 2
Blencho, 14
Blot, 174
Bloxam, 11
Blundell, 124
Blyth, 87, 102, 107
Boak, 82
Bocher, 110
Bokvyle, 4
Bolham, 30
Bomber, 136
Bonde, 93
Bonfoy, 175
Boniface, 31
Bonner, 92
Booth, 39, 115, 140
Boothby, 55
Boothe, 173
Borstall, 14
Bothe, 140
Botolph, 91, 115
Boton, 30

INDEX I.—PERSONS.

Botulfus, 61
Bouchereau, 116
Bourn, 93
Bowdon, 79
Bowen, 137
Bowker, 191, 203
Bowley, 88
Boxall, 57
Bracher, 122
Bradehurst, 187
Bradford, 173
Bradley, 146, 151
Bradyll, 1
Braibroc, 30
Brampton, 102
Brando, 55
Brecknock, 116, 117
Brereton, 161
Brewster, 30
Brice, 147
Brictmer, 123
Bridgeman, 143, 148
Bridges, 9
Brigham, 195
Brightmore, 26
Bringhurst, 131, 132, 133
Britefelde, 4
Brity, 174
Brocksopp, 29, 34
Brockwell, 76
Broome, 24
Brown, 66, 123, 148, 190
Browne, 24, 79, 110, 142, 153
Brownlow, 193
Brownrig, 195
Bruce, 191, 192
Bryggys, 123
Bryngton, 186
Buck, 187, 204
Buckingham, 56
Bud, 108
Budd, 3
Buddel, 93
Bull, 9, 101
Burges, 107
Burgess, 110, 115
Burgh, 93
Burgo, 14, 66, 78
Burgoyn, 66
Burne, 48
Burroughs, 122
Burrowe, 48
Burton, 191
Butcher, 89, 124
Butler, 58, 63

Cairon, 116
Calah, 61
Caleto, 55
Callow, 152

Campbell, 93
Campe, 40
Candidus, 46
Capstaffe, 24
Carleton, 57
Carlisle, 211
Carnall, 141
Carr, 181, 204
Carter, 3, 30
Caryer, 137
Carysfort, 147, 164
Casewik, 123
Caster, 48
Castor, 117
Castr, 48
Catell, 89
Cato, 191
Cautley, 117
Celredus, 55
Ceolred, 121
Chambers, 48, 56, 62, 87, 88, 145
Chaplin, 12
Chapman, 30, 79, 195, 196
Charles I, 56
Charles II, 56, 173
Charleton, 193
Charlton, 204
Charwelton, 117
Chateres, 122
Chesham, 193
Cheswick, 209
Cheyle, 93
Cheyne, 79
Chichele, 79
Child, 137, 138, 191, 196
Childerhouse, 102
Childers, 99
Childs, 174
Chiltenden, 137
Christian, 42
Chune, 133
Clapham, 98
Clapton, 114
Clare, 92
Clark, 12, 72, 96
Clarke, 23, 89
Clathery, 115
Claughton, 161
Clavering, 15, 57
Clayton, 57
Clement, 78, 131, 132, 153
Clerke, 84
Cleypoole, 64
Clifton, 54, 173
Clinton, 190
Cloppwell, 186
Clopton, 12, 117, 195
Clyff, 61
Clyffe, 48
Cobley, 12

Cœur-de-Lion, 192
Coke, 12
Cole, 20, 181
Coles, 155, 156
Collier, 66
Collins, 182
Coltman, 54
Colvile, 4
Colynson, 14
Comme, 186
Coo, 21
Cook, 99, 110, 112, 210
Cooke, 35, 127, 137, 153, 167
Cooper, 133, 159, 160, 161
Cope, 139
Copmanford, 195
Cornelius, 76
Cory, 195, 198
Cosin, 58, 61
Cotton, 135, 181
Courtney, 153, 212
Coveney, 195, 198
Covergrave, 78
Covetre, 48
Cowley, 122
Cowling, 177, 181
Cowper, 57, 78, 79
Cox, 34, 150
Craddock, 195
Crane, 181, 194
Crayton, 102
Creed, 173
Crimble, 61
Cromwell, 122, 171, 173
Crosier, 93
Crow, 54
Crowland, 124, 126
Croylade, 48
Croyland, 48, 55, 66, 123
Cumberland, 15, 56, 60, 61, 66, 70, 161
Cupper, 30
Currer, 93
Curtes, 72
Curteys, 3, 14
Curthop, 57
Cuthbaldus, 55

Dalyson, 14
Danois, 116, 120
Darby, 53, 88, 127
Daumo, 30
David, 114, 117
Davie, 109
Davis, 130
Davys, 15, 30, 57
Daw, 109
Dawkins, 12
Day, 181
Dayson, 187

INDEX I.—PERSONS.

215

Deacon, 29, 54, 61
Deboo, 116
Dee, 14, 56, 209
Deeping, 56, 117
Delacree, 79
Delarue, 27, 34, 209
Delenoy, 116
Delf, 110
Denham, 164
Denis, 141
Denson, 174, 177
Deping, 66
Desborow, 136
Descamps, 116
Descow, 181
Devie, 193, 195, 200
Dickens, 130
Dickenson, 28, 29, 76, 133, 158, 161
Dickins, 159
Diconson, 93
Digbye, 137
Dinham, 164
Disney, 79
Dobson, 33, 34, 60, 106
Dodyngton, 14
Dollman, 91
Dornell, 116
Doscrile, 4
Doughty, 195
Douglas, 191
Dove, 14, 56, 123
Drake, 147
Dranfield, 195
Draper, 191
Driden, 152, 155, 156, 157, 177, 179
Dryden, 58, 176
Dudley, 14
Dunne, 187
Dunstan, 45
Du Perrier, 112
Duport, 58, 61
Durance, 116
Dyer, 108
Dykelun, 66

Eaton, 76
Eayre, 81, 106, 111, 112, 133, 145
Edenford, 14
Ederston, 66
Edgar, 45, 55, 113, 114, 171
Edgcomb, 66
Edis, 147, 159
Edmonds, 187
Edred, 123, 126
Edward, 55, 61, 123
Edward I, 55
Edward II, 145

Edward IV, 123
Edward VI, 192
Edwards, 157, 166, 169
Egar, 116
Egbaldus, 55
Egelric I, 123
Egelric II, 123
Elfricus, 61
Elizabeth, 48, 57, 192
Ellesworth, 102
Elliott, 34
Ellis, 40, 52, 193, 204
Ellys, 204
Elm, 66
Elsinus, 11, 55
Emeley, 137
Emelton, 141
Empson, 194
English, 20, 181
Ennyle, 177
Ernulphus, 55
Esdall, 142, 153
Ethelbald, 121, 126
Ethelwold, 113
Evans, 60, 137, 174
Everard, 123
Exeter, 48
Eyre, 204

Faber, 161
Fellowes, 177, 179, 181, 182, 183
Fenwick, 56
Fereby, 142
Ferrar, 15, 204
Ferrers, 173, 181, 182
Fiscampo, 66
Fish, 1
Fisher, 30, 161
Fitzwarin, 104
Fitzwilliam, 1, 2, 4, 5, 7, 8, 9, 11, 34, 42, 44, 54, 140
Fitzwilliams, 4
Flahau, 116
Fletcher, 57
Fletton, 207
Florentius, 61
Fludd, 187
Flynte, 79
Forbes, 177
Fordham, 211
Forman, 30
Forster, 101, 102, 110, 142, 161, 195, 196, 211
Fossdyke, 123
Foster, 79, 131, 132
Fovargue, 82, 116
Fowke, 153
Fowler, 115
Fraunces, 164

Fraunceys, 30
Fraxino, 78
Freeman, 34, 58, 148
Freer, 187
French, 166
Freston, 78
Frisby, 146
Fulcard, 117
Fuller, 167, 169
Fyrth, 137
Fysher, 211

Gaches, 116
Gainthropp, 194
Gallant, 187
Galloway, 140
Garforth, 93
Garner, 173
Garrat, 24
Gascoigne, 30, 79
Gates, 100, 102, 108, 110
Gayton, 14, 66, 209, 210
Geddyng, 123
Gedney, 186
Gee, 58
Genge, 56
Gibbon, 195
Gibbs, 52, 54, 177
Gibson, 4, 79, 83, 135, 139, 142
Giddings, 142
Gilbert, 30, 117
Giles, 2
Gillon, 173
Giraud, 116
Girdlestone, 90, 117, 209, 210
Glazier, 53
Gloucester, 48
Glovernin, 131
Glynton, 48
Goche, 124
Godeman, 117
Godewyk, 109
Godewyke, 109
Godfrey, 51, 55, 123
Godric, 123
Godricus, 55
Gold, 39
Goodman, 54, 146
Goodwin, 130
Goodwinn, 84
Goodyn, 159
Gordon, 66, 152, 153, 210
Gowin, 89
Grantham, 48
Grave, 78
Gravell, 195
Grawley, 88
Gray, 148
Grazier, 70

INDEX I.—PERSONS.

Green, 4, 99, 109
Gregory, 29, 30, 52, 148, 150
Greue, 12
Greenhill, 65, 66
Griffin, 83, 209
Griffinus, 66
Griffith, 102
Ground, 100, 106, 112, 211
Grounde, 211
Grymesby, 4
Gryndell, 30
Grystewe, 48
Guerin, 116
Guibbon, 26
Gunterus, 117
Gunton, 25, 27, 30, 54, 209
Guthlac, 63, 121, 122, 125, 126, 128

Hacke, 211
Haddon, 117
Hake, 107, 211
Haldure, 110
Hall, 141, 181
Halles, 4
Halywell, 153
Hamerton, 79, 137
Hammerson, 52
Hamserley, 102
Hanbury, 24
Hanger, 167
Hanns, 173
Hans, 88
Harbottill, 169
Harby, 14
Hardey, 147
Hardy, 173
Hare, 30, 92, 93, 142
Hargrave, 80
Harley, 116
Harlton, 48
Harman, 4
Harold, 113
Harrison, 110, 115
Harry, 13, 14
Harvey, 52, 177
Harwedon, 79, 102
Hawelye, 77
Hawkeman, 53
Hawkings, 34
Hawkins, 21, 153, 167, 211
Hawmile, 82
Hawtrey, 102
Haycock, 131
Hechyn, 92
Hedda, 11, 45, 52, 55, 121
Hegham, 93, 96
Heiton, 141
Helpeston, 93

Helpo, 91
Hendry, 173
Henry, 204
Henry II, 55
Henry III, 55
Henry VI, 123
Henry VIII, 8, 171
Henshaw, 15, 21, 56
Henson, 76, 81, 159
Herberd, 211
Herbert, 53, 117
Herke, 72
Herlyngton, 145
Hertford, 48
Hervey, 105, 113
Hervy, 14, 66
Hetley, 26, 146, 151
Heverardus, 113
Hewett, 155
Hewitt, 152
Hickes, 66
Hickling, 127
Hill, 30
Hilles, 2
Hills, 4
Hinchcliffe, 15, 57
Hinscote, 96
Hobbes, 56
Hochyn, 92
Hoddye, 136
Hodgeson, 14
Hodgson, 3, 4, 209
Holbech, 117
Holbeche, 48
Holderness, 55, 62
Holmes, 116
Hopkinson, 82, 148, 149
Horsham, 30
Hotot, 55
Houghton, 66
House, 105
Howland, 56
Howlatt, 195
Hubbersty, 93
Hudson, 124
Hugel, 116
Hughes, 60, 89
Hugo, 30
Hume, 177
Hunt, 117, 137, 153
Huntly, 140
Huppax, 24
Hurd, 15
Hurry, 101
Hutchinson, 23, 100
Hutton, 15
Huxley, 174
Hydson, 79

Ikleburgh, 102
Image, 30, 34

Ingulf, 64, 113, 128
Inkerson, 77
Ireland, 65
Irthlingburgh, 133
Islep, 117
Iwardby, 122
Ivo, 113
Ixem, 93

Jackson, 57, 147
James, 30, 60, 66, 69
James I, 57, 143
Jeanes, 193, 198
Jeffery, 14, 137, 194, 209
Jefferys, 89
Jeffrey, 187
Jembelin, 116
Jenning, 194
Jeune, 57
Joffrid, 123, 124, 125
John, 117
Johns, 179
Johnson, 30, 83, 88, 106, 112
Jollis, 24
Jones, 79, 110, 180, 196, 210
Jordan, 185
Judkin, 129

Katherine, 48
Kay, 30
Keble, 4
Kelfull, 109
Kempthorne, 161
Ken, 66
Kennett, 4, 11, 15, 47, 56, 58, 60, 66, 99, 148
Kent, 100
Kenulphus, 55, 123, 124, 126
Kerby, 14
Kermihil, 100
Keteriche, 146, 167, 169
Keteryng, 48
Kettlewell, 66
Kidder, 58, 195
King, 12, 82, 136, 137, 187
Kinge, 4
Kinsius, 61
Kipling, 49, 58, 59
Kirby, 129
Kirketon, 117, 211
Kirton, 7, 48, 56, 62
Kisbee, 203
Kisby, 129
Knipe, 166, 167, 169
Knowles, 26, 53, 93
Kyneburgha, 10, 11, 45
Kynesman, 30
Kyng, 79

INDEX I.—PERSONS.

Kyniswitha, 11
Kynwolmersh, 14
Kyrketon, 148, 211
Kyrkton, 48
Kyrktun, 48
Kyrton, 102

Labyr, 101
Lacy, 53
Lamb, 15, 57, 58, 66, 210
Lambe, 201
Lamberd, 136
Lambert, 173
Lammin, 53
Lampkin, 76
Laney, 15, 56
Lanfranc, 126
Langeford, 14
Langtoft, 78
Lany, 79
Latimer, 148
Latymer, 57
Lauderdale, 66
Laurence, 156
Lavin, 76
Lawrance, 146
Lawrence, 34, 97
Laxton, 79, 193
Layng, 4, 20
Leafield, 36
Leahair, 116
Leaves, 102
Ledbeater, 146
Lee, 146, 187, 204
Le Fevre, 116
Lefsinus, 117
Lefsius, 117
Lefwinus, 117
Le Houcq, 116
Le Leu, 116
Lemon, 175
Leofricus, 55
Leofwyn, 108
Le Pla, 116
Lernoult, 187
Lesueur, 116
Le Tal, 116
Levit, 91
Lewis, 137
Leycester, 14
Lezygham, 48
Lilley, 54
Lincoln, 48, 66, 200
Lindesay, 55
Lindsay, 14, 56, 209
Lindsell, 4
Litlington, 123, 126
Llewellyn, 66, 148, 211
Lloyd, 15, 56, 79, 81
Lockier, 49, 58
Lodington, 78

Lodynton, 102
Loftes, 115
Lomes, 112
London, 48, 55, 62
Long, 134
Longchamp, 123
Longe, 105
Loomes, 101
Love, 171
Lovin, 52, 54
Low, 82
Lowe, 205
Lowry, 29
Lucy, 181
Luffenham, 123
Luvedon, 66
Lyne, 48
Lynton, 110
Lyon, 159

Mac Duggle, 88
Machon, 195
Macklen, 24
Madan, 15, 57, 60
Magnaville, 171
Makernesse, 195, 196
Mallason, 24
Manbye, 77
Mandeville, 58
Mandevyle, 110
Mansco, 61
Mansfield, 53
Mange, 116
March, 123
Margetts, 176
Marriott, 186
Marsh, 15, 57, 60, 69
Marshal, 175
Marshall, 14, 21, 29, 30
Marsham, 146, 148
Martin, 23, 46
Mary, 57, 88, 192
Mary of Scots, 48, 52, 57, 62
Marys, 14
Mason, 29, 89, 102, 110, 112
Masons, 23
Massingarb, 116
Mast, 175
Matilda, 126
Matthias, 55
Mawdesley, 177
Mayden, 14
Mc Douall, 60
Mears, 112, 184
Mees, 110
Melsintown, 185
Melton, 14, 51, 93
Meltun, 48
Meriton, 57

Merry, 40
Messenger, 4
Messynger, 4
Mews, 52
Middleton, 173
Mildmay, 193, 200, 201
Millicent, 142
Mills, 90, 142
Milner, 148
Milton, 34
Moigne, 100
Monk, 49, 58, 66
Montfort, 203
Moore, 102, 106, 107, 110, 112, 140, 210
Mopsey, 12
Morcot, 55
More, 14, 52, 92
Mores, 102
Morgan, 153
Morpeth, 211
Morrys, 48
Morton, 65, 70
Mortun, 48
Mossop, 93
Mott, 177
Moulton, 117
Mountsteven, 77, 78, 82
Mountstevinge, 12
Murcott, 117
Murrey, 53
Mythingesby, 78

Nassington, 14, 195
Naturas, 48, 79
Neal, 174
Neale, 141
Negus, 100
Nelson, 177, 187
Neve, 33, 130, 145, 148, 211
Nevill, 57, 210
Newcomb, 82
Newcome, 148, 187
Newton, 66, 102
Nicolas, 56
Nigel, 107
Noble, 109
Noppe, 4
Norris, 8, 69, 127, 144, 150, 198
Northburg, 137
Northburgh, 14
Nottyngham, 48, 79
Nouman, 141
Nuscote, 96

Oddam, 29
Offly, 174
Old, 153, 167, 211, 212
Orby, 124
Orme, 29, 61, 107, 143

INDEX I.—PERSONS.

Ormesby, 14
Orton, 48
Osborn, 74, 106
Osketyl, 123
Othebothe, 66
Overall, 174
Overton, 51, 56, 123, 126

Paddy, 24
Pagitt, 27
Pain, 174
Palady, 14
Paley, 53, 93
Palmer, 57, 141
Palyngton, 66
Pancke, 26
Panke, 30
Parker, 52, 56, 72, 124, 180
Parsons, 15, 57, 66
Parys, 47
Patrick, 55, 58, 66, 99
Payne, 72, 100, 187
Peach, 146, 153
Peada, 45
Peckard, 58, 187, 204
Pega, 63
Peirse, 14, 56, 57
Peirson, 109
Pell, 146
Pelle, 211
Penda, 10
Pendelton, 4
Penn, 60, 88, 89, 90, 190
Pennington, 137
Penny, 84
Percy, 4
Pern, 124
Person, 84
Peter, 141
Peters, 194
Petit, 195, 196
Petye, 131
Peverel, 177
Phelips, 4
Philippa, 171
Philipp, 79
Phillips, 174
Philpot, 93
Pickard, 177
Pickeryng, 24
Pierson, 109
Pigott, 152, 157, 175, 176
Pindar, 177
Pleynson, 109
Pocklington, 52, 193
Pole, 48, 56
Pollard, 193, 195
Pond, 24
Pooley, 160, 180
Pope, 2, 58, 102

Porter, 33
Postlethwayte, 124
Potts, 1
Pratt, 30, 34, 60, 66, 79, 99, 102
Preston, 4, 204
Priest, 174
Proby, 160, 164, 186, 190, 204
Provost, 116
Pufferett, 48
Pusa, 55
Pykeryng, 79
Pykwell, 14
Pyndar, 54
Pytteman, 66

Radcliffe, 195
Radwell, 23
Rainbow, 58
Rainer, 23
Ralph, 117
Ramsey, 48, 55, 56, 117
Randall, 109, 172
Ravey, 4
Rawlins, 23, 27
Rawlyns, 14
Rawson, 173
Rayment, 204
Raynbill, 14, 79
Read, 112, 115
Reade, 107
Rede, 148
Reeve, 147
Remigius, 166
Repyngbam, 14
Reve, 153
Reynolds, 24, 58, 60, 89, 110, 112
Richard I, 55, 145
Richard II, 126
Richardson, 47, 137
Richerson, 52
Ris, 117
Robert, 114, 117, 123
Robertson, 167
Robertus, 78
Robins, 173, 177
Robinson, 24, 146
Rogers, 23, 137, 138
Rokeby, 192
Ronds, 209
Roper, 194
Rowe, 92
Rudstow. 109
Russell, 115, 122
Ryall, 48, 117
Rydell, 79
Ryder, 142
Rydley, 66
Ryley, 78, 79, 123

Sais, 46, 47, 55
Salman, 34
Salmon, 193, 195, 200
Sambrook, 34
Sampson, 173, 177
Sancroft, 66
Sandford, 4
Sandiver, 124
Sandivers, 117
Sanford, 4
Sapcote, 164
Sappcottes, 160
Sappcotts, 164, 165
Saunders, 58, 187
Savage, 187
Sawyer, 137
Saxulphus, 55
Scambler, 23, 56
Scarlet, 54, 62
Schardelow, 4
Schutz, 79
Sciebo, 127
Scot, 195
Scott, 74, 103, 104, 128
Scribo, 124
Searle, 124, 177, 181
Seby, 160
Sedgewicke, 4
S. Edmunds, 55
Selby, 21, 100
Serocold, 93
Seymour, 140
Shappett, 130
Sharman, 145, 147
Sharpe, 175
Shaw, 146, 166
Shellit, 115
Shelstone, 12
Shepe, 130
Shepherd, 34
Sherman, 173
Sherwood, 52
Shrewsbury, 139
Sigee, 116
Simpcox, 34
Sinke, 193
Siward, 126
Siwardus, 117, 123
Skakylton, 141
Skeels, 90
Skelton, 137
Skiner, 175
Skrimshire, 37
Sloper, 159
Slowe, 142
Smeaton, 76
Smith, 53, 93, 96, 102, 104, 137, 142, 179, 193, 198
Smyth, 13, 30, 66, 131, 132, 133, 142, 173, 181, 195

INDEX I.—PERSONS.

210

Smythe, 110, 173
Smythies, 195, 198
Solomon, 117
Southampton, 140
Southgate, 148, 151, 167
Spaldynge, 89
Sparby, 195
Sparke, 55, 89
Spaulding, 77
Spayn, 194
Speechley, 101
Speechly, 140
Spinkes, 14, 66, 137, 210
Spinks, 12
Sprung, 173
Squier, 66
Squire, 34, 191
Stamford, 78
Standish, 48, 89, 131
Stanford, 117
Stanton, 14, 66
Starkye, 108
Starling, 195
Stavenesby, 66
Stene, 79
Stephen, 55
Stephenson, 161
Stevyns, 66
Stevynson, 29
Stewart, 137
Stiles, 82
Stimpson, 146, 173
St. John, 39, 49, 199
Stockewith, 177
Stona, 112
Stone, 90
Story, 174
Stow, 48
Stowkes, 23
Strickland, 49
Stringer, 187
Strong, 34, 60
Stubbs, 136, 137, 138
Stuke, 177
Styles, 77, 124, 187, 190
Sudbery, 147
Sudbury, 106
Suthwik, 4
Sutton, 35, 55
Suttun, 48
Swane, 64
Swannock, 93
Sweeby, 96
Swynscoe, 24
Sybely, 14

Taillor, 4
Talbot, 23, 139
Tanfield, 14
Tapton, 93
Tarrant, 58, 60

Tatym, 167
Taylor, 60, 137, 138, 141, 180
Tempest, 30
Tench, 153
Tennant, 142, 143
Terrick, 15, 57
Thacker, 204
Theed, 204
Theodore, 113, 123
Thirkell, 177
Thirlby, 30
Thomas, 42, 57, 58, 89, 142
Thompson, 117
Thorndon, 110
Thorne, 137
Thoroldus, 55
Thornton, 48
Thorp, 1, 35, 93, 122, 123
Thorpe, 2
Thresser, 177
Thurnell, 90
Tidmarsh, 176
Tigardine, 116
Tompson, 70, 131, 185, 195
Topping, 99, 100, 101, 102, 104, 110, 112
Tournay, 60
Towers, 14, 28, 56, 57
Treton, 93
Trygg, 30
Tully, 66
Tunny, 52
Tunstall, 137
Turketyl, 123, 124, 126
Turner, 9, 161, 166
Turton, 58, 60
Tydde, 29
Tyrington, 4
Tytley, 64, 66

Underwood, 100, 107, 112, 115
Upton, 123, 204
Usill, 116
Utting, 64

Vangalloway, 100
Vasey, 142
Vaudeberk, 116
Vaughan, 93
Vaux, 164
Vecti, 55
Veer, 4
Villars, 37
Virgilius, 14
Vokes, 131, 132, 133
Voy, 185

Wager, 30, 137

Wake, 93
Wakelin, 140, 187, 205, 207
Waldegrave, 99
Waldeve, 123
Waldron, 30
Walker, 123
Waller, 102
Wallis, 180
Walmesford, 30
Walpooll, 48
Walsham, 28, 130, 131, 133, 136, 195, 204
Walsingham, 110
Walter, 117, 134
Walton, 174
Ward, 131, 132, 137
Warde, 14, 66, 79
Waring, 30, 60, 148, 150
Warner, 90
Warren, 65
Warriner, 34
Warrok, 30
Warwick, 173, 198
Water-Newton, 117
Watervile, 4
Waterville, 1, 31, 46, 55
Wates, 206
Watford, 30
Watson, 137
Wattkin, 96
Webster, 70, 74, 100, 137
Weddred, 30
Welbye, 108
Welles, 30, 123
Wells, 93, 117, 167
Wellton, 24
Were, 37
Wermingham, 30
Westmoreland, 193, 200
Weston, 79, 191
Whalley, 142, 143
Whelpdale, 66
Whiston, 14, 177
Whitbrooke, 170
White, 15, 20, 28, 56, 66
Whitehall, 66
Whitehead, 195, 196
Whitfeild, 4
Whitfeld, 9
Whitmore, 134
Whitstones, 107, 131
Whittewell, 66
Whittlesey, 112, 117
Whittyngton, 148
Whitwell, 82
Whyt, 102
Wigmore, 79
Wilcoke, 131
Wilcox, 173
Wildbore, 75, 207

Wilford, 14
Wilkes, 109
Wilkinson, 30, 195
Willan, 161
William, 24, 30, 93, 113, 126
Williams, 66, 171
Williamson, 24, 30, 79, 148
Willowes, 53
Wiltshey, 102
Wiltshire, 66
Winchley, 12
Wing, 90, 211
Wingfield, 12
Winstanley, 13
Wirmington, 78
Wisbech, 117
Wisditch, 173
Wiseman, 107
Witham, 14
Witlesey, 102
Wodeham, 110

Wodham, 172
Wolfe, 66
Wolfenden, 195
Wollaston, 66, 79, 131, 210
Wolloure, 4
Wolmer, 4
Wolsey, 8
Womack, 194
Wood, 23
Woodcrofte, 66
Woodford, 55
Woodfowl, 211
Woodward, 52
Woolley, 177
Workman, 66
Worseleye, 93
Wortley, 138
Wright, 14, 20, 131, 133, 136, 142, 203, 204, 205, 207, 209
Writte, 175
Wryght, 79

Wulgatus, 64, 123
Wulketyl, 123, 124
Wyldbore, 3, 29, 34, 71
Wylde, 30
Wyllkes, 109
Wyllson, 102
Wylson, 93, 109
Wyman, 142
Wynde, 177
Wynslowe, 93
Wysbeche, 68
Wysbyche, 48
Wytham, 14
Wyttilbury, 1, 93
Wyttylbyri, 9

Yarwell, 136, 139
Yaxley, 114, 117
Yearwell, 136
Yeoman, 4
York, 209
Young, 130

Index 2.—Places.

Abbot's Ripton, Hun., 204
Achurch, Nhants, 4, 30
Addington, Sus., 58
Alderkirk, Lin., 57
Alderminster, Wor., 131
Algiers, 100
Aliwal, 104
Alligny, Burgundy, 158
Allington, Dev., 158
Allington, Kent, 168
ALWALTON, Hun., 30, 141, 145—151, 207, 210, 211
Ambrosden, Ber., 56
Anjou, 55
Arthingworth, Nhants., 15
Ashford, Derb., 7
Ashford, Lei., 76
Ashley, Ber., 57
Astwick, Bed., 1
Australia, 164
Averham, Not., 58
Axholme, Isle of, Lin., 185

Bainton, Nhants., 92
Bampton, Ox., 56
Bangor, 58
Barbadoes, 54
Barnack, Nhants., 57, 66, 78, 91, 98

Basingchurch, Han., 159
Baston, Lin., 169
Bath, 196
Bath and Wells, 56, 195
Battersea, 58
Beavois, 55
Beccles, Suf., 109
Benefield, Nhants., 58, 117
Beverley, Yor., 137
Birmingham, 57
Blisworth, Nhants., 15
Bocking, Es., 57
Bodmin, Cor., 207
Bordeaux, 140
Boston, Lin., 91
Botsford, Lei., 56
Bottisham, Cam., 142, 153
BOTTLEBRIDGE, Hun., 52, 91, 135—137
Bowton, Lit., Lei., 194
Bradwell, Es., 143
Brancepeth, Dur., 58
Brecksh., 84
Bridgenorth, Sal., 109, 137, 159, 194
Brinckton, Hun., 176
Bringhurst, Nhants., 90
Bristol, 57, 67

Brixworth, Nhants., 96, 210
Brockley, Som., 82
Broseby, 130
Brosley, Sal., 157
Broughton, Nhants., 160
Bruern, Ox., 139
Buckingham, 56
Buriton, Han., 56
Burton, 55
Burton Cogles, Lin., 148
Burton-on-Stather, Lin., 194
Bury, Hun., 172, 179
Bury S. Edmunds, 15, 107

Cadbury, N., Som., 195
Calcott, Hun., 148
Cambridge, 9, 15, 21, 34, 52, 56, 57, 58, 66, 71, 78, 82, 91, 93, 108, 131, 140, 143, 144, 148, 153, 167, 169, 193, 195, 198, 201, 204
Cambsh., 100, 163
Canons Ashby, Nhants., 156
Canterbury, 15, 30, 53, 55, 58, 71, 112

INDEX II.—PLACES. 221

Carlisle, 53, 58, 93
Cartmel, Lan., 93
CASTOR, Nhants., 4, 10—21, 46, 56, 66, 78, 79, 102, 137, 151, 153, 160, 168, 209, 211
Charlton, Nhants., 90
Chatteris, Cam., 175
Cherry Hinton, Cam., 100, 140
Chester, 12, 57, 159
Chesterford, Lit., Es., 58
CHESTERTON, Hun., 10, 131, 137, 151—157, 162, 211, 212
Chichester, 33, 56, 66
Churton, Nhants., 57
Clapham, Bed., 172
Clonfert, 161
Colombo, 161
Colyngham, Nhants., 66
Compiegne, 120
Compton Gifford, Dev., 212
Conington, Lin., 79
Connington, Cam., 58
Connington, Hun., 20
Cornwall, 91, 111
Cottingham, Nhants., 15
Cotton End, Nhants., 109
Coventry, 55, 137
Cowbit, Lin., 136
Cranford, Nhants., 30
Creton, Nhants., 30
CROWLAND, Lin., 55, 63, 68, 70, 113, 121—128, 170, 211
Culross, 102
Cumberland, 35

Dalston, Cum., 58
Dandelyon, Ken., 106
Darlington, Dur., 130
Deeping, Market, Lin., 1, 117, 122
Deeping, W., Lin., 4, 79
Dembleby, Nhants, 90
Denton, Hun., 58
Derby, 114
Derbysh., 7
Devonsh., 111
Dormundceastre, 10
Down, 87, 102, 117
Downham, Nor., 33, 60, 74, 106
Dublin, 108, 192
Dukinfield, Che., 102
Dunnington, Cam., 57
Durham, 57, 58, 61, 84, 140
Durobrivæ, 10, 145, 151

Eapley, Staf., 194
Easton, G., Nhants, 90
Eastree, Cam., 101
Ecton, Nhants., 20, 58
Edinburgh, 194
Eddystone, Dev., 13
Eldernell, Cam., 101, 102, 107, 211
Elme, Cam., 108
Elmly, Wor., 159
Elsworth, Cam., 191, 194
ELTON, Hun., 147, 158—165, 212
Ely, Cam., 12, 56, 57, 58, 63, 90, 96, 105, 108, 126, 160
Emneth, Cam., 108
Eriswell, Suf., 103
Ermine Street, 151, 184
Essex, 25
Estreye, Cam., 211
Etton, Nhants., 93, 148, 189
Everton, 148
Evesham, Wor., 123
EYE, Nhants, 87—91, 116, 117, 210

FARCET, Hun., 146, 182, 192, 199—203
Fechamp, Normandy, 66
Fenstanton, Hun., 185, 190
Fiskerton, Lin., 30, 66
FLETTON, Hun., 58, 187, 192, 203—207
Flootburgh, Lan. 194
Fornham, Suf., 39
Fotheringay, Nhants., 52, 158, 159, 164
Framlingham, Suf., 56
France, 166
Freston, Suf., 123

Gasley, 180
Gayton, Nhants., 15, 58
Gidding, Lit., Hun., 204
Giggleswick, Yor., 93
Gimingham, Nor., 58
GLINTON, Nhants., 30, 64, 65, 71—75
Gloucester, 56, 67
Godmanchester, Hun., 175
Good Hope, Cape of, 104
Grafton, Regis, Nhants., 56
Grantham, Lin., 79
Greasborough, Yor., 204
Greenwich, 57
Gretford, Lin., 161

Greton, Nhants., 148
Gretworth, 161
Guilsborough, Nhants., 191
Gunthorpe, Nhants., 76, 77
Gunvile, 141

Haddon, Hun., 142, 152, 153, 156, 159
Hadley, Suf., 57
Hales, Sal., 25
Halifax, Yor., 192
Halvergate, Nor., 107
Hamelden (Hamilton), Rutl., 66, 148
Hansworth, 58
Harlow, Es., 194
Harpole, Nhants., 15
Harrow, Mid., 58
Harwich, Es., 150, 194
Hatfield, Hert., 57, 210
Halton, W., Lin., 57
Haxey, Lin., 57, 102
Hedon, Yor., 108, 159
HELPSTON, Nhants., 91—98, 165, 170
Hemelden, 137
Hereford, 56
Herefsh., 7, 84
Heston, Mid., 13
Heydon, Es., 56
Hilton, Hun., 185
Hinchinbrooke, Hun., 173
Holcot, Nhants., 15
Holland, 49, 115, 192
Holm-Cultram, Cum., 211
Holme, Yor., 58
Holwel, Bed., 66
Horton, Dor., 191
Houghton - le - Spring, Dur., 56
Howden, Yor., 104
Hungary, 160
Huntingdon, 56, 91, 112, 141, 148, 152, 161, 173, 174, 175, 181, 193
Hunts., 131, 146, 151, 155, 156, 157, 163, 164, 181

Impington, Cam., 107
Ingham, 66
Inniskilling, 160
Ireland, 9
Irthlingborough, Nhants., 30, 133
Isleham, Cam., 200

Jersey, 57

Kerkley, Suf., 200

19

INDEX II.—PLACES.

Kesteven, Lin., 2
Kilmore, 100
Kimbolton, Hun., 48
Kirksanton, Cam., 160

Lamberhurst, Sus., 58
Lancash., 194
Lavant, E., Sus., 56
Lavington, Lin., 20
Laxton, Nhants., 93
Leicester, 15, 30, 127
Leicestersh., 166
Leifield, 78
Leominster, Heref., 123
Leverington, Cam., 124
Lichfield, 15, 55, 56, 57, 121, 137, 160
Lincoln, 15, 16, 30, 53, 56, 57, 58, 66, 70, 75, 84, 89, 124, 131, 135, 137, 141, 148, 151, 155, 177
Lincolnsh., 35, 147
Lithuania, 159
Littleport, 130
Llandaff, 15, 56, 57
London, 1, 2, 3, 8, 24, 27, 54, 56, 57, 90, 91, 143, 148, 151, 159, 163, 184; Aldgate, 56; Allhallows, Barking, 66—Lombard st., 56—London Wall, 57; Blackfriars, 195; Bloomsbury, 58; Camberwell, 9; Charterhouse, 56, 58; Clerkenwell, 9; Drury Lane, 100; Dyers' Hall, 160; Goldsmiths' Hall, 185; Hammersmith, 56; Hampstead, 110; Kensington, S., 62; Lambeth, 56; Old Fish st., 68; S. Andrew, Holborn, 56—Undershaft, 8; S. Anne, Aldersgate, 58; S. Bartholomew the Great, 200--the Less, 56; S. Benet, Gracechurch, 71—Fink, 71; —Paul's Wharf, 71;— Sherchog, 71; S. Christopher, 56; S. Faith, 66; S. Gregory, 56; S. Helen, 195; S. Laurence, Pountney, 57; S. Martin, 15, 159—Outwich, 195; S. Mary, Aldermary, 56 — le Strand, 58; Smithfield, 104; S. Paul's cathedral, 2, 56, 57, 82, 137,

160—Covent Garden, 58, 195; Walbrook, 66; Whitechapel, 194
Longthorpe, Nhants., 4, 22, 35—30, 85, 87
Lusiburge, 147
Lutterworth, Lei., 160
Luton, Bed., 194

Machanes, 12, 160
Maharajpoor, 104
Malmesbury, Wil., 25
Malsingham, G., Nor., 163
Manfield, Yor., 4
Marholm, Nhants., 1—10, 20, 37, 39, 83, 121, 140, 209
Market Harborough, Lei., 194
Maxey, Nhants., 24, 30, 67
Medehamsted, 22, 113
Mediterranean, 13
Melford, Long, Suf., 194
Mercia, 10, 46, 63, 121
Mersh Gibbon, Buc., 57
Middleholm, 131
Middlesex, 140
Milan, 125
Milton, Cam., 194
Milton, Nhants., 2, 8, 10, 25
Molesworth, Hun., 209
Monte Casino, 71
Morborne, Hun., 110
Morcott, Rut., 4
Moulton, Nhants., 57
Moulton, Nor., 107

Nassaburgh, 82
Nayland, Suf., 210
Nene, 134, 145, 151, 165
Newark, Nott, 56
Newborough, Nhants., 137
Newbottle, Nhants., 90
Newcastle-on-Tyne, 57
Niend Savage, Sal., 157
Norfolk, 14, 52, 75, 166
Normancross, 184, 191
Normandy, 55, 66
Northall, 56
Northam, Nhants., 88
Northampton, 15, 24, 34, 57, 58, 60, 66, 92, 97, 134, 160
Northants., 130, 151, 156, 200
Northborough, Nhants., 64, 72, 90, 204
Northumbria, 10, 54
Norton, 66
Norwich, 12, 56, 57, 58, 86

Nottingham, 56
Notts., 204

Orange, 12, 160
Orton Longville, Hun., 15, 52, 79, 134—140, 144, 150, 153, 188, 211
Orton Waterville, Hun., 140—145, 153, 154
Oundle, Nhants., 30, 67, 159, 161
Overston, Nhants., 30
Oxford, 1, 9, 15, 30, 56, 57, 66, 67, 148, 161, 165, 175, 204
Oxfordsh., 159

Pagham, Sus., 56
Pampisford, Cam., 107
Paris, 177
Paston, Nhants., 4, 15, 75—83, 84, 210
Peakirk, Nhants., 12, 30, 57, 58, 63—70, 72, 74, 78, 85, 123, 148, 161, 209, 211
Peninsula, 104
Perth Marston, 130
Peterborough, 2, 12, 63, 65, 82, 91, 98, 116, 122, 145, 173, 184, 195, 199, 200, 210. Abbots, 8, 11, 31, 35, 55—56, 73, 113; Angel inn, 24; Bishops, 10, 23, 28, 29, 56—57, 60, 83, 99; Boroughbury, 24, 42; Bridge, 29, 106; Cathedral, 4, 14, 15, 16, 29, 45—63, 66, 72, 78, 89, 93, 107, 126, 131, 142, 151, 167, 209; Chancellor, 15, 58; Chapter, 65, 146; Chorister, 29; Cowgate, 34; Crawthorne hill, 24; Deans, 57—58, 187, 195, 204; Dog and doublet, 109; Dogsthorpe, 26, 78, 84; King's school, 5, 30, 31, 52, 55, 58, 78, 82, 85, 80, 131, 135, 148; Layclerk, 29; Market-cross, 26; Minor-canons, 89, 90, 93, 102, 110, 131, 148; Mulloryes Pits, 23; Northgate, 4; Prebendaries, 4, 15, 29, 34, 58, 60, 66, 67, 70, 79, 137, 148, 161; Precentors, 15, 30, 148; Priestgate,

209; Registrar, 89; Reten Rowe, 29; Sacrist, 23, 42, 123; S. John Baptist, 22—35, 36, 84, 133, 148, 209, 210; S. Mark, 40—42; S. Mary, 42—44; Sexton barns, 130; Westgate, 23, 133; Westwood, 24, 35; Woodgrounds, 24
Pightesley (Pitchley), Nhants., 15, 30
Pluckley, Ken., 210
Plymouth, Dev., 212
Poland, Gr., 194
Poland, Lower, 160
Poland-Prussia, 194
Polebrook, Nhants., 15, 79
Pond's bridge, Cam. 182
Postland, Lin., 122
Preston, 156

Quebeck, 147

Rabye, Lin., 141
Raine, Ess., 195
RAMSEY, Hun., 113, 123, 158, 170—182, 192; S. Mary, 182—184
Rayley, 66
Rheims, 166
Ripon, 159
Rochester, 55, 56, 58, 112
Rome, 56
Rouen, 192
Royston, Hert., 152
Rushton, Nhants., 30
Rutland, 3
Rye, Sus., 56, 57

S. Adde, Sal., 15
Saffron Walden, Es., 56
S. Albans, Hert., 55, 123
Salisbury, 66
Salop, 108
Sarum, 15, 56, 57, 58, 66, 117, 137, 209
S. Asaph, 57
Saxted, Suf., 56
Scotland, 100
S. Davids, 15, 193
S. Ebrulph, 123
Sedgfield, Dur., 56
Selling, Ken., 204
S. Helena, 161
Shireland, 130
Shottesbrook, Ber., 56
Sibson, Lei., 56
Sibson, Nhants., 146
Sierra Leone, 137

Singlesholt, Nhants, 68
S. Ives, Hun., 56, 176
S. Neots, Hun., 55, 76, 110, 145, 180
Soham, Cam., 56, 160
Somersham, Hun., 102, 109
Southwark, Sur., 194
Southwell, Not., 61, 204
Southwick, Nhants., 194
Spalding, Lin., 128, 148
Spilsby, Lin., 130
Staines, Mid., 58
Stamford, Lin., 9, 56, 75, 124, 141
STANGROUND, Hun., 58, 144, 192—199, 200, 201, 202, 205
Stanton Barry, Buc., 58
Stanway, Es., 57
Stanwick, Nhants., 15, 70
Stathern, Lei., 56
Staverton, Nhants., 160
Stedham, Sus., 56
Steyford, Lin., 182
Stilton, Hun., 147
Stoke-by-Nayland, Suf., 210
Stow, Lin., 15
Suffolk, 88, 91
Sunderland, Dur., 193
Switzerland, 12
Syresham, Nhants., 15

Tansover, Nhants., 148
Tanworth, War., 58
Teversham, Cam., 57
Thanet, Ken., 196
Thetford, Nor., 66
THORNEY, Cam., 55, 99, 102, 104, 105, 107, 112, 113—120, 131, 152, 166, 170, 185, 192, 193, 199, 210, 211
Thornhaugh, Nhants., 211
Thrapston, Nhants., 159
Tidworth, N., Wil., 58
Towcester, Nhants., 130
Turfen, Hun., 172
Twickenham, Mid., 57
Twywell, Nhants., 93

Uffington, Lin., 15
Ugmeare, Hun., 172

Wales, 25
Walsoken, Nor., 211
Walthamstow, Es., 56, 133
Walton, Nor., 200
Walton, Nhants., 77
Wansford, Nhants., 29

Wappenham, Nhants., 15
Ware, Hert., 30
Waresley, Hun., 52
Waterloo, 104, 153
WATER NEWTON, Hun., 146, 153, 165—170, 211
Watlingford, Hert., 142
Wearmouth, 71
Welburn, 66
Wells, Som., 195
WERRINGTON, Nhants., 76, 77, 83—86
Westminster, 48, 56, 57, 58, 67
Weston Colville, Cam., 15
Weston Favell, Nhants., 15
Whaplode Drove, Lin., 124
Wheaton-Aston, Staf., 194
WHITTLESEY, Cam., 114, 146, 154, 175, 182, 189, 201; S. Andrew, 99, 101, 102, 107—112, 210, 211; S. Mary, 18, 98—107, 117, 131, 195, 210, 211
Whitwell, Der., 58
Wickford, Es., 56
Willoughby, Not., 57
Winchester, 55, 56, 57, 117, 146
Windsor, 52, 57, 58
Winteringham, Lin., 79
Wisbech, Cam., 52, 66, 102, 115, 210
Wistow, Hun., 174, 175
Witham-on-the-Hill, Lin., 60
Witney, Ox., 27
Wonston, Han., 129
Woodcroft., Nhants., 124
Woodford, Nhants., 30, 191
Wood Newton, Nhants., 105
WOODSTON, Hun., 107, 129—134, 153, 196
Wooller, Nhumb., 160
Worcester, 57, 117
Wrotham, Ken., 58

Yarmouth, Nor., 9
YAXLEY, Hun., 26, 114, 129, 147, 153, 184—192, 199, 204
Yaxley, Suf., 185
Yedingham, Yor., 4
Yelden, Bed., 52
York, 55, 56, 57, 58, 61, 108, 123, 140, 184, 194

Index 3.—Matters.

Abbots, quarrels of, 113
Achievements, 7, 139, 164
Almsbox, ancient, 19
Almshouses, 3, 54, 78, 82, 100
Altarpiece removed, 33
Altars, 50, 84, 102
Attendance at church, enforced, 26
Aumbries, 19, 67, 85, 94, 162, 168, 189, 190, 197, 202

Barn, ancient, 42
Beadle's uniform, 26
Bells, inscribed, 8, 20, 33, 60, 69, 74, 81, 90, 96, 106, 111, 127, 133, 139, 144, 150, 155, 163, 169, 180, 184, 190, 198, 202, 206
Ben Barr, a prophet, 98
Benefactions, 3, 14, 24, 28, 55, 58, 65, 77, 84, 89, 92, 101, 109, 116, 123, 131, 133, 136, 137, 140, 142, 148, 157, 160, 176, 177, 182, 183, 186, 195, 201, 204
Bequests for ringers, 29, 92; lamp, 14; image, 65, 69; roodlight, 72; saying Lord's prayer, 29
Bible, ancient, 3
Brasses, 8, 36, 61, 79, 120, 145, 191, 198
Briefs, collections on, 2, 12, 25, 76, 108, 130, 159, 194, 200
Burials, in woollen, 2, 52, 84, 185; of hearts, 55, 191, 192; costly, 56; of queens, 48, 52

Cattle plague, 130
Cenotaph, 140
Chantries, 1, 141
Chapel, desecrated, 70; demolished, 49, 88, 101, 114

Charles I., portrait of, 32
Choir of cathedral reseated, 49
Christian names, unusual, 12, 25, 76, 108, 141, 169, 174, 204
Church destroyed, 135; removed, 30, 35
Churchwardens' books, 12, 25, 64, 65, 84, 92, 130, 147, 152, 166, 175, 186
Churchyard, dilapidated, 186
Clock, 21, 53, 105
Coffin, stone, 95, 127, 157, 164, 170
Coffin-lids, engraved, 20, 21, 75, 97, 104, 127, 133, 164, 180, 181, 191
Coinage, 26
Comet, 113
Consecration deed, 87, 102
Constable's books, 12, 166
Corbels, grotesque, 73, 110
Crewel, what, 27
Crosses, churchyard, 21, 92, 165, 173, 181, 198, 207; village, 39, 97, 128, 192; floor 20, 59, 60, 81, 96, 180, 198; on headstones, 97, 98, 105; finial, 20, 40, 44, 139
Crucifix, 33
Custom, old, 7, 12, 13, 86

Darnix, what, 13
Deaths, sudden (accidents or suicides), 23, 24, 52, 76, 89, 91, 100, 108, 115, 122, 129, 130, 141, 143, 149, 159, 166, 172, 173, 174, 175, 185, 193
Dedication-stone, 15
Dedications, unusual, 10, 63, 70, 71, 121, 166; changed, 89, 172
Deviation in chancel and nave, 58, 103, 198

Domestic architecture, 39, 135
Duel, 24

Earthquake, 125
Ejectments from benefices, 15, 30, 48, 56, 57, 58, 79, 137, 153, 161, 186, 187, 195
Embroidery, ancient, 32
Erasmus, paraphrase of, 13
Etymologies of places, 10, 22, 35, 63, 71, 75, 83, 87, 91, 98, 113, 121, 129, 134, 135, 140, 145, 151, 158, 165, 184, 185, 192, 199, 203
Exchequer tally, 27
Executions, 12, 23, 24, 56, 57

Faculties, 27
Fairs, 55, 140, 184
Fanon, what, 27
Fellowships founded, 56, 78, 82
Fen drainage, 115, 123, 193, 199
Fires, 2, 23, 45, 54, 76, 141, 159, 160, 173, 174, 175, 194
Floods, 2, 54, 65, 113
Fomart (fulimire), 147
Fonts, 7, 21, 38, 41, 44, 52, 68, 73, 74, 81, 86, 105, 132, 142, 144, 154, 162, 179, 183, 206
Foundation stone, 36
France, kings of, 106
French names, 112, 116; prisoners, 191
Frescoes, 7, 19, 103, 138, 190
Friars, 8
Front, cathedral, 47, 50, 59
Funeral garland, 7

Galilee, 30

INDEX III.—MATTERS.   225

Geese, wild, 147
Glass, stained, ancient, 7, 48, 49, 50, 68, 81, 119, 122, 138, 164, 179, 197; modern, 44, 69, 60, 90, 102, 118, 183, 191, 197, 198
Greek epitaphs, 61, 82
Guilds, 23

Heronry, 25

Inventories of church goods, 3, 13, 28, 37, 51, 65, 72, 77, 84, 89, 92, 101, 109, 130, 136, 142, 148, 160, 194

King's evil, 54

Latten, what, 3
Lawsuit, 65, 124
Letterns, 43, 51, 67, 68, 74, 162, 179
Librarian, 151
Library, 33, 48, 55, 107, 196
Lightning, 21, 24
Litany-desk at cathedral, 54
Livings augmented, 99, 131, 185, 193, 199, 200,

Markets, 26, 184
Marriage by laymen, 2, 130
Martyrs, 15, 113
Mayneport, what, 77
Miracle, 102
Monuments, cumbrous, 9, 61, 156; inscriptions on, 9, 10, 20, 21, 34, 39, 55, 56, 70, 75, 82, 96, 97, 107, 110, 112, 127, 132, 133, 134, 138, 139, 140, 149, 151, 155, 156, 163, 169, 181, 191, 192, 196, 198, 203, 205; pyramidal, 11, 45, 52; lost, 9, 30, 47, 60, 79, 133, 193; tasteful, 10, 134, 184; destroyed, 61; effigies on, 5, 61, 62, 75, 82, 104, 139, 169, 172

Mortuary, 66, 76, 177
Murders, 71, 150, 174; confession of, 72

Nest, 7, 83
Nonjurors, 12, 56, 66, 89, 134

Occupations, singular, 52, 53, 136, 146, 147, 185

Penance, 108
Pillory, 54
Piscinas, 19, 38, 67, 73, 85, 94, 104, 105, 111, 113, 153, 162, 168, 179, 189, 197, 202
Plague, 23, 24, 25, 26, 115, 159, 173, 194
Plate, 27, 44, 54, 56, 101, 116, 122, 130, 160, 176, 186, 201
Pound, 147, 148, 166
Procurations, what, 1
Protestant refugees, 12, 112, 115, 116
Pulpit, a fine one, 144, 154
Punning mottoes, 123, 181
Purprise, what, 199
Priest's chamber, 199

Rebus, 7, 8
Registers, 2, 11, 23, 51, 64, 71, 76, 83, 88, 99, 108, 115, 122, 129, 130, 141, 146, 152, 158, 166, 172, 185, 193, 200, 203
Roodloft, an original, 84
Roodloft window, 103, 143, 154
Roofs, 7, 18, 32, 41, 43, 48, 50, 59, 67, 73, 81, 86, 90, 105, 110, 118, 126, 143, 144, 188; stone, 33, 126
Roman stations, 10, 151

Scarlett, old, 54, 62, 63
Scholarships founded, 1, 56, 201
Schools, 29, 65, 103, 105, 131, 160, 177, 201
Screen, altar, 48

Screens, 7, 67, 68, 73, 81, 95, 105, 111, 120, 138, 154, 170, 183, 188, 197, 205
Seats, good, 41, 43, 69, 73, 103, 132, 183, 190; bad, 32, 118, 146, 150, 154, 206; erection of, 27, 49; original, 6, 38, 94, 162, 190, 206
Sedilia, 19, 73, 80, 94, 111, 138, 150, 162, 168, 179, 189, 197
Shrine, 119
Slavery, 2, 12, 160, 200
Spires of cathedral, not same height, 47
Squints, 94, 162
Stone figures, 17, 120, 125, 126, 170
Stone seats, 85, 94, 138, 144, 169, 196, 202
Storm, the great, 12, 13, 160, 195
Stoups, 95, 168
Sun-dials, 82, 151, 191
Supremacy of king acknowledged, 48
Synodals, what, 1

Taffeta, what, 13
Threepenny tax, 100, 166
Tiffany, what, 27
Tiles, remarkable, 94
Tithe book, 77
Tobacco, 54, 147, 175
Tower destroyed, 132
Tradition, parish, 78
Triangular bridge, 127, 128

Union of benefices, deed for, 135

Wainscot, what, 77
Whipping, 12, 193
Wills, old, 14, 23, 29, 65, 66, 72, 78, 79, 84, 89, 92, 100, 107, 122, 142, 155, 177, 186
Woodwork, inscription on, 18
Workshop, cathedral used as, 49

20

Index 4.—Authors quoted.

Abstract of charitable donations
Archæological institute, report

Bacon's essays
Bacon's liber regis
Baker's Northamptonshire
Baker's Northamptonshire glossary
Bloxam's architecture
Bloxam's letter to Northampton mercury
Bloxam's paper, Archæol. inst.
Botfield's cathedral libraries
Brand's antiquities
Bridges' Northamptonshire
Britton's Peterborough
Burns' foreign refugees
Burns' parish registers

Calamy's ministers ejected
Cassan's bishops of Bath and Wells
Chalmer's biographical dictionary
Chambers' book of days
Churches of Cambridgeshire
Clement's church notes MS.
Cole's MS.
Cotton MS.
Cowel's glossary
Craddock's Peterborough cathedral

Davys' Peterborough cathedral

Derby's Iliad
Domesday book
Dryden's poems
Dugdale's monasticon
Dyer's reports

East Anglian
Ecclesiologist
Edward confessor, life of
Elliot's paper, Arch. soc., Nhants.
Essex's church notes MS.

Fuller's worthies

Gentleman's magazine
Gough's monuments
Gough's MS.
Granger's wonderful museum
Gunton's Peterborough

Harleian MS.
Hone's every day book
Hone's year book
Hyett's sepulchral memorials

Ingulf's chronicle

James's Northamptonshire
Johnson's dictionary

Kennett's register and chronicle
Kennett's MS.
Kerrich church notes MS.
Kettlewell, life of

Liber albus
Lewis's isle of Tenet
Lukis's church bells

Martineau's history of the peace
Masters's Corpus Christi college
Moore's paper, Arch. Soc. Lin.
Morton's Northamptonshire
Murray's cathedrals

Nicolas's testamenta vetusta
Notes and queries

Paley's Peterborough cathedral
Paley's parish churches
Parker's glossary of architecture
Parker's domestic architecture
Parliamentary enquiry on registers
Parliamentary inquisition
Peterborough advertiser

Shakspere's plays
Speed's history
Spelman's glossary
Steele's MS.
Strype's memorials

Taylor's words and places
Timbs's curiosities of London

Valor ecclesiasticus

Walcott's memorials of Peterborough
Walker's sufferings of the clergy
Willis's cathedrals

PRINTED BY E. T. HAMBLIN, NARROW STREET, PETERBOROUGH.

www.ingramcontent.com/pod-product-compliance
Lightning Source LLC
Chambersburg PA
CBHW032049230426
43672CB00009B/1536